BBC

DOCTOR WHO

THE TWELFTH DOCTOR

GHOST STORIES

"Great superhero action."
GEEK GIRL PROJECT

"Does anyone ever really know what to expect from a Time Lord? Rhetorical question. Of course not. If you're a *Doctor Who* fan, it's a must-buy."
GRAPHIC POLICY

"Crisp, clean, and nicely animated action. 4 out of 5!"
NERDLY

"The color art by Dijjo Lima proves fantastic, well-suiting the bright, four-color aesthetic of the story."
KABOOOOOM!

"Welcome back, Doctor!"
CHUCK'S COMIC OF THE DAY

"Extremely well-balanced and paced extremely well."
CAPELESS CRUSADER

"Ivan Rodriguez displays an aptitude for bringing superhero-based artistry to life."
THAT'S NOT CURRENT

"Interesting character development, sharp dialogue, colorful and impressive artwork!"
BLOGTOR WHO

"The characterization is consistent with what was shown on TV [...] the art is gorgeous and detailed."
GAMING TREND

"Reminiscent of Pixar's *The Incredibles*!"
GEEK.COM

TITAN COMICS

SENIOR COMICS EDITOR
Andrew James

COLLECTION EDITOR
Lauren Bowes

ASSISTANT EDITORS
Jessica Burton & Amoona Saohin

TITAN EDITORIAL
Lauren McPhee

COLLECTION DESIGNER
Andrew Leung

PRODUCTION ASSISTANT
Natalie Bolger

PRODUCTION SUPERVISOR
Maria Pearson

PRODUCTION CONTROLLER
Peter James

SENIOR PRODUCTION CONTROLLER
Jackie Flook

ART DIRECTOR
Oz Browne

SENIOR SALES MANAGER
Steve Tothill

PRESS OFFICER
Will O'Mullane

COMICS BRAND MANAGER
Chris Thompson

ADS & MARKETING ASSISTANT
Tom Miller

DIRECT SALES & MARKETING MANAGER
Ricky Claydon

COMMERCIAL MANAGER
Michelle Fairlamb

HEAD OF RIGHTS
Jenny Boyce

PUBLISHING MANAGER
Darryl Tothill

PUBLISHING DIRECTOR
Chris Teather

OPERATIONS DIRECTOR
Leigh Baulch

EXECUTIVE DIRECTOR
Vivian Cheung

PUBLISHER
Nick Landau

Special thanks to Steven Moffat, Brian Minchin, Mandy Thwaites, Matt Nicholls, James Dudley, Edward Russell, Derek Ritchie, Scott Handcock, Kirsty Mullan, Kate Bush, Julia Nocciolino and Ed Casey for their invaluable assistance.

BBC WORLDWIDE

DIRECTOR OF EDITORIAL GOVERNANCE
Nicholas Brett

DIRECTOR OF CONSUMER PRODUCTS AND PUBLISHING
Andrew Moultrie

HEAD OF UK PUBLISHING
Chris Kerwin

PUBLISHER
Mandy Thwaites

PUBLISHING CO-ORDINATOR
Eva Abramik

For rights information
contact Jenny Boyce
jenny.boyce@titanemail.com

DOCTOR WHO: GHOST STORIES
HB ISBN: 9781785861697
SB ISBN: 9781785861703

Published by Titan Comics, a division of Titan Publishing Group, Ltd. 144 Southwark Street, London, SE1 0UP.

A CIP catalogue record for this title is available from the British Library.
First edition: October 2017.

10 9 8 7 6 5 4 3 2 1

Printed in China.

Titan Comics does not read or accept unsolicited DOCTOR WHO submissions of ideas, stories or artwork.

BBC

DOCTOR WHO

THE TWELFTH DOCTOR

GHOST STORIES

WRITER: GEORGE MANN

ARTISTS: IVAN RODRIGUEZ, PASQUALE QUALANO & DENNIS CALERO

COLORIST: DIJJO LIMA

LETTERS: RICHARD STARKINGS AND COMICRAFT'S JIMMY BETANCOURT

BBC

DOCTOR WHO

THE TWELFTH DOCTOR

THE DOCTOR

A rogue Time Lord of Gallifrey. Never cruel or cowardly, he champions the oppressed across time and space. Adventure and travel are what he lives for – and danger always has a way of finding him!

GRANT

Thanks to the alien gemstone he absorbed into his body as a child, Grant can fly, is invulnerable and super-strong, and doesn't feel silly dressed up in a tight leather costume to fight crime in New York City.

LUCY

A top journalist and investigator, Lucy has a keen head for secrets and a sharp line in incisive prose. Mother of Jennifer, and now married to Grant, thanks to their adventure with the Doctor eight years ago.

PREVIOUSLY...

Together, the Doctor, Lucy, and Grant defeated the nefarious forces of Harmony Shoal. The world saved, and his love for Lucy reciprocated, Grant put away the costume, and the Doctor left Grant and Lucy to their new life together.

But the Doctor is terrible for picking at loose ends...

When you've finished reading this collection, please email your thoughts to doctorwhocomic@titanemail.com

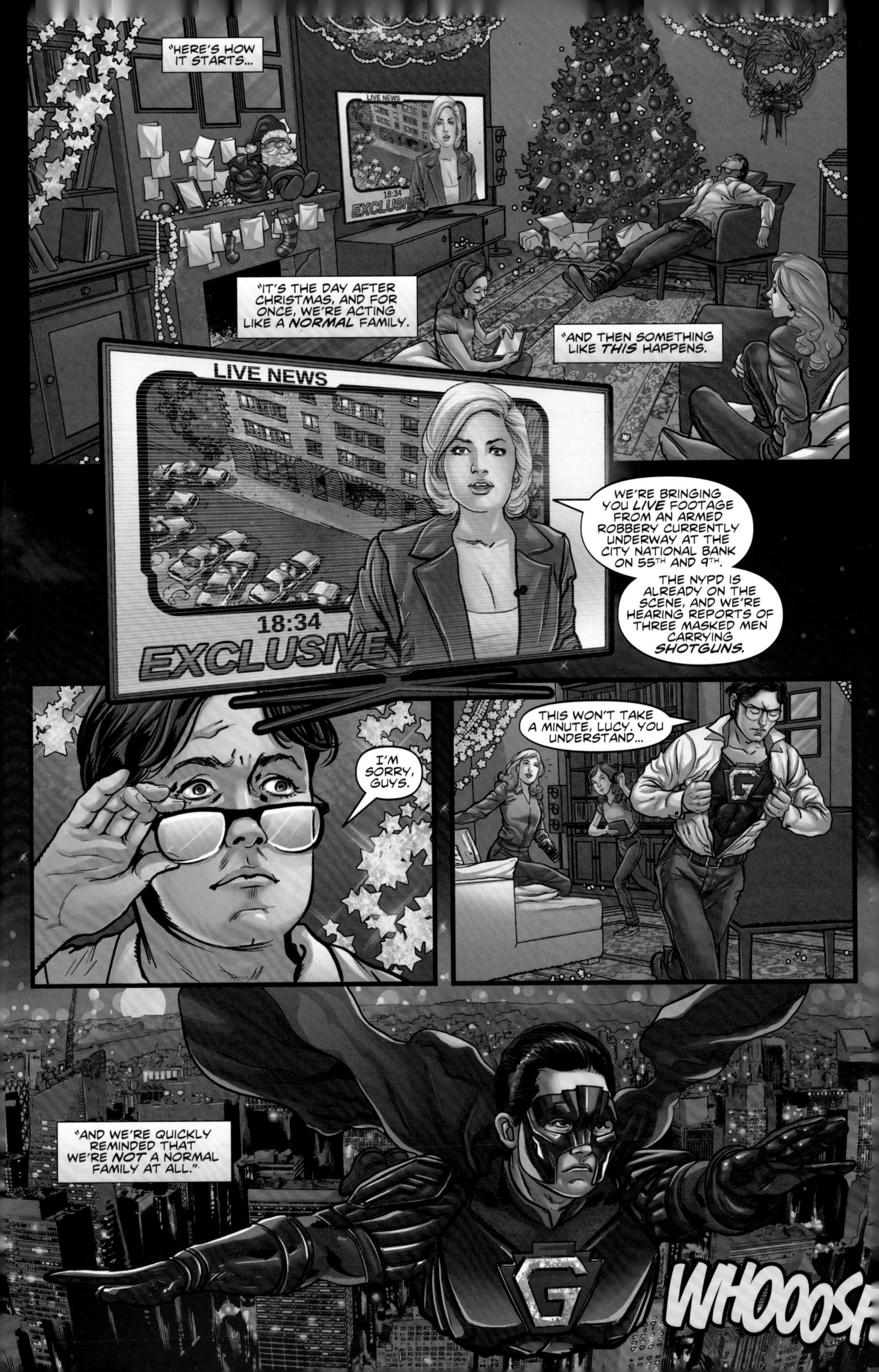
"HERE'S HOW IT STARTS...
LIVE NEWS
EXCLUSIVE
"IT'S THE DAY AFTER CHRISTMAS, AND FOR ONCE, WE'RE ACTING LIKE A *NORMAL* FAMILY.
"AND THEN SOMETHING LIKE *THIS* HAPPENS.
LIVE NEWS
18:34
EXCLUSIVE
WE'RE BRINGING YOU *LIVE* FOOTAGE FROM AN ARMED ROBBERY CURRENTLY UNDERWAY AT THE CITY NATIONAL BANK ON 55TH AND 9TH.
THE NYPD IS ALREADY ON THE SCENE, AND WE'RE HEARING REPORTS OF THREE MASKED MEN CARRYING *SHOTGUNS*.
I'M SORRY, GUYS.
THIS WON'T TAKE A MINUTE, LUCY. YOU UNDERSTAND...
"AND WE'RE QUICKLY REMINDED THAT WE'RE *NOT* A NORMAL FAMILY AT ALL."
WHOOOSH

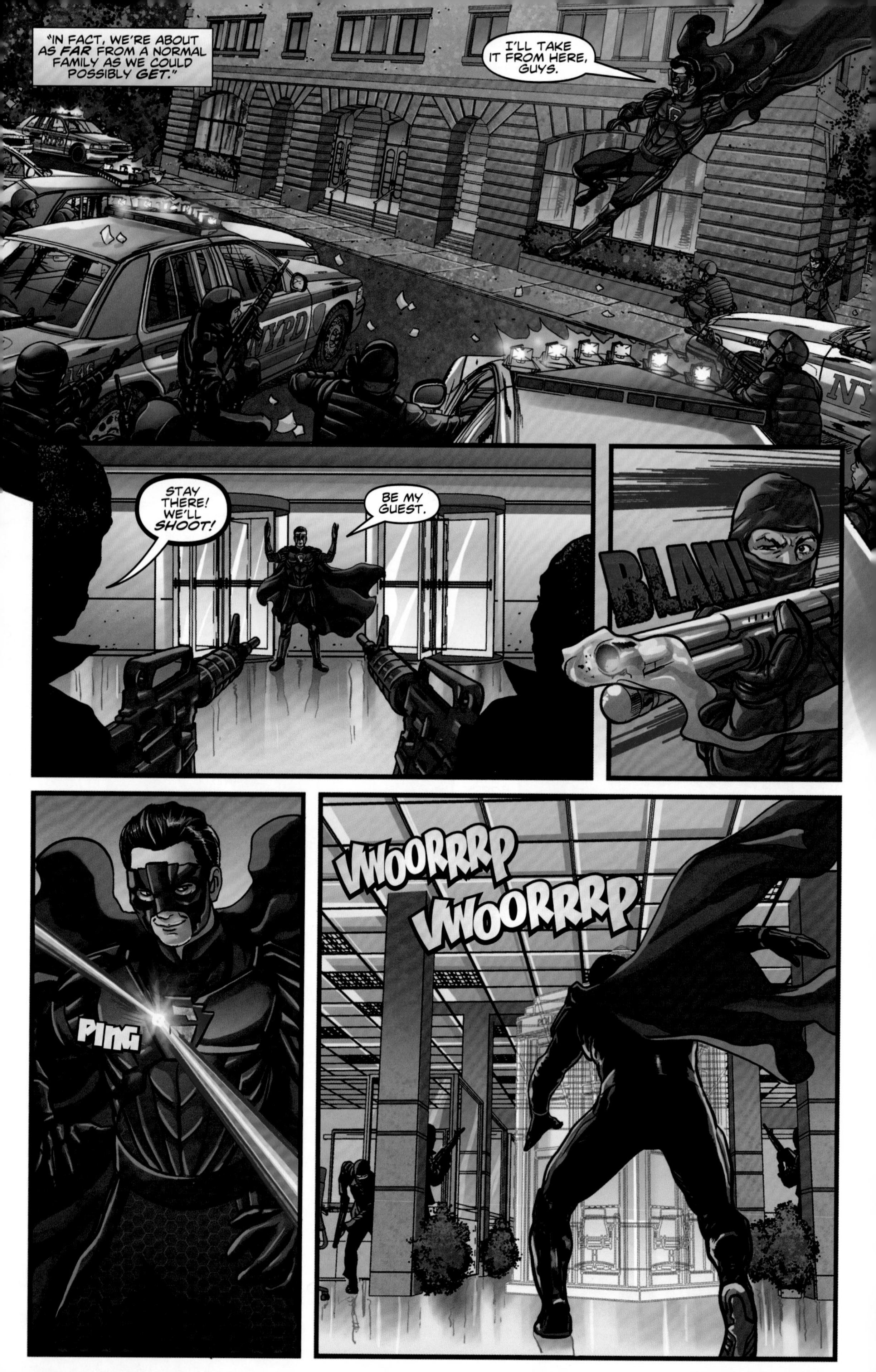
"IN FACT, WE'RE ABOUT AS FAR FROM A NORMAL FAMILY AS WE COULD POSSIBLY GET."
I'LL TAKE IT FROM HERE, GUYS.
NYPD
STAY THERE! WE'LL SHOOT!
BE MY GUEST.
BLAM!
PING
VWOORRRP
VWOORRRP

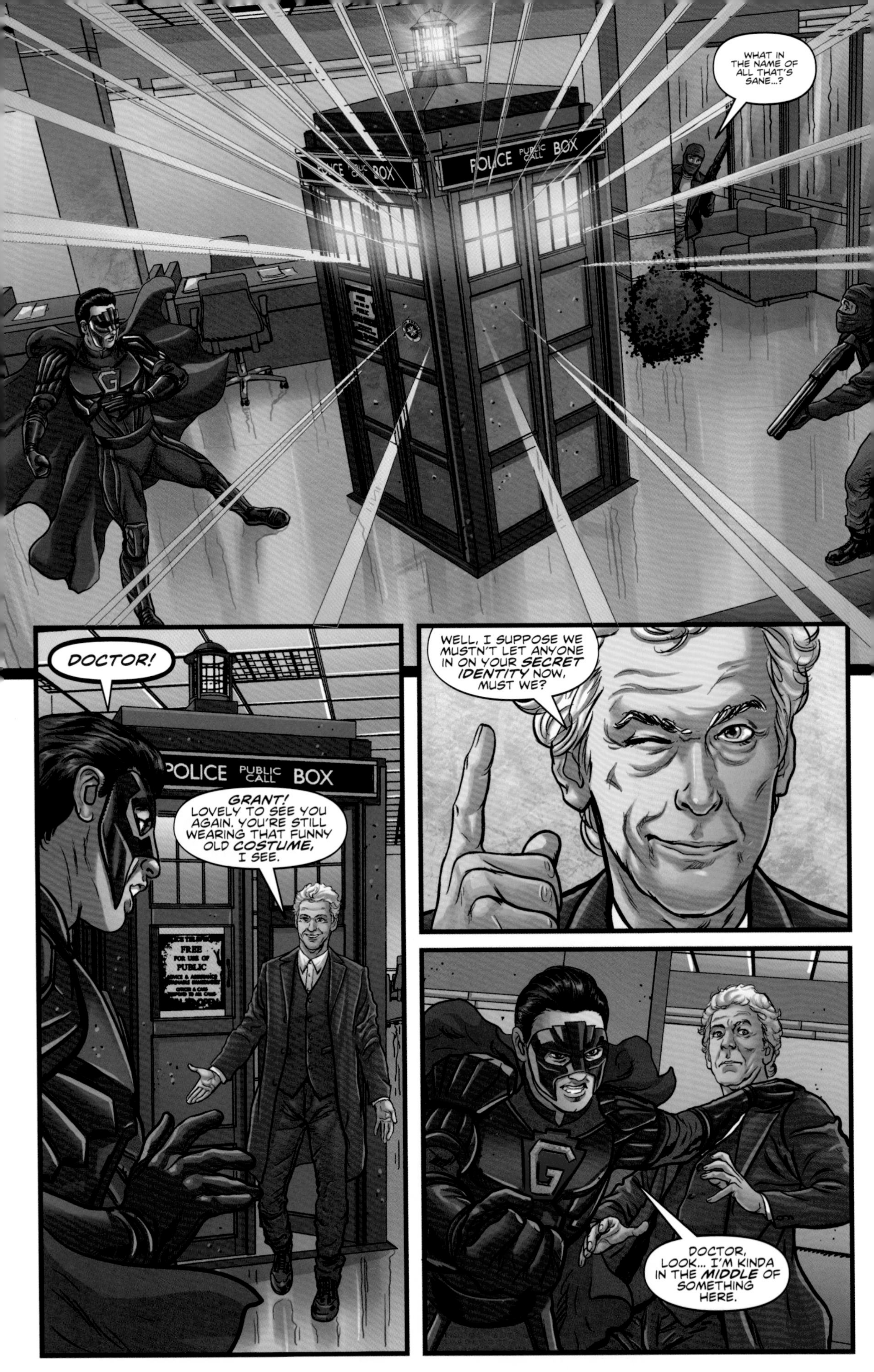

POLICE PUBLIC CALL BOX
WHAT IN THE NAME OF ALL THAT'S SANE...?
DOCTOR!
POLICE PUBLIC CALL BOX
GRANT! LOVELY TO SEE YOU AGAIN. YOU'RE STILL WEARING THAT FUNNY OLD COSTUME, I SEE.
FREE FOR USE OF PUBLIC
WELL, I SUPPOSE WE MUSTN'T LET ANYONE IN ON YOUR SECRET IDENTITY NOW, MUST WE?
DOCTOR, LOOK... I'M KINDA IN THE MIDDLE OF SOMETHING HERE.

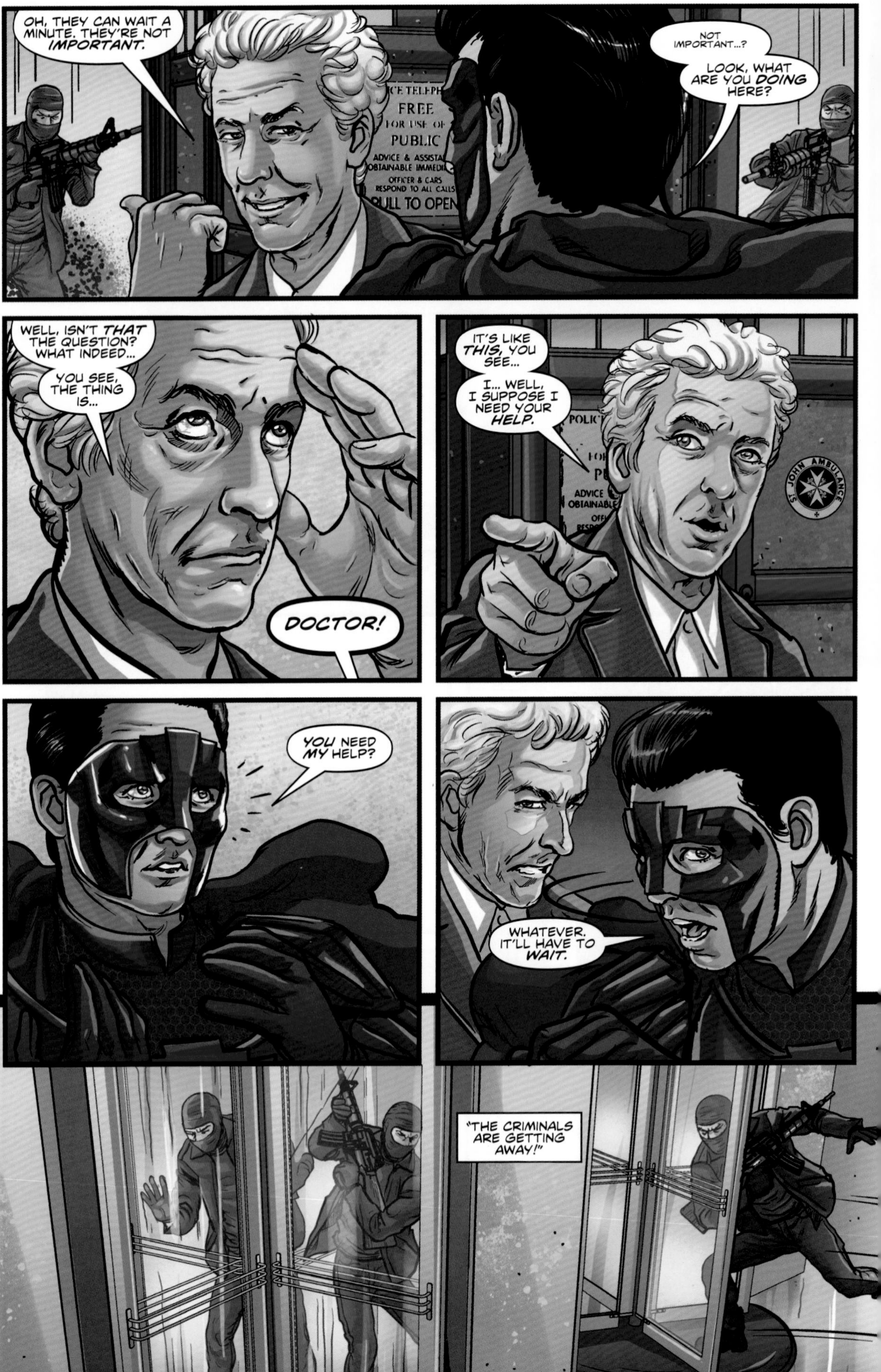
OH, THEY CAN WAIT A MINUTE. THEY'RE NOT IMPORTANT.
FREE FOR USE OF PUBLIC ADVICE & ASSISTA OBTAINABLE IMMEDI OFFICER & CARS RESPOND TO ALL CALLS PULL TO OPEN
NOT IMPORTANT...?
LOOK, WHAT ARE YOU DOING HERE?
WELL, ISN'T THAT THE QUESTION? WHAT INDEED...
YOU SEE, THE THING IS...
DOCTOR!
IT'S LIKE THIS, YOU SEE...
I... WELL, I SUPPOSE I NEED YOUR HELP.
ST. JOHN AMBULANCE
YOU NEED MY HELP?
WHATEVER. IT'LL HAVE TO WAIT.
"THE CRIMINALS ARE GETTING AWAY!"

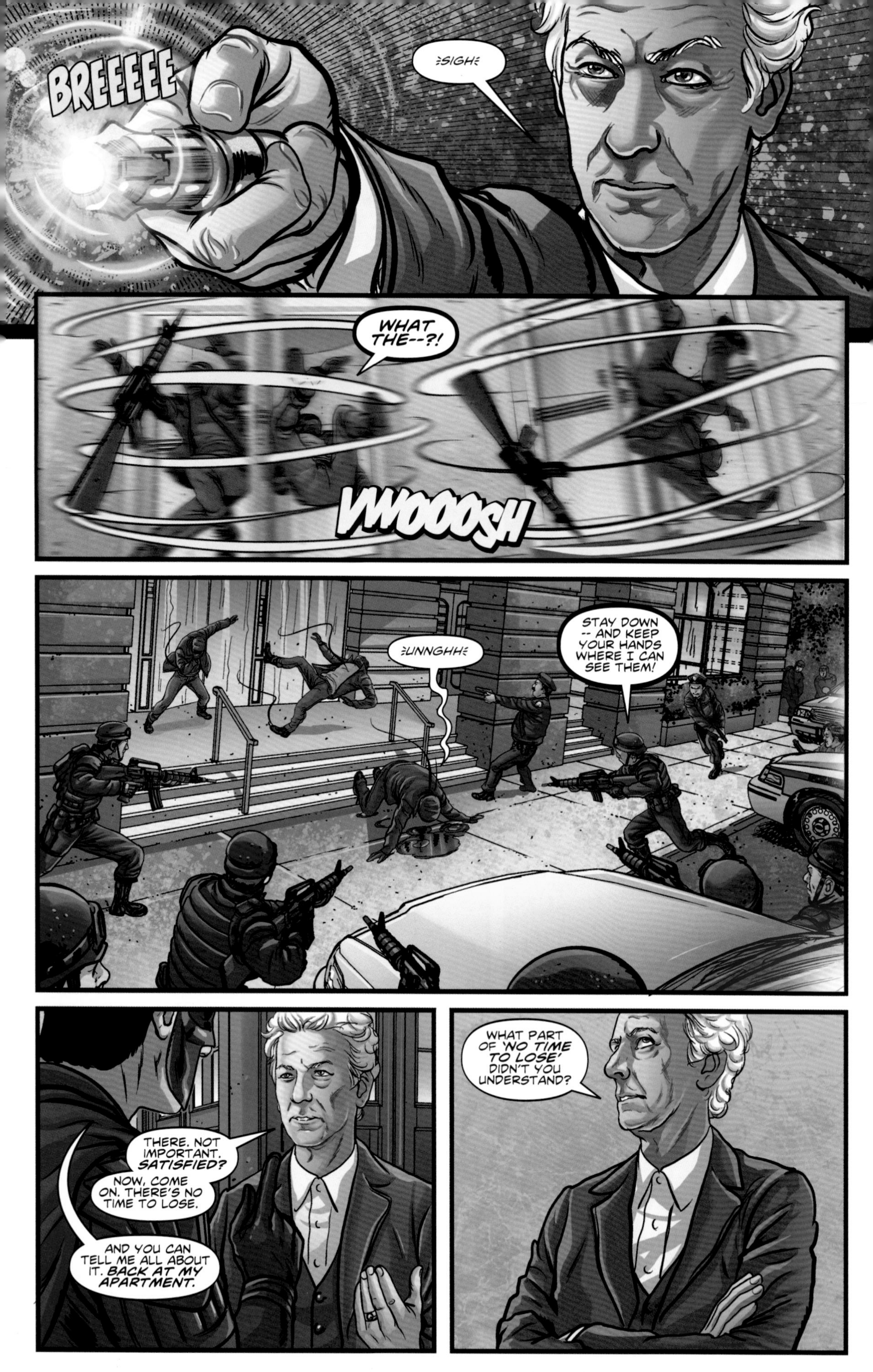
BREEEEE
SIGH
WHAT THE--?!
VWOOOSH
UNNGHH
STAY DOWN -- AND KEEP YOUR HANDS WHERE I CAN SEE THEM!
THERE. NOT IMPORTANT. SATISFIED?
NOW, COME ON. THERE'S NO TIME TO LOSE.
AND YOU CAN TELL ME ALL ABOUT IT. BACK AT MY APARTMENT.
WHAT PART OF 'NO TIME TO LOSE' DIDN'T YOU UNDERSTAND?

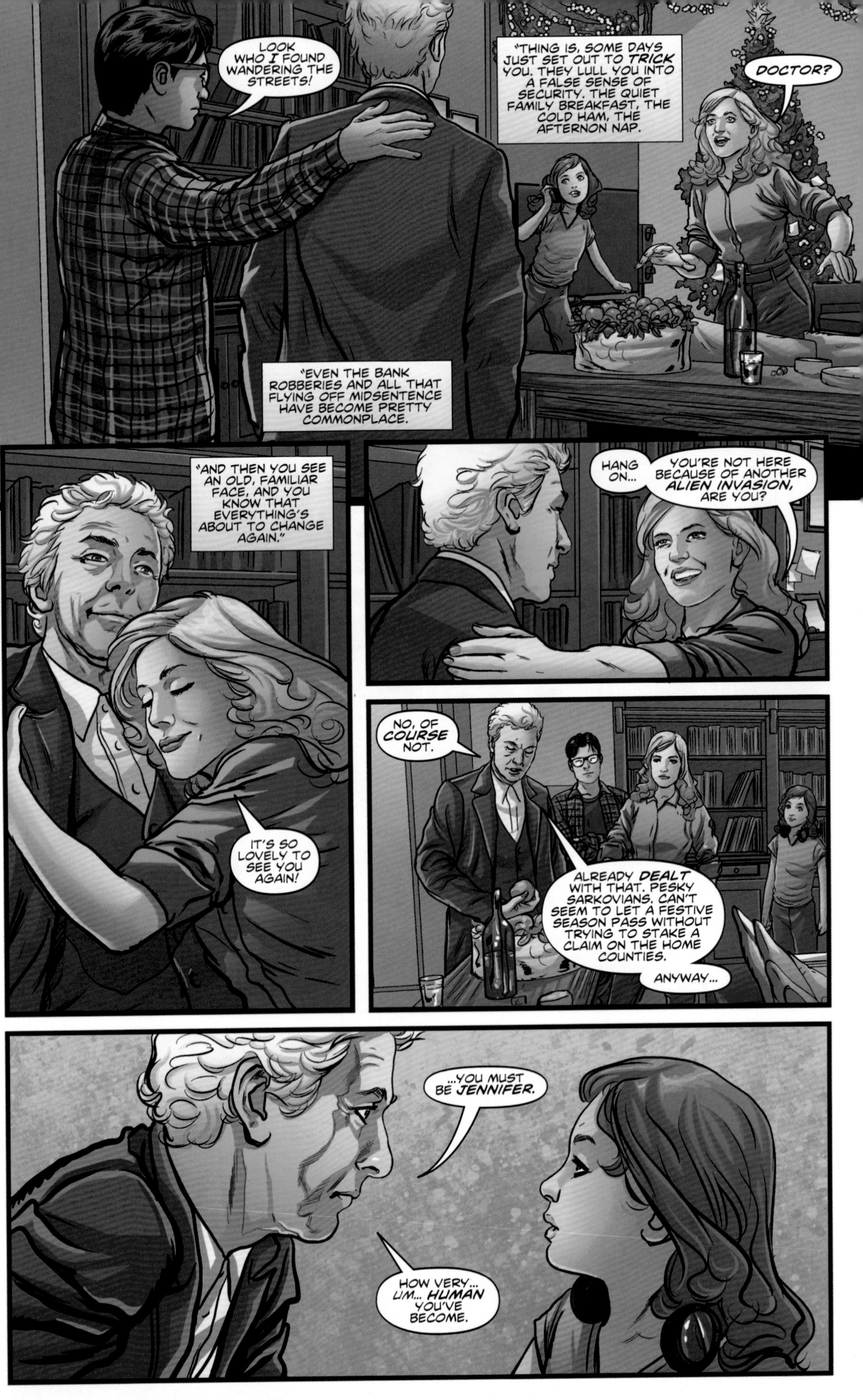
LOOK WHO *I* FOUND WANDERING THE STREETS!
"THING IS, SOME DAYS JUST SET OUT TO *TRICK* YOU. THEY LULL YOU INTO A FALSE SENSE OF SECURITY. THE QUIET FAMILY BREAKFAST, THE COLD HAM, THE AFTERNON NAP.
DOCTOR?
"EVEN THE BANK ROBBERIES AND ALL THAT FLYING OFF MIDSENTENCE HAVE BECOME PRETTY COMMONPLACE.
"AND THEN YOU SEE AN OLD, FAMILIAR FACE, AND YOU KNOW THAT EVERYTHING'S ABOUT TO CHANGE AGAIN."
IT'S SO LOVELY TO SEE YOU AGAIN!
HANG ON...
YOU'RE NOT HERE BECAUSE OF ANOTHER *ALIEN INVASION,* ARE YOU?
NO, OF *COURSE* NOT.
ALREADY *DEALT* WITH THAT. PESKY SARKOVIANS. CAN'T SEEM TO LET A FESTIVE SEASON PASS WITHOUT TRYING TO STAKE A CLAIM ON THE HOME COUNTIES.
ANYWAY...
...YOU MUST BE *JENNIFER.*
HOW VERY... UM... *HUMAN* YOU'VE BECOME.

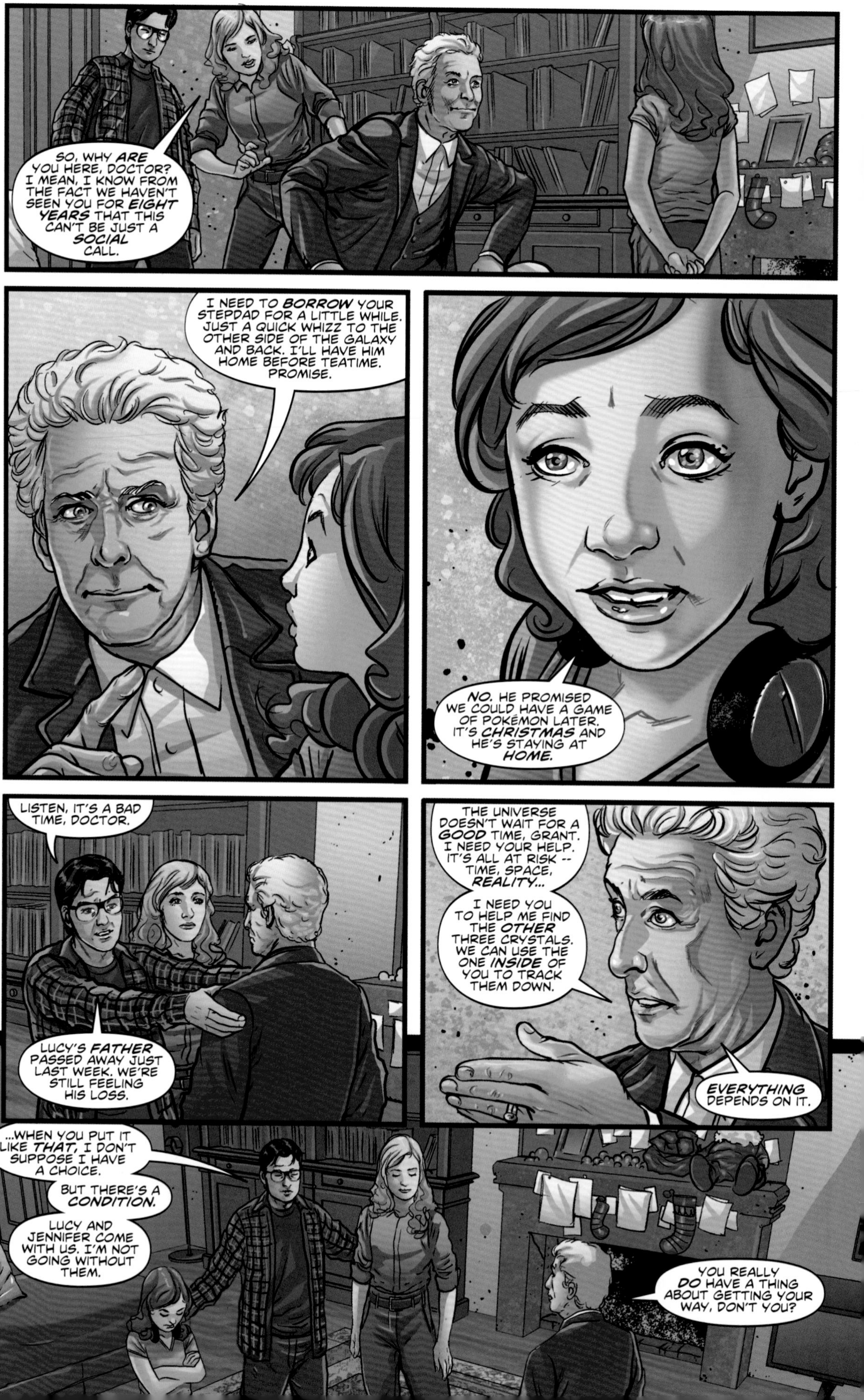
SO, WHY ARE YOU HERE, DOCTOR? I MEAN, I KNOW FROM THE FACT WE HAVEN'T SEEN YOU FOR EIGHT YEARS THAT THIS CAN'T BE JUST A SOCIAL CALL.
I NEED TO BORROW YOUR STEPDAD FOR A LITTLE WHILE. JUST A QUICK WHIZZ TO THE OTHER SIDE OF THE GALAXY AND BACK. I'LL HAVE HIM HOME BEFORE TEATIME. PROMISE.
NO. HE PROMISED WE COULD HAVE A GAME OF POKÉMON LATER. IT'S CHRISTMAS AND HE'S STAYING AT HOME.
LISTEN, IT'S A BAD TIME, DOCTOR.
LUCY'S FATHER PASSED AWAY JUST LAST WEEK. WE'RE STILL FEELING HIS LOSS.
THE UNIVERSE DOESN'T WAIT FOR A GOOD TIME, GRANT. I NEED YOUR HELP. IT'S ALL AT RISK -- TIME, SPACE, REALITY...
I NEED YOU TO HELP ME FIND THE OTHER THREE CRYSTALS. WE CAN USE THE ONE INSIDE OF YOU TO TRACK THEM DOWN.
EVERYTHING DEPENDS ON IT.
...WHEN YOU PUT IT LIKE THAT, I DON'T SUPPOSE I HAVE A CHOICE.
BUT THERE'S A CONDITION.
LUCY AND JENNIFER COME WITH US. I'M NOT GOING WITHOUT THEM.
YOU REALLY DO HAVE A THING ABOUT GETTING YOUR WAY, DON'T YOU?

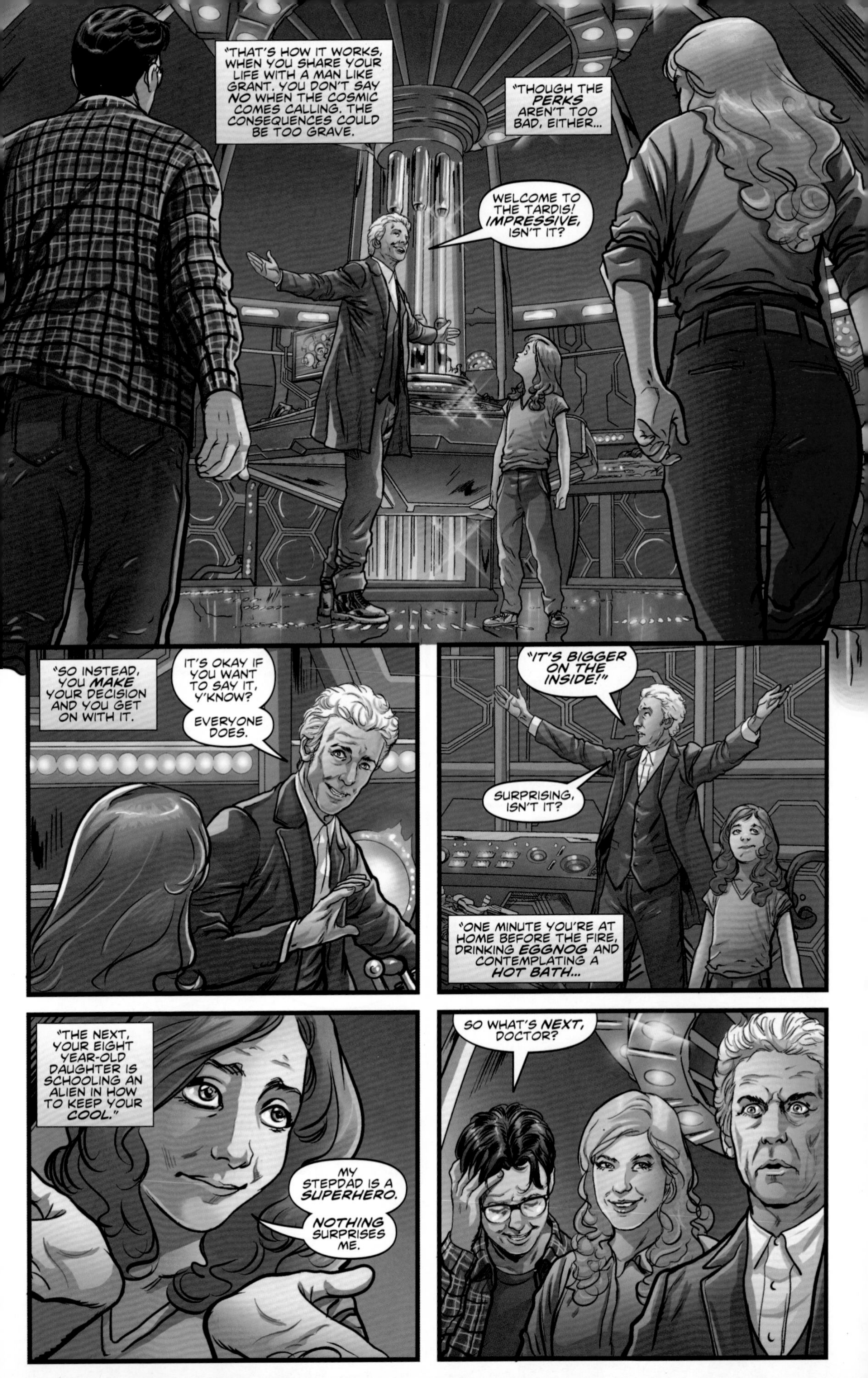
"THAT'S HOW IT WORKS, WHEN YOU SHARE YOUR LIFE WITH A MAN LIKE GRANT. YOU DON'T SAY NO WHEN THE COSMIC COMES CALLING. THE CONSEQUENCES COULD BE TOO GRAVE.
"THOUGH THE PERKS AREN'T TOO BAD, EITHER...
WELCOME TO THE TARDIS! IMPRESSIVE, ISN'T IT?
"SO INSTEAD, YOU MAKE YOUR DECISION AND YOU GET ON WITH IT.
IT'S OKAY IF YOU WANT TO SAY IT, Y'KNOW?
EVERYONE DOES.
"IT'S BIGGER ON THE INSIDE!"
SURPRISING, ISN'T IT?
"ONE MINUTE YOU'RE AT HOME BEFORE THE FIRE, DRINKING EGGNOG AND CONTEMPLATING A HOT BATH...
"THE NEXT, YOUR EIGHT YEAR-OLD DAUGHTER IS SCHOOLING AN ALIEN IN HOW TO KEEP YOUR COOL."
MY STEPDAD IS A SUPERHERO.
NOTHING SURPRISES ME.
SO WHAT'S NEXT, DOCTOR?

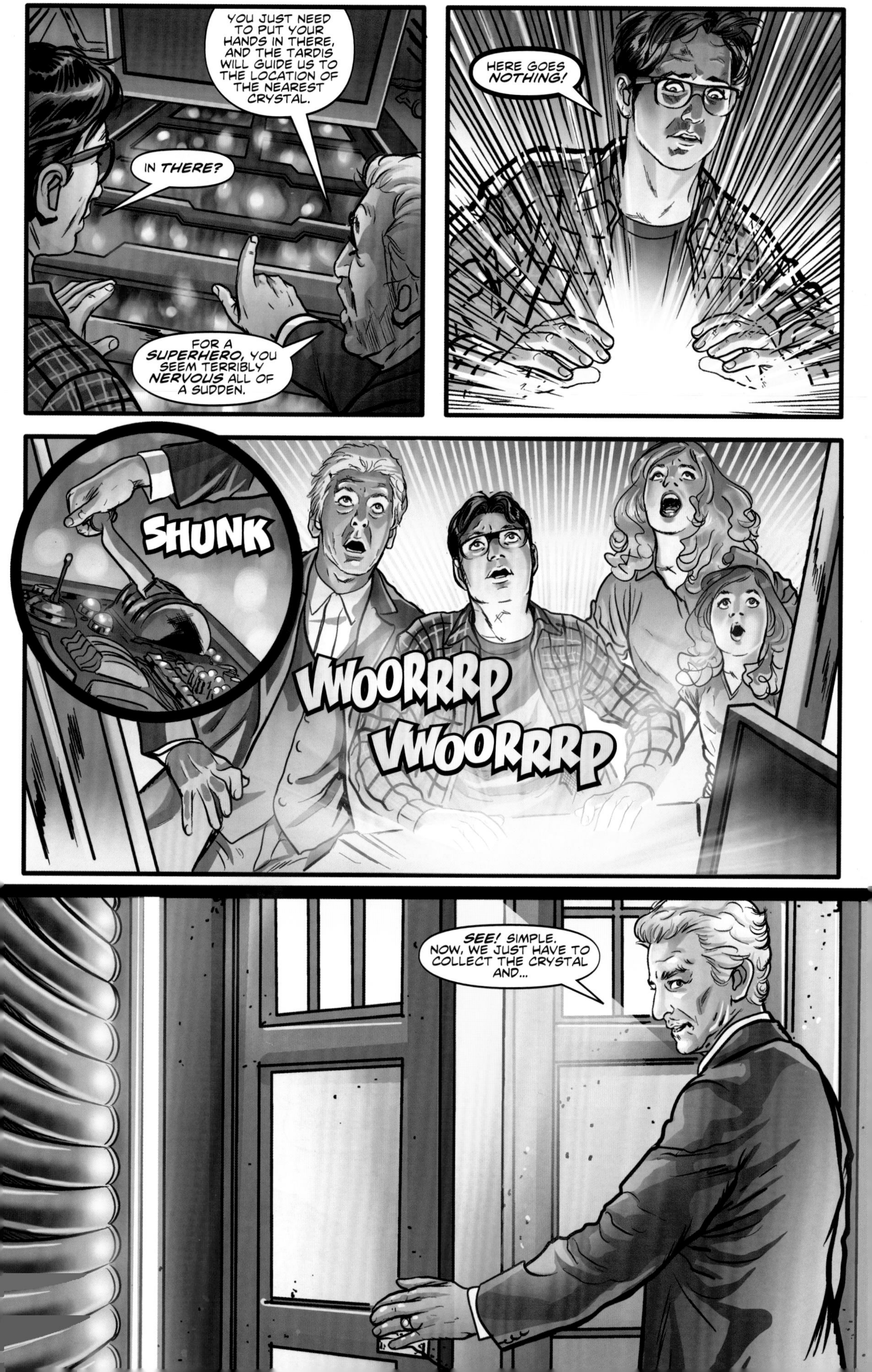

YOU JUST NEED TO PUT YOUR HANDS IN THERE, AND THE TARDIS WILL GUIDE US TO THE LOCATION OF THE NEAREST CRYSTAL.
IN THERE?
FOR A SUPERHERO, YOU SEEM TERRIBLY NERVOUS ALL OF A SUDDEN.
HERE GOES NOTHING!
SHUNK
VWOORRRP
VWOORRRP
SEE! SIMPLE. NOW, WE JUST HAVE TO COLLECT THE CRYSTAL AND...

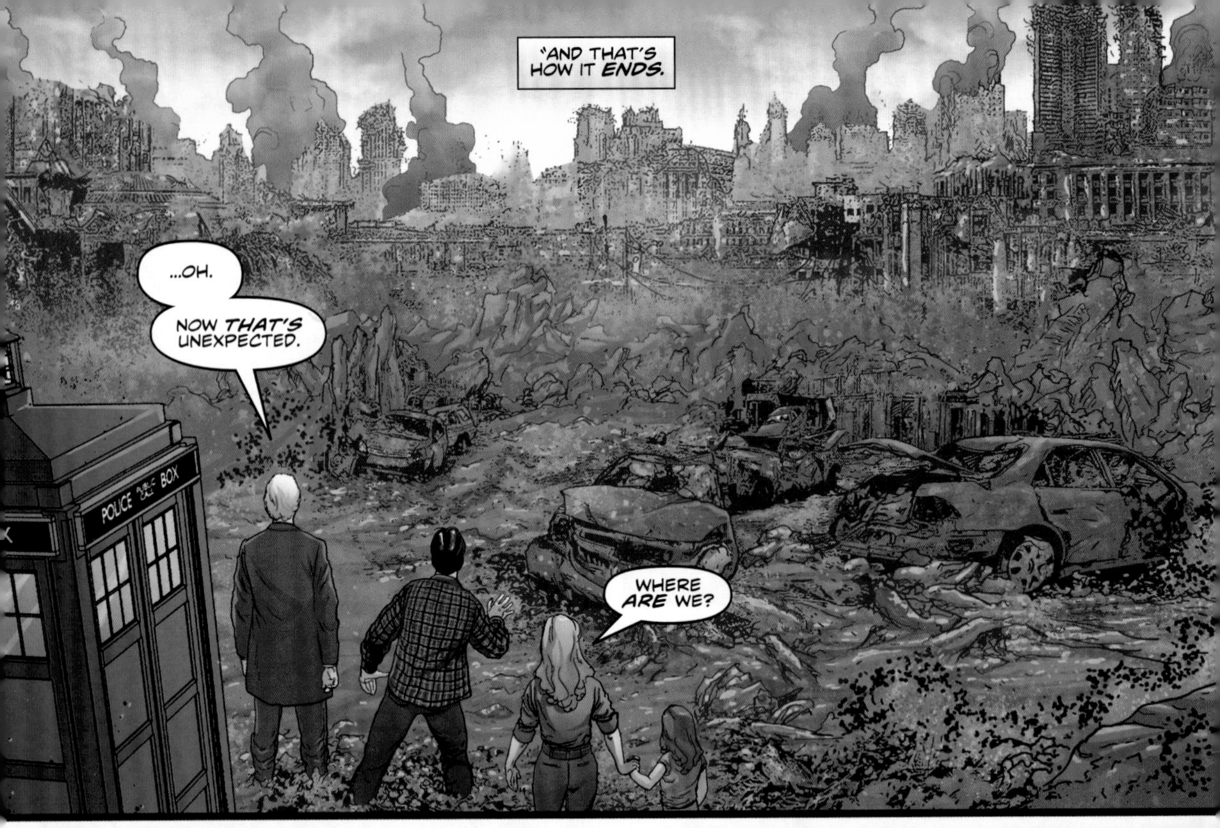
"AND THAT'S HOW IT ENDS.
...OH.
NOW THAT'S UNEXPECTED.
WHERE ARE WE?

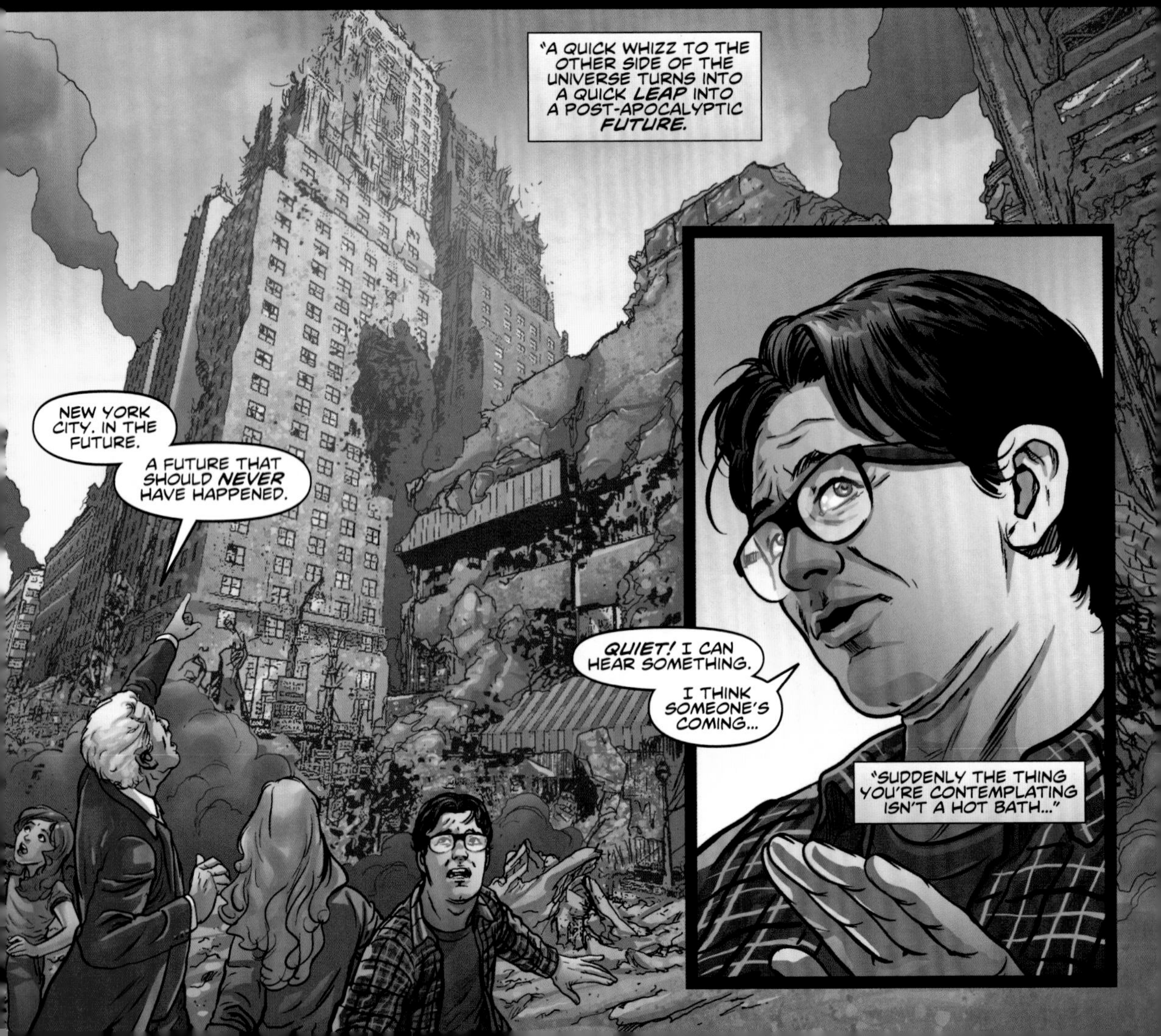
"A QUICK WHIZZ TO THE OTHER SIDE OF THE UNIVERSE TURNS INTO A QUICK LEAP INTO A POST-APOCALYPTIC FUTURE.
NEW YORK CITY. IN THE FUTURE.
A FUTURE THAT SHOULD NEVER HAVE HAPPENED.
QUIET! I CAN HEAR SOMETHING.
I THINK SOMEONE'S COMING...
"SUDDENLY THE THING YOU'RE CONTEMPLATING ISN'T A HOT BATH..."

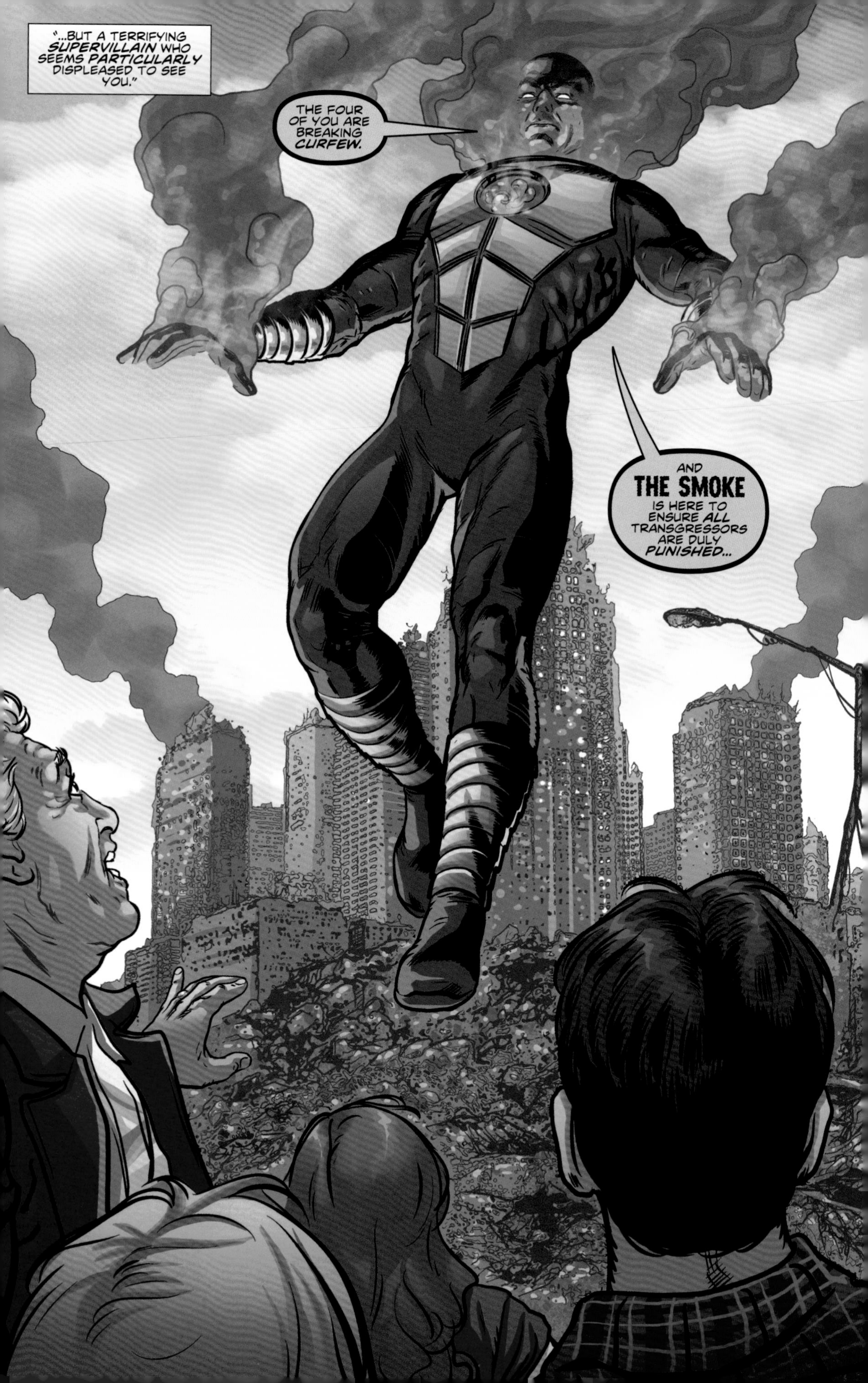
"...BUT A TERRIFYING SUPERVILLAIN WHO SEEMS PARTICULARLY DISPLEASED TO SEE YOU."
THE FOUR OF YOU ARE BREAKING CURFEW.
AND THE SMOKE IS HERE TO ENSURE ALL TRANSGRESSORS ARE DULY PUNISHED...

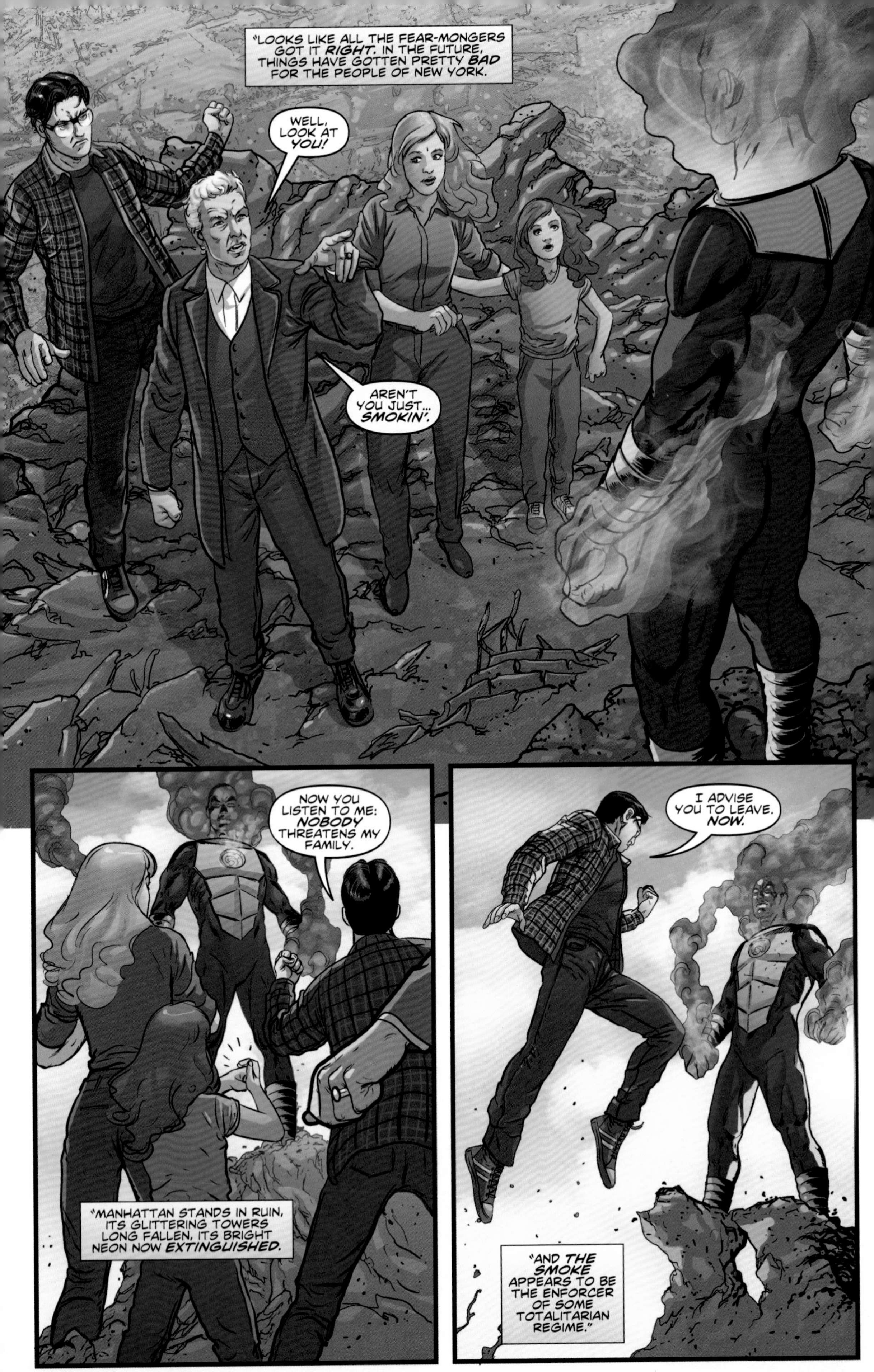
"LOOKS LIKE ALL THE FEAR-MONGERS GOT IT RIGHT. IN THE FUTURE, THINGS HAVE GOTTEN PRETTY BAD FOR THE PEOPLE OF NEW YORK.
WELL, LOOK AT YOU!
AREN'T YOU JUST... SMOKIN'.
NOW YOU LISTEN TO ME: NOBODY THREATENS MY FAMILY.
"MANHATTAN STANDS IN RUIN, ITS GLITTERING TOWERS LONG FALLEN, ITS BRIGHT NEON NOW EXTINGUISHED.
I ADVISE YOU TO LEAVE. NOW.
"AND THE SMOKE APPEARS TO BE THE ENFORCER OF SOME TOTALITARIAN REGIME."

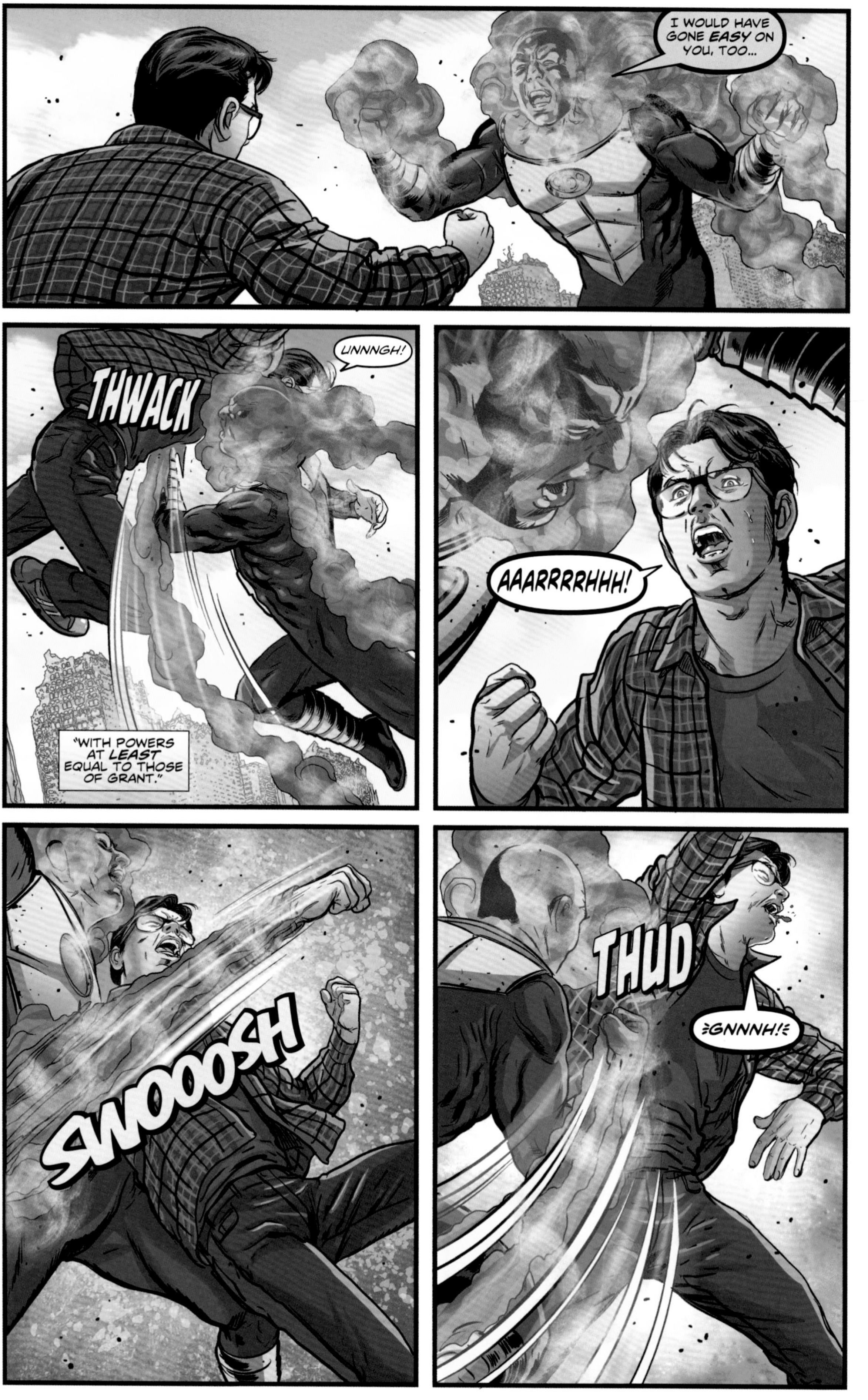
I WOULD HAVE GONE EASY ON YOU, TOO...
THWACK
UNNNGH!
"WITH POWERS AT LEAST EQUAL TO THOSE OF GRANT."
AAARRRRHHH!
SWOOOSH
THUD
GNNNH!

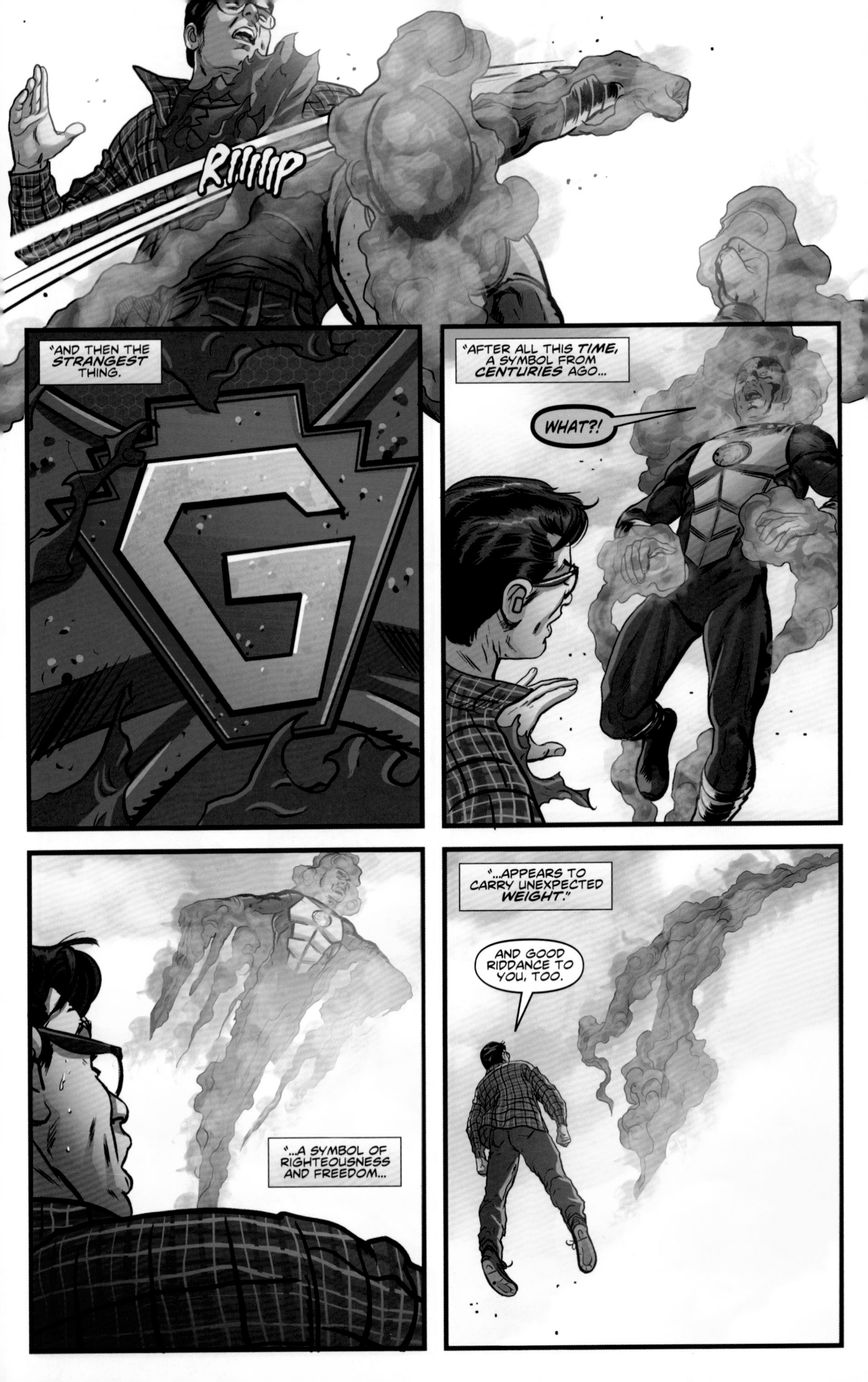
RIIIIP
"AND THEN THE STRANGEST THING.
"AFTER ALL THIS TIME, A SYMBOL FROM CENTURIES AGO...
WHAT?!
"...A SYMBOL OF RIGHTEOUSNESS AND FREEDOM...
"...APPEARS TO CARRY UNEXPECTED WEIGHT."
AND GOOD RIDDANCE TO YOU, TOO.

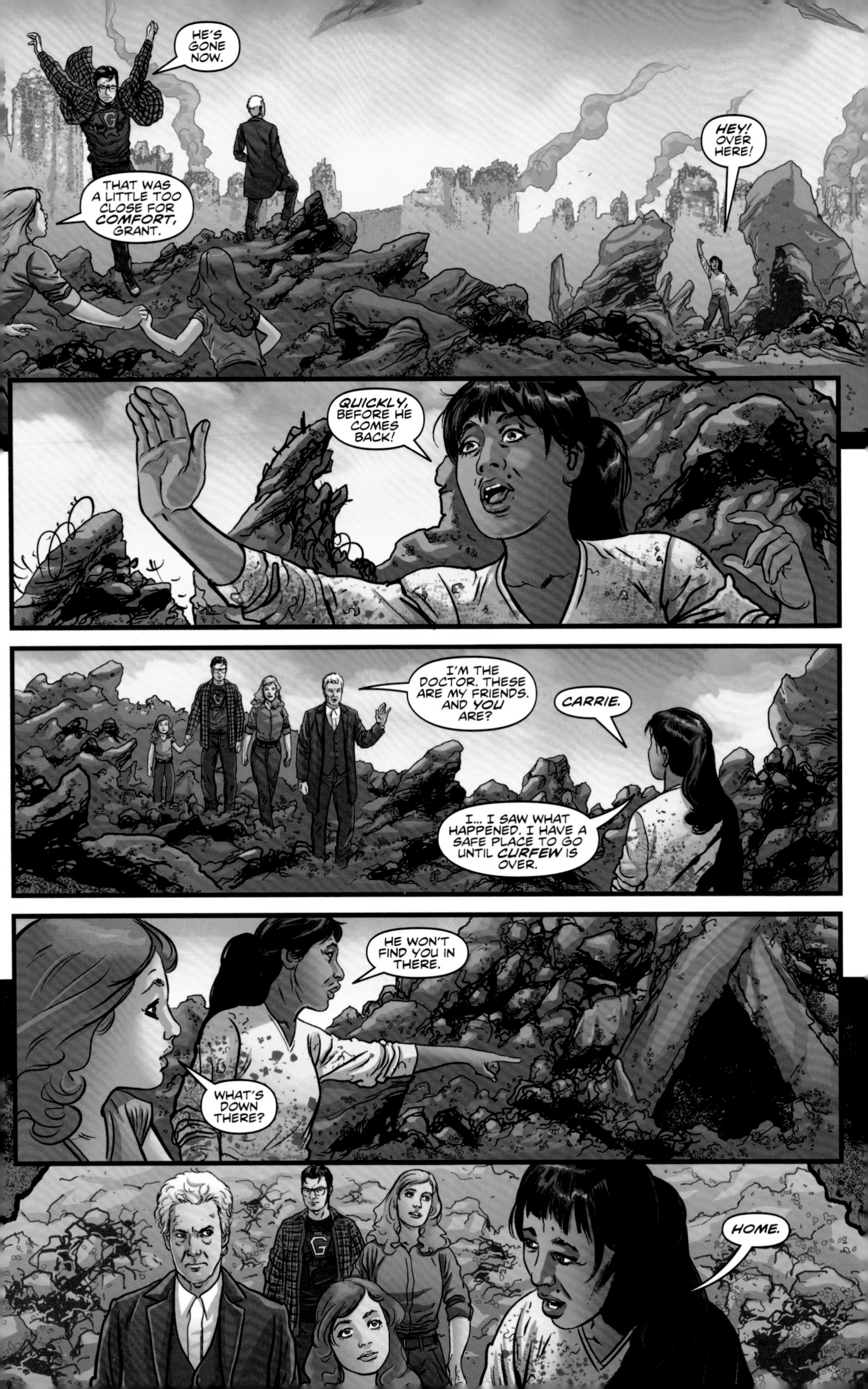
HE'S GONE NOW.
THAT WAS A LITTLE TOO CLOSE FOR COMFORT, GRANT.
HEY! OVER HERE!
QUICKLY, BEFORE HE COMES BACK!
I'M THE DOCTOR. THESE ARE MY FRIENDS. AND YOU ARE?
CARRIE.
I... I SAW WHAT HAPPENED. I HAVE A SAFE PLACE TO GO UNTIL CURFEW IS OVER.
HE WON'T FIND YOU IN THERE.
WHAT'S DOWN THERE?
HOME.

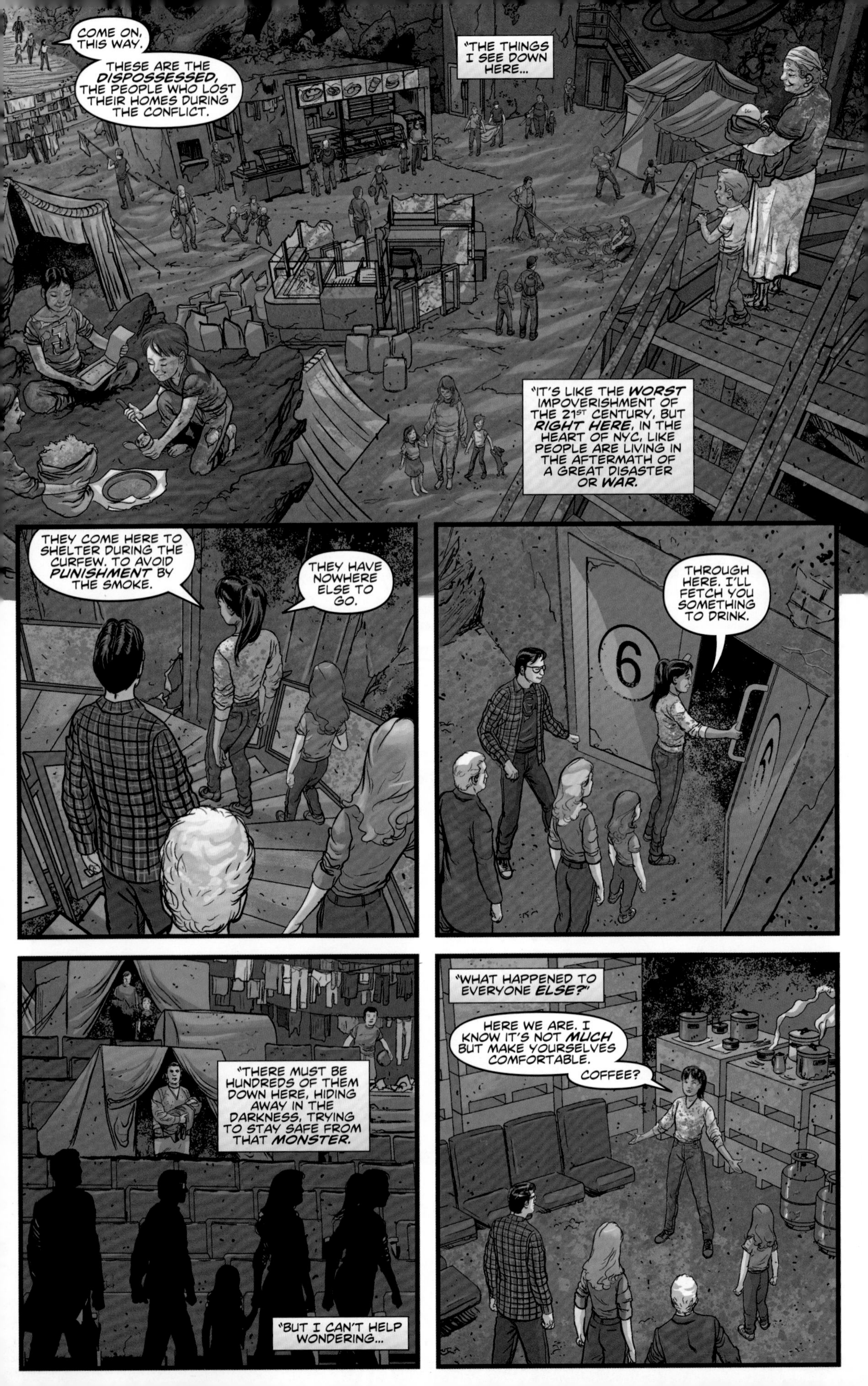
COME ON, THIS WAY.
THESE ARE THE DISPOSSESSED, THE PEOPLE WHO LOST THEIR HOMES DURING THE CONFLICT.
"THE THINGS I SEE DOWN HERE...
"IT'S LIKE THE WORST IMPOVERISHMENT OF THE 21ST CENTURY, BUT RIGHT HERE, IN THE HEART OF NYC, LIKE PEOPLE ARE LIVING IN THE AFTERMATH OF A GREAT DISASTER OR WAR.
THEY COME HERE TO SHELTER DURING THE CURFEW. TO AVOID PUNISHMENT BY THE SMOKE.
THEY HAVE NOWHERE ELSE TO GO.
THROUGH HERE. I'LL FETCH YOU SOMETHING TO DRINK.
"THERE MUST BE HUNDREDS OF THEM DOWN HERE, HIDING AWAY IN THE DARKNESS, TRYING TO STAY SAFE FROM THAT MONSTER.
"BUT I CAN'T HELP WONDERING...
"WHAT HAPPENED TO EVERYONE ELSE?"
HERE WE ARE. I KNOW IT'S NOT MUCH BUT MAKE YOURSELVES COMFORTABLE.
COFFEE?

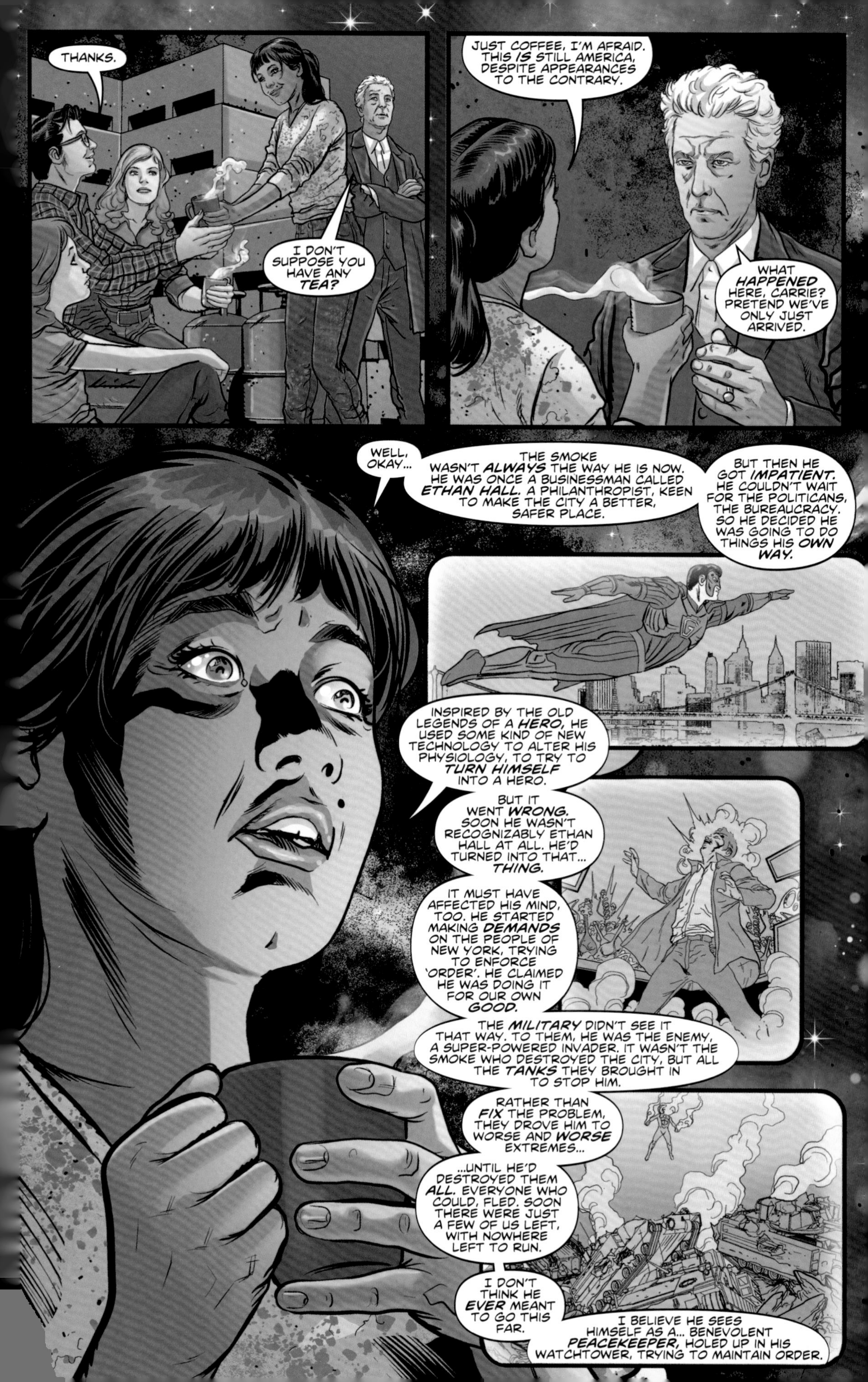
THANKS.
I DON'T SUPPOSE YOU HAVE ANY TEA?
JUST COFFEE, I'M AFRAID. THIS IS STILL AMERICA, DESPITE APPEARANCES TO THE CONTRARY.
WHAT HAPPENED HERE, CARRIE? PRETEND WE'VE ONLY JUST ARRIVED.
WELL, OKAY...
THE SMOKE WASN'T ALWAYS THE WAY HE IS NOW. HE WAS ONCE A BUSINESSMAN CALLED ETHAN HALL. A PHILANTHROPIST, KEEN TO MAKE THE CITY A BETTER, SAFER PLACE.
BUT THEN HE GOT IMPATIENT. HE COULDN'T WAIT FOR THE POLITICANS, THE BUREAUCRACY. SO HE DECIDED HE WAS GOING TO DO THINGS HIS OWN WAY.
INSPIRED BY THE OLD LEGENDS OF A HERO, HE USED SOME KIND OF NEW TECHNOLOGY TO ALTER HIS PHYSIOLOGY, TO TRY TO TURN HIMSELF INTO A HERO.
BUT IT WENT WRONG. SOON HE WASN'T RECOGNIZABLY ETHAN HALL AT ALL. HE'D TURNED INTO THAT... THING.
IT MUST HAVE AFFECTED HIS MIND, TOO. HE STARTED MAKING DEMANDS ON THE PEOPLE OF NEW YORK, TRYING TO ENFORCE 'ORDER'. HE CLAIMED HE WAS DOING IT FOR OUR OWN GOOD.
THE MILITARY DIDN'T SEE IT THAT WAY. TO THEM, HE WAS THE ENEMY, A SUPER-POWERED INVADER. IT WASN'T THE SMOKE WHO DESTROYED THE CITY, BUT ALL THE TANKS THEY BROUGHT IN TO STOP HIM.
RATHER THAN FIX THE PROBLEM, THEY DROVE HIM TO WORSE AND WORSE EXTREMES...
...UNTIL HE'D DESTROYED THEM ALL. EVERYONE WHO COULD, FLED. SOON THERE WERE JUST A FEW OF US LEFT, WITH NOWHERE LEFT TO RUN.
I DON'T THINK HE EVER MEANT TO GO THIS FAR.
I BELIEVE HE SEES HIMSELF AS A... BENEVOLENT PEACEKEEPER, HOLED UP IN HIS WATCHTOWER, TRYING TO MAINTAIN ORDER.

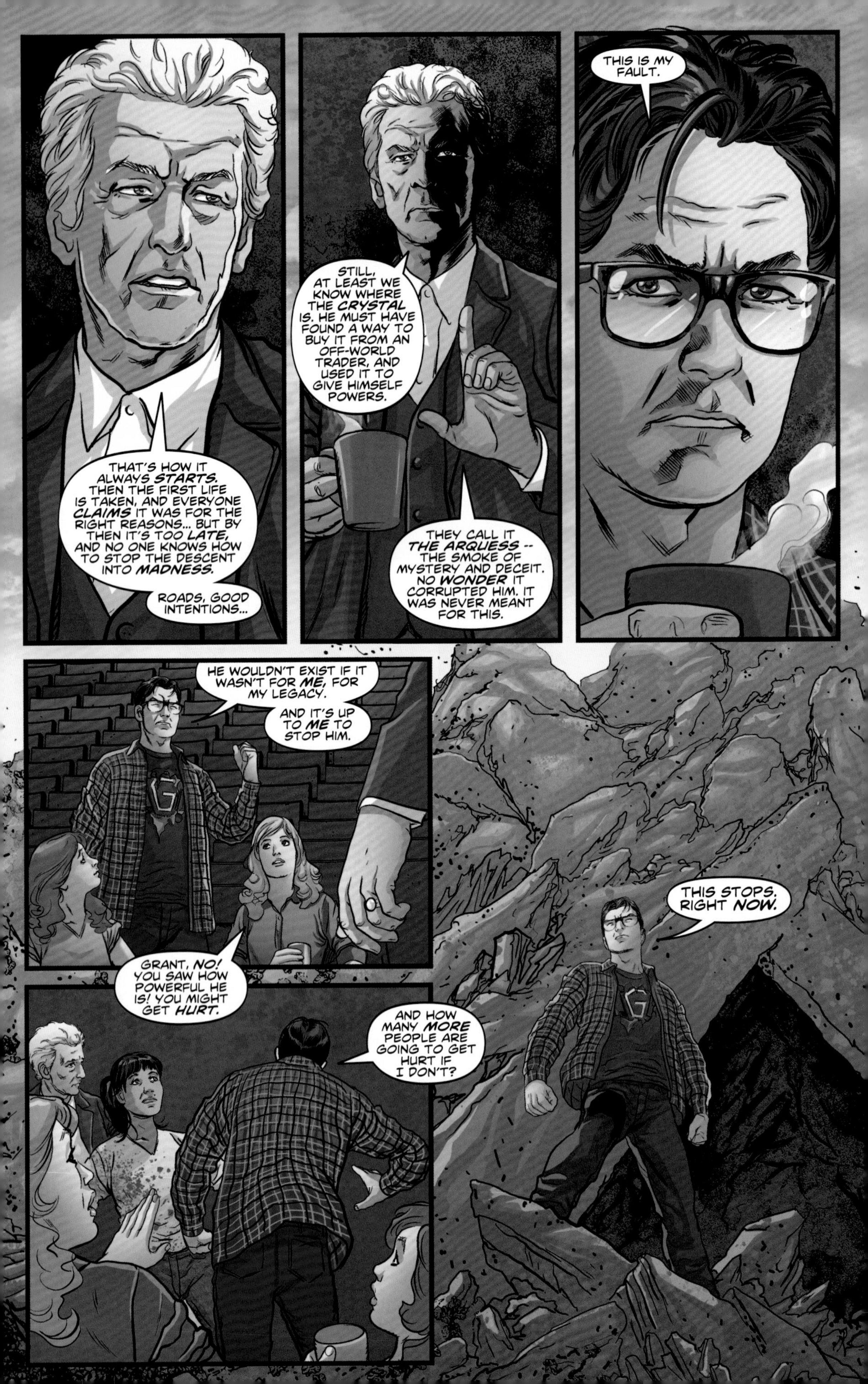
THAT'S HOW IT ALWAYS STARTS. THEN THE FIRST LIFE IS TAKEN, AND EVERYONE CLAIMS IT WAS FOR THE RIGHT REASONS... BUT BY THEN IT'S TOO LATE, AND NO ONE KNOWS HOW TO STOP THE DESCENT INTO MADNESS.
ROADS, GOOD INTENTIONS...
STILL, AT LEAST WE KNOW WHERE THE CRYSTAL IS. HE MUST HAVE FOUND A WAY TO BUY IT FROM AN OFF-WORLD TRADER, AND USED IT TO GIVE HIMSELF POWERS.
THEY CALL IT THE ARQUESS -- THE SMOKE OF MYSTERY AND DECEIT. NO WONDER IT CORRUPTED HIM. IT WAS NEVER MEANT FOR THIS.
THIS IS MY FAULT.
HE WOULDN'T EXIST IF IT WASN'T FOR ME, FOR MY LEGACY.
AND IT'S UP TO ME TO STOP HIM.
GRANT, NO! YOU SAW HOW POWERFUL HE IS! YOU MIGHT GET HURT.
AND HOW MANY MORE PEOPLE ARE GOING TO GET HURT IF I DON'T?
THIS STOPS. RIGHT NOW.

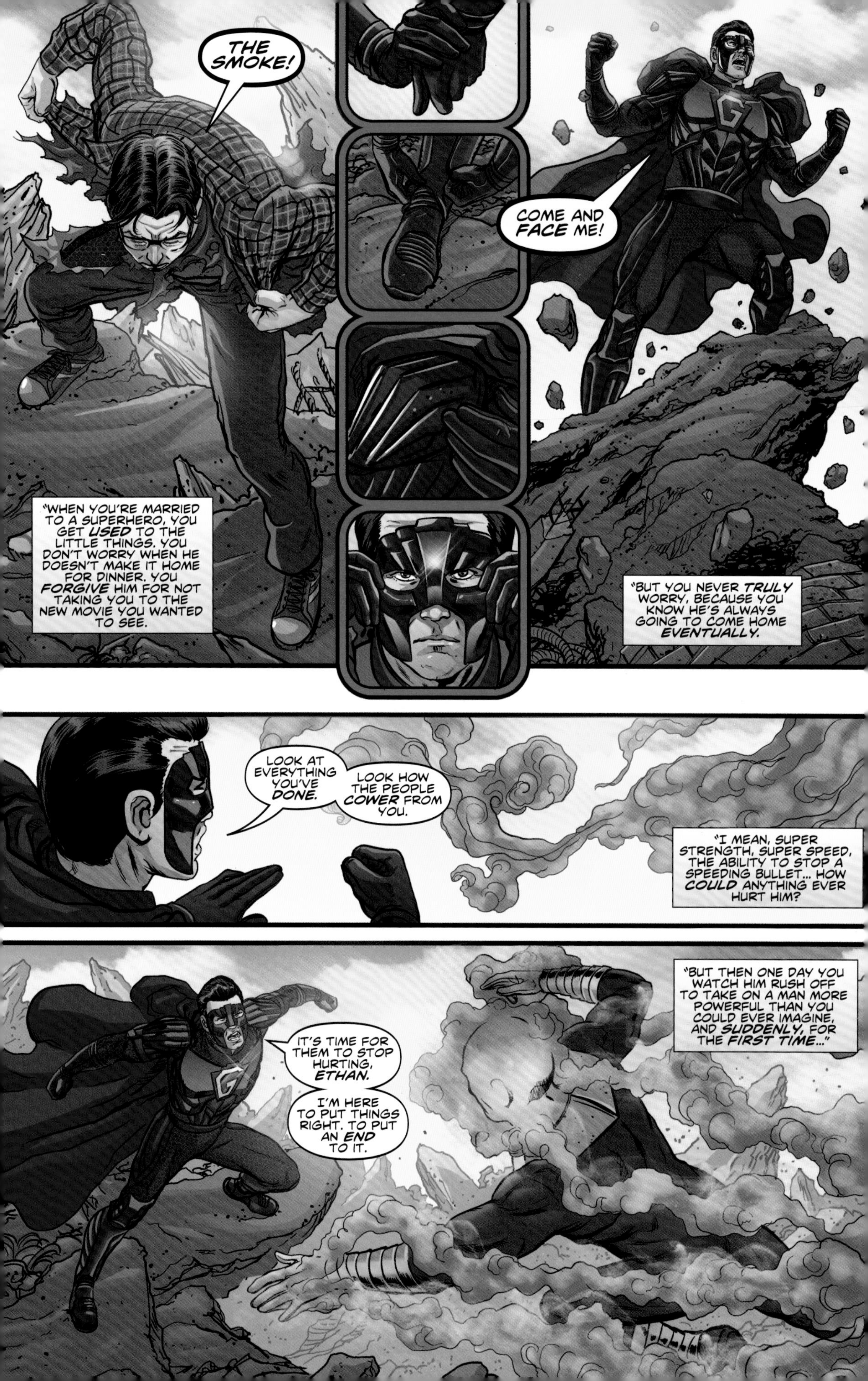
THE SMOKE!
"WHEN YOU'RE MARRIED TO A SUPERHERO, YOU GET USED TO THE LITTLE THINGS. YOU DON'T WORRY WHEN HE DOESN'T MAKE IT HOME FOR DINNER. YOU FORGIVE HIM FOR NOT TAKING YOU TO THE NEW MOVIE YOU WANTED TO SEE.
COME AND FACE ME!
"BUT YOU NEVER TRULY WORRY, BECAUSE YOU KNOW HE'S ALWAYS GOING TO COME HOME EVENTUALLY.
LOOK AT EVERYTHING YOU'VE DONE.
LOOK HOW THE PEOPLE COWER FROM YOU.
"I MEAN, SUPER STRENGTH, SUPER SPEED, THE ABILITY TO STOP A SPEEDING BULLET... HOW COULD ANYTHING EVER HURT HIM?
"BUT THEN ONE DAY YOU WATCH HIM RUSH OFF TO TAKE ON A MAN MORE POWERFUL THAN YOU COULD EVER IMAGINE, AND SUDDENLY, FOR THE FIRST TIME..."
IT'S TIME FOR THEM TO STOP HURTING, ETHAN.
I'M HERE TO PUT THINGS RIGHT. TO PUT AN END TO IT.

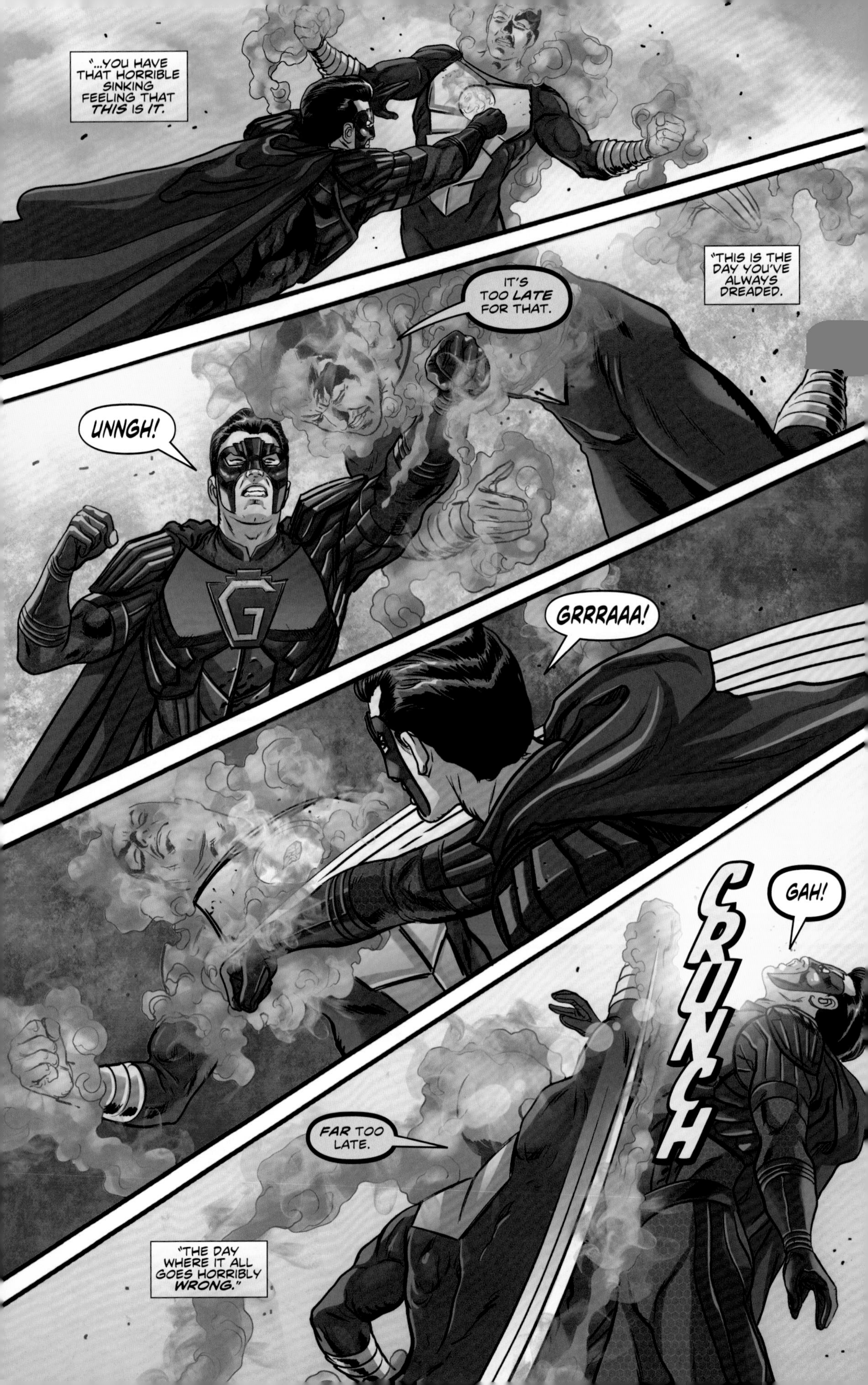
"...YOU HAVE THAT HORRIBLE SINKING FEELING THAT THIS IS IT.
"THIS IS THE DAY YOU'VE ALWAYS DREADED.
IT'S TOO LATE FOR THAT.
UNNGH!
GRRRAAA!
CRUNCH
GAH!
FAR TOO LATE.
"THE DAY WHERE IT ALL GOES HORRIBLY WRONG."

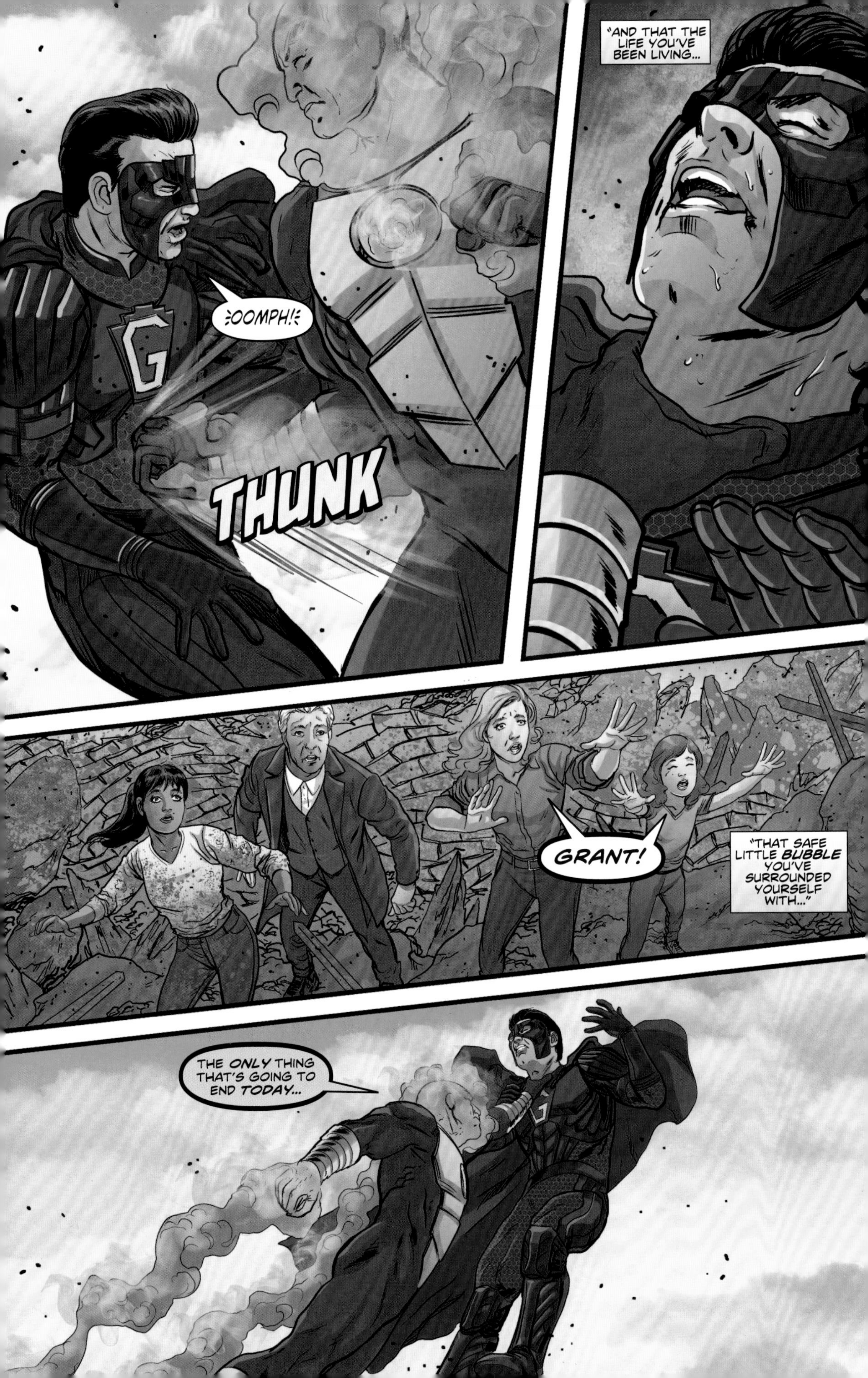
OOMPH!
THUNK
"AND THAT THE LIFE YOU'VE BEEN LIVING...
GRANT!
"THAT SAFE LITTLE BUBBLE YOU'VE SURROUNDED YOURSELF WITH..."
THE ONLY THING THAT'S GOING TO END TODAY...

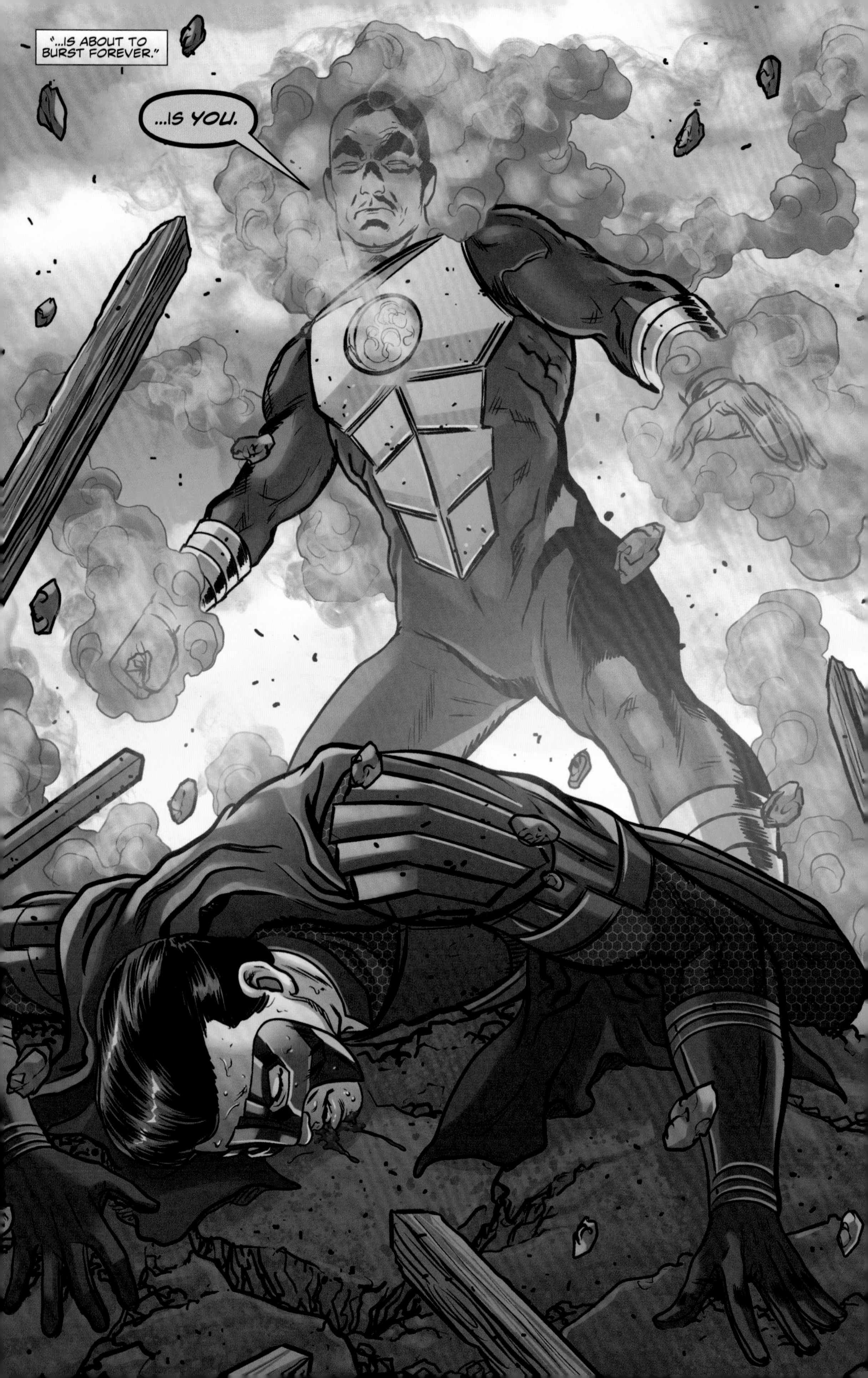
"...IS ABOUT TO BURST FOREVER."
...IS YOU.

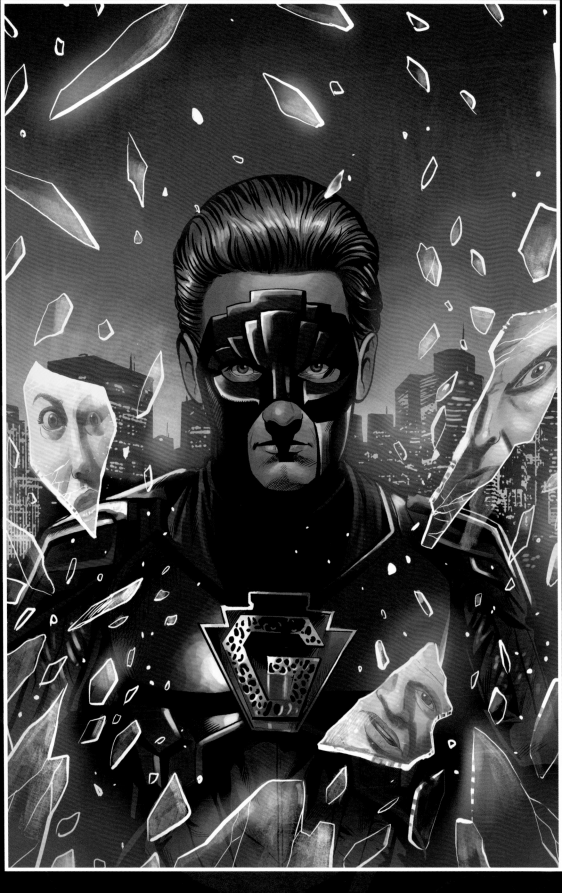

#1 Cover A: MARIANO LACLAUSTRA

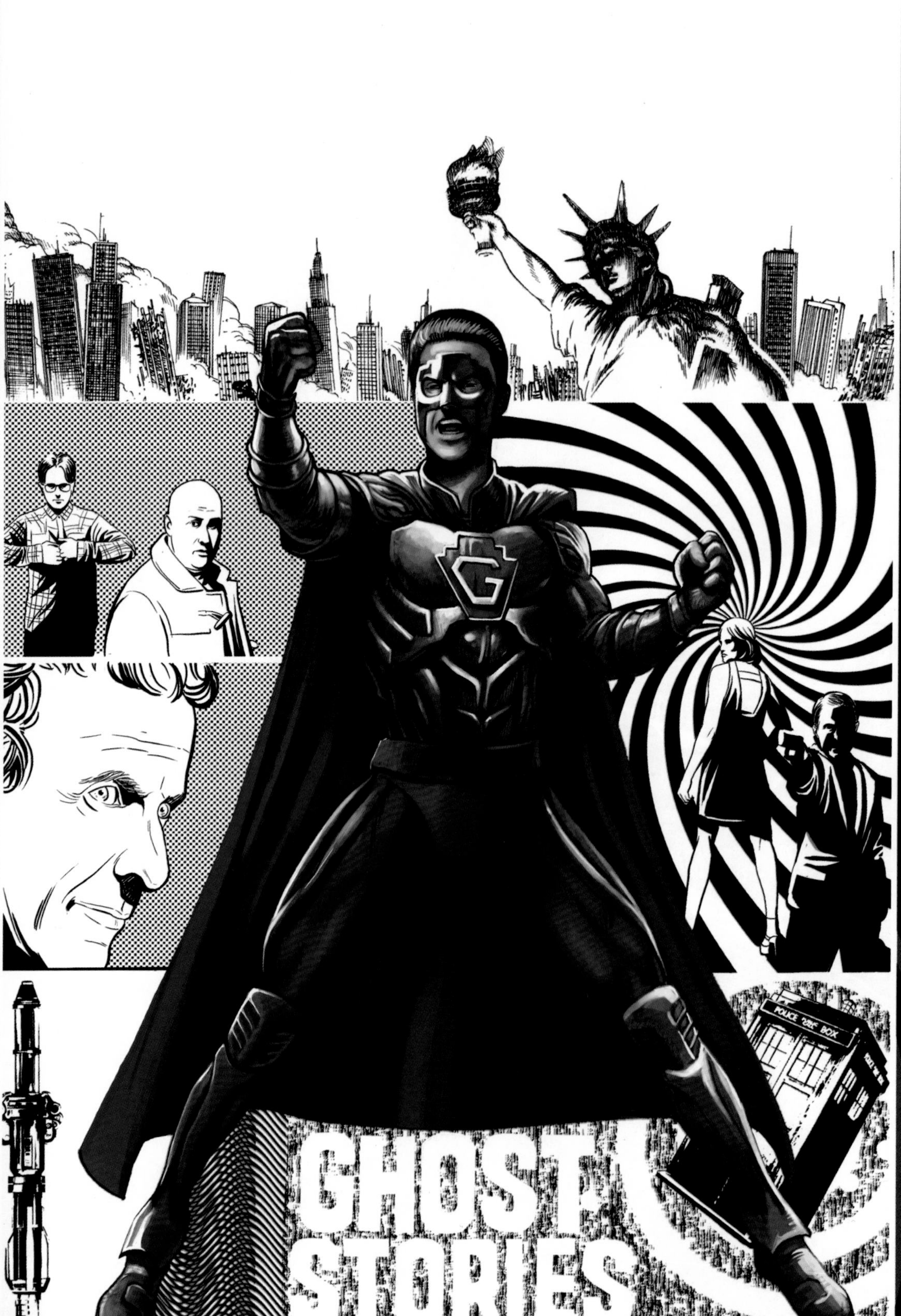
POLICE BOX
GHOST STORIES
BRITO-LACLAUSTRA

#2 Cover A: MARIANO LACLAUSTRA & PIER BRITO

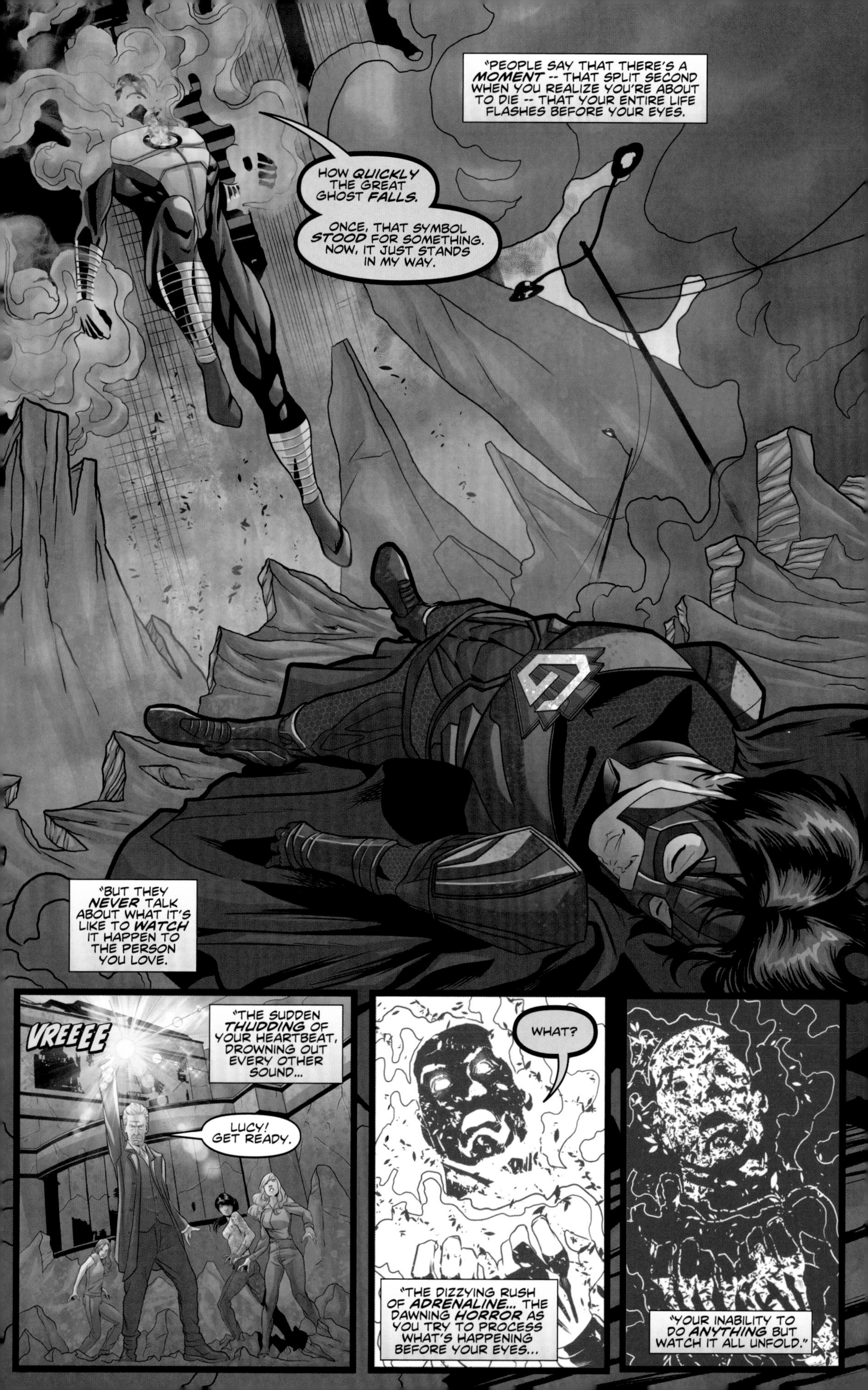
"PEOPLE SAY THAT THERE'S A MOMENT -- THAT SPLIT SECOND WHEN YOU REALIZE YOU'RE ABOUT TO DIE -- THAT YOUR ENTIRE LIFE FLASHES BEFORE YOUR EYES.
HOW QUICKLY THE GREAT GHOST FALLS.
ONCE, THAT SYMBOL STOOD FOR SOMETHING. NOW, IT JUST STANDS IN MY WAY.
"BUT THEY NEVER TALK ABOUT WHAT IT'S LIKE TO WATCH IT HAPPEN TO THE PERSON YOU LOVE.
VREEEE
"THE SUDDEN THUDDING OF YOUR HEARTBEAT, DROWNING OUT EVERY OTHER SOUND...
LUCY! GET READY.
WHAT?
"THE DIZZYING RUSH OF ADRENALINE... THE DAWNING HORROR AS YOU TRY TO PROCESS WHAT'S HAPPENING BEFORE YOUR EYES...
"YOUR INABILITY TO DO ANYTHING BUT WATCH IT ALL UNFOLD."

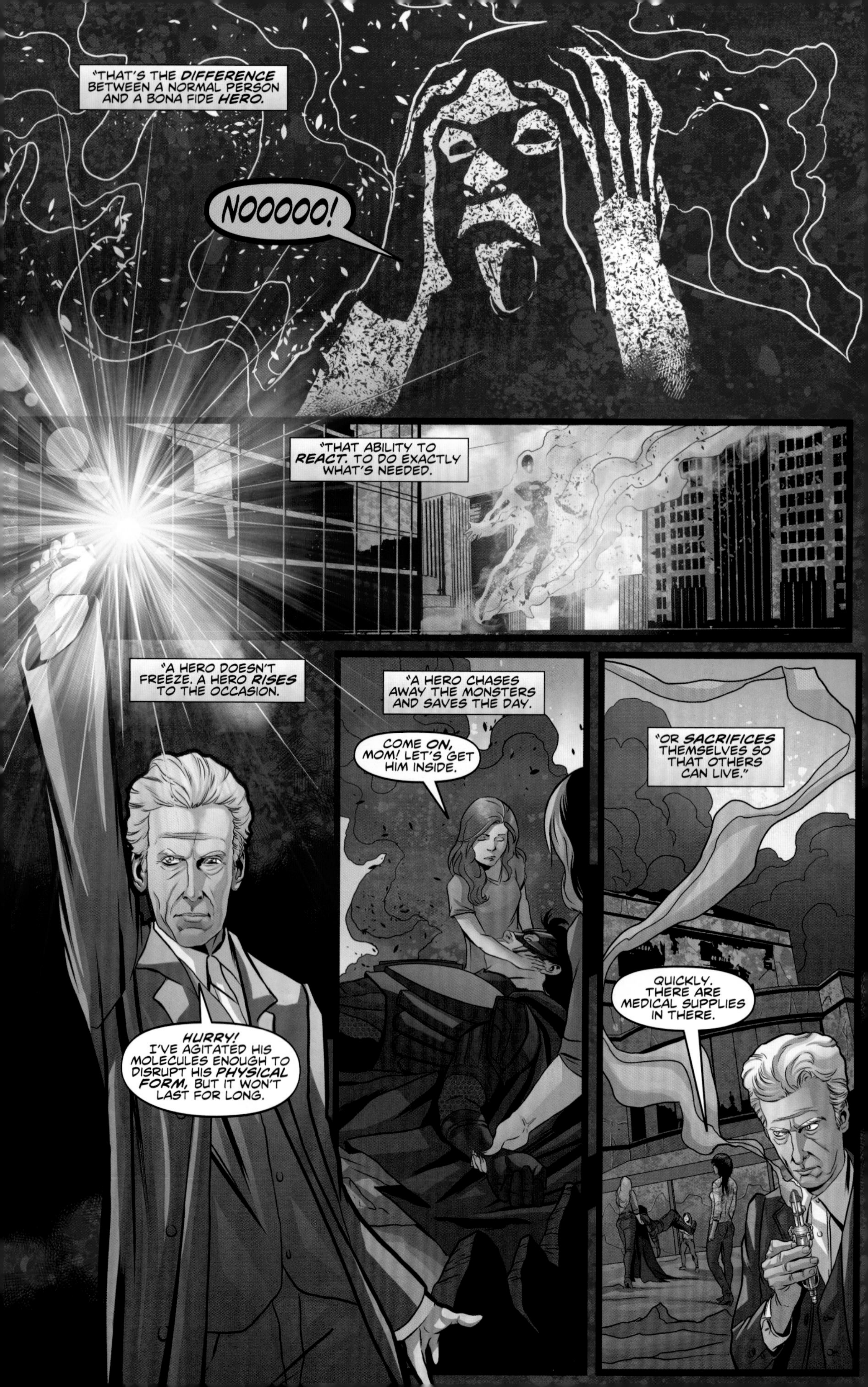
"THAT'S THE DIFFERENCE BETWEEN A NORMAL PERSON AND A BONA FIDE HERO.
NOOOOO!
"THAT ABILITY TO REACT. TO DO EXACTLY WHAT'S NEEDED.
"A HERO DOESN'T FREEZE. A HERO RISES TO THE OCCASION.
HURRY! I'VE AGITATED HIS MOLECULES ENOUGH TO DISRUPT HIS PHYSICAL FORM, BUT IT WON'T LAST FOR LONG.
"A HERO CHASES AWAY THE MONSTERS AND SAVES THE DAY.
COME ON, MOM! LET'S GET HIM INSIDE.
"OR SACRIFICES THEMSELVES SO THAT OTHERS CAN LIVE."
QUICKLY. THERE ARE MEDICAL SUPPLIES IN THERE.

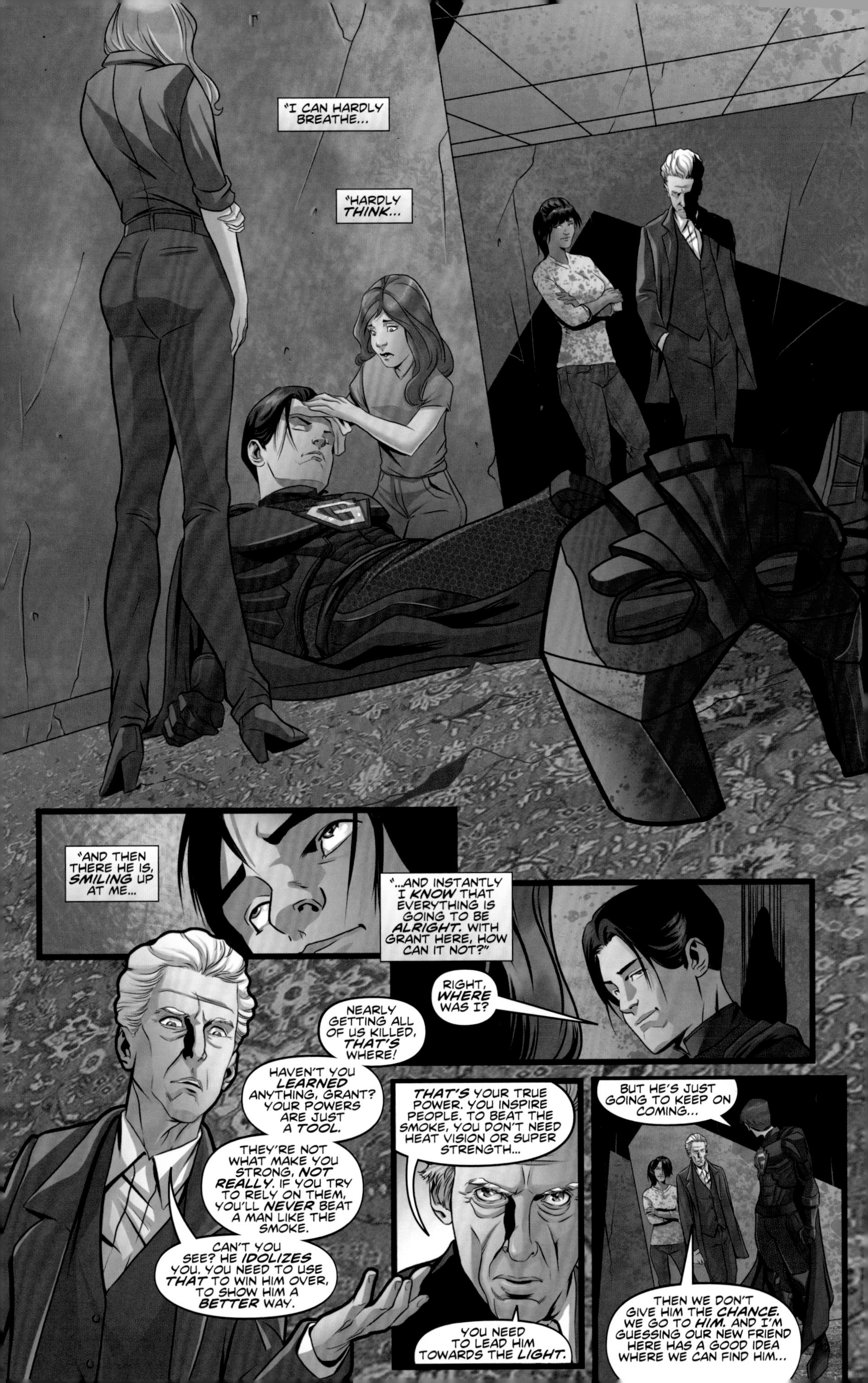
"I CAN HARDLY BREATHE...
"HARDLY THINK...
"AND THEN THERE HE IS, SMILING UP AT ME...
"...AND INSTANTLY I KNOW THAT EVERYTHING IS GOING TO BE ALRIGHT. WITH GRANT HERE, HOW CAN IT NOT?"
RIGHT, WHERE WAS I?
NEARLY GETTING ALL OF US KILLED, THAT'S WHERE!
HAVEN'T YOU LEARNED ANYTHING, GRANT? YOUR POWERS ARE JUST A TOOL.
THEY'RE NOT WHAT MAKE YOU STRONG, NOT REALLY. IF YOU TRY TO RELY ON THEM, YOU'LL NEVER BEAT A MAN LIKE THE SMOKE.
CAN'T YOU SEE? HE IDOLIZES YOU. YOU NEED TO USE THAT TO WIN HIM OVER, TO SHOW HIM A BETTER WAY.
THAT'S YOUR TRUE POWER. YOU INSPIRE PEOPLE. TO BEAT THE SMOKE, YOU DON'T NEED HEAT VISION OR SUPER STRENGTH...
YOU NEED TO LEAD HIM TOWARDS THE LIGHT.
BUT HE'S JUST GOING TO KEEP ON COMING...
THEN WE DON'T GIVE HIM THE CHANCE. WE GO TO HIM. AND I'M GUESSING OUR NEW FRIEND HERE HAS A GOOD IDEA WHERE WE CAN FIND HIM...

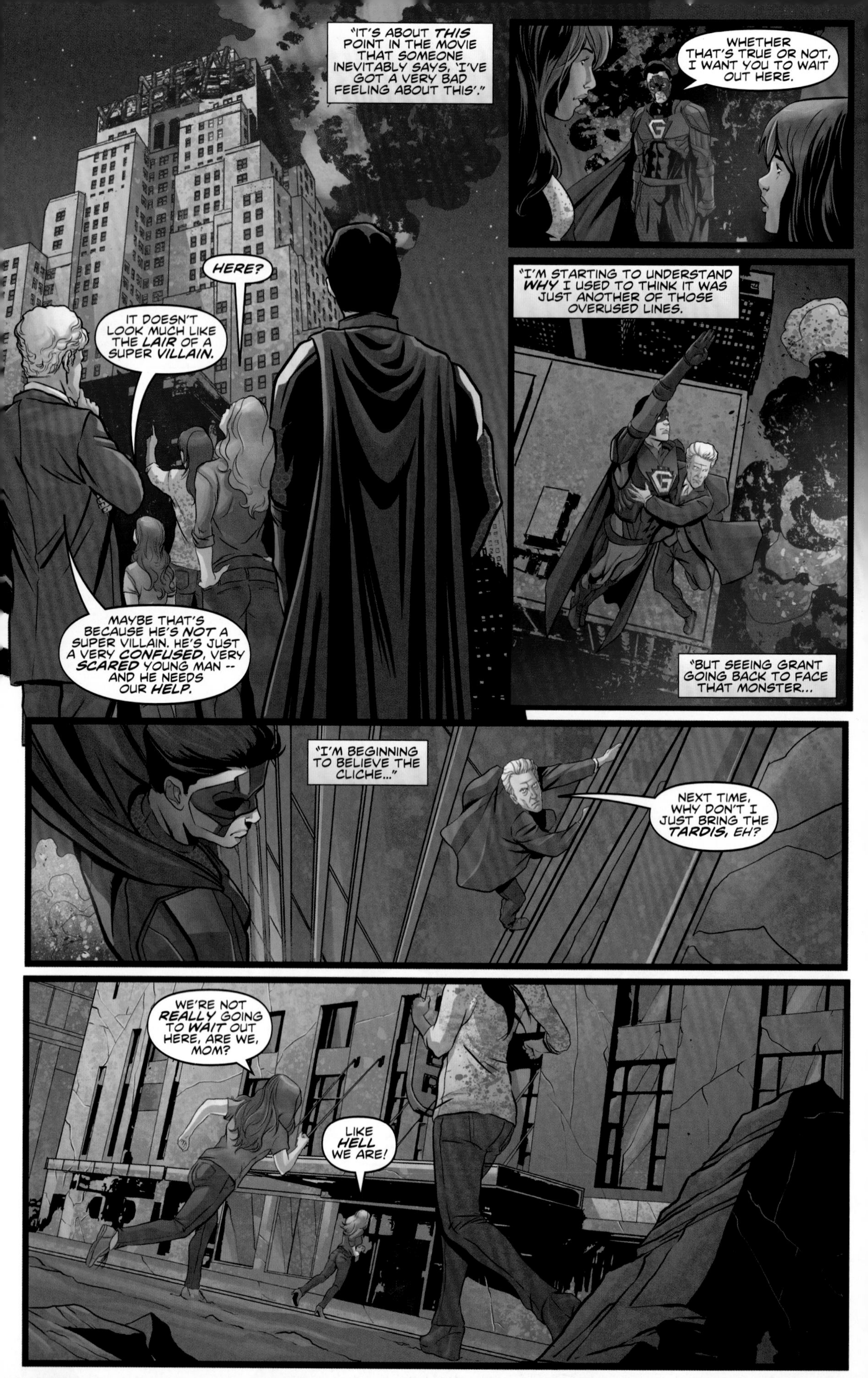
"IT'S ABOUT THIS POINT IN THE MOVIE THAT SOMEONE INEVITABLY SAYS, 'I'VE GOT A VERY BAD FEELING ABOUT THIS'."
HERE?
IT DOESN'T LOOK MUCH LIKE THE LAIR OF A SUPER VILLAIN.
MAYBE THAT'S BECAUSE HE'S NOT A SUPER VILLAIN. HE'S JUST A VERY CONFUSED, VERY SCARED YOUNG MAN -- AND HE NEEDS OUR HELP.
WHETHER THAT'S TRUE OR NOT, I WANT YOU TO WAIT OUT HERE.
"I'M STARTING TO UNDERSTAND WHY I USED TO THINK IT WAS JUST ANOTHER OF THOSE OVERUSED LINES.
"BUT SEEING GRANT GOING BACK TO FACE THAT MONSTER...
"I'M BEGINNING TO BELIEVE THE CLICHE..."
NEXT TIME, WHY DON'T I JUST BRING THE TARDIS, EH?
WE'RE NOT REALLY GOING TO WAIT OUT HERE, ARE WE, MOM?
LIKE HELL WE ARE!

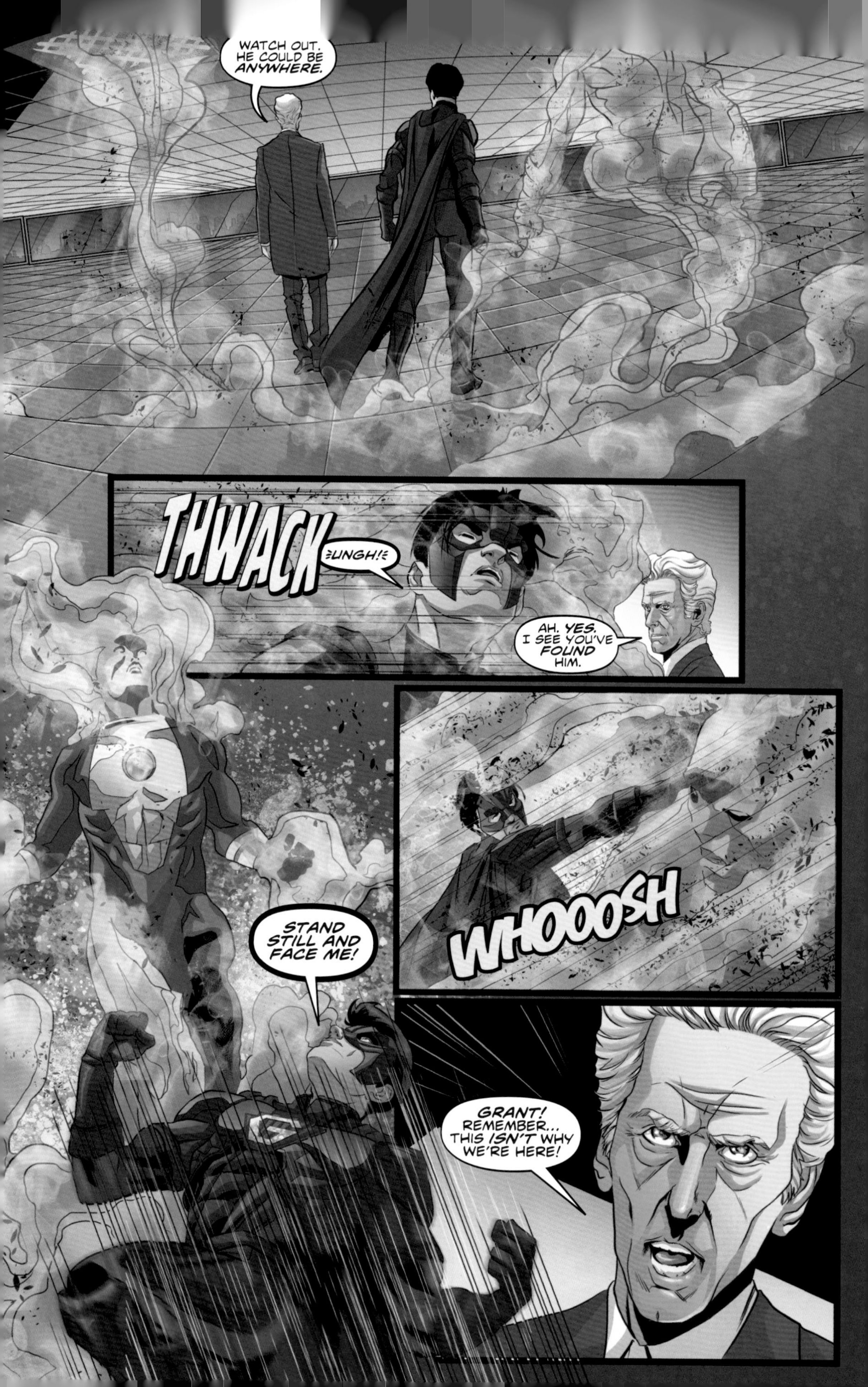
WATCH OUT. HE COULD BE ANYWHERE.
THWACK
UNGH!
AH. YES. I SEE YOU'VE FOUND HIM.
WHOOOSH
STAND STILL AND FACE ME!
GRANT! REMEMBER... THIS ISN'T WHY WE'RE HERE!

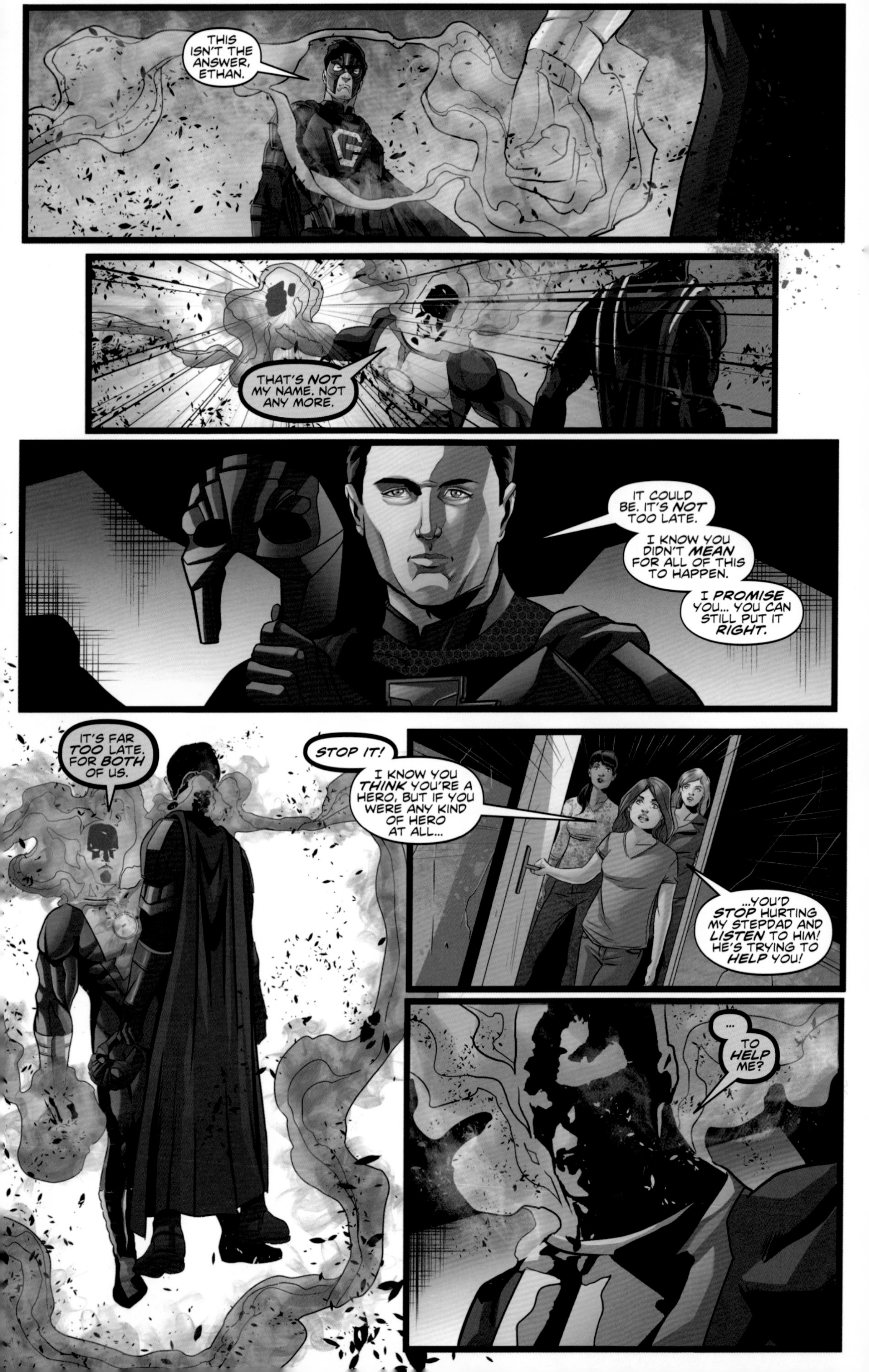
THIS ISN'T THE ANSWER, ETHAN.
THAT'S NOT MY NAME. NOT ANY MORE.
IT COULD BE. IT'S NOT TOO LATE.
I KNOW YOU DIDN'T MEAN FOR ALL OF THIS TO HAPPEN.
I PROMISE YOU... YOU CAN STILL PUT IT RIGHT.
IT'S FAR TOO LATE. FOR BOTH OF US.
STOP IT!
I KNOW YOU THINK YOU'RE A HERO, BUT IF YOU WERE ANY KIND OF HERO AT ALL...
...YOU'D STOP HURTING MY STEPDAD AND LISTEN TO HIM! HE'S TRYING TO HELP YOU!
... TO HELP ME?

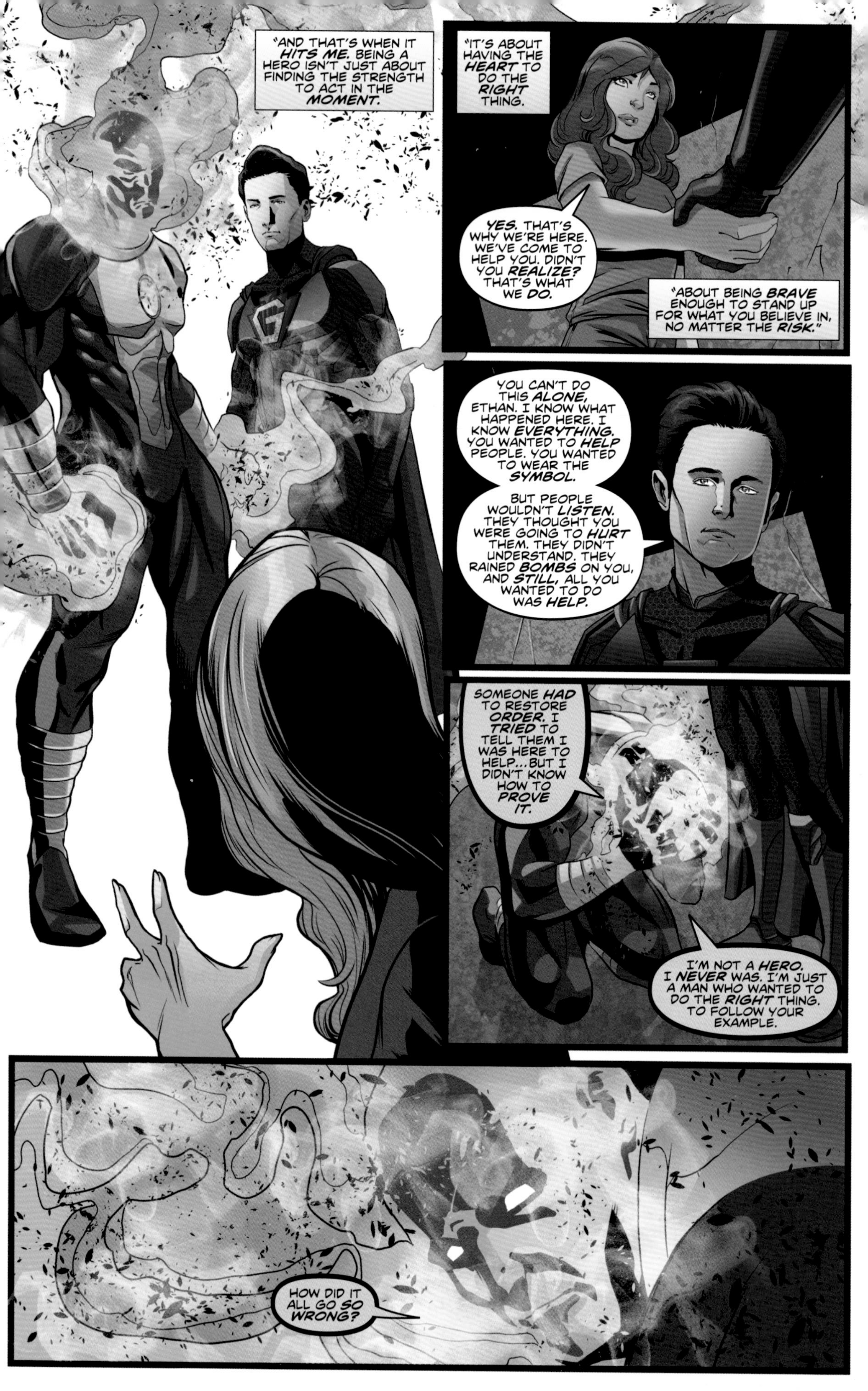
"AND THAT'S WHEN IT HITS ME. BEING A HERO ISN'T JUST ABOUT FINDING THE STRENGTH TO ACT IN THE MOMENT.
"IT'S ABOUT HAVING THE HEART TO DO THE RIGHT THING.
YES. THAT'S WHY WE'RE HERE. WE'VE COME TO HELP YOU. DIDN'T YOU REALIZE? THAT'S WHAT WE DO.
"ABOUT BEING BRAVE ENOUGH TO STAND UP FOR WHAT YOU BELIEVE IN, NO MATTER THE RISK."
YOU CAN'T DO THIS ALONE, ETHAN. I KNOW WHAT HAPPENED HERE. I KNOW EVERYTHING. YOU WANTED TO HELP PEOPLE. YOU WANTED TO WEAR THE SYMBOL.
BUT PEOPLE WOULDN'T LISTEN. THEY THOUGHT YOU WERE GOING TO HURT THEM. THEY DIDN'T UNDERSTAND. THEY RAINED BOMBS ON YOU, AND STILL, ALL YOU WANTED TO DO WAS HELP.
SOMEONE HAD TO RESTORE ORDER. I TRIED TO TELL THEM I WAS HERE TO HELP... BUT I DIDN'T KNOW HOW TO PROVE IT.
I'M NOT A HERO. I NEVER WAS. I'M JUST A MAN WHO WANTED TO DO THE RIGHT THING. TO FOLLOW YOUR EXAMPLE.
HOW DID IT ALL GO SO WRONG?

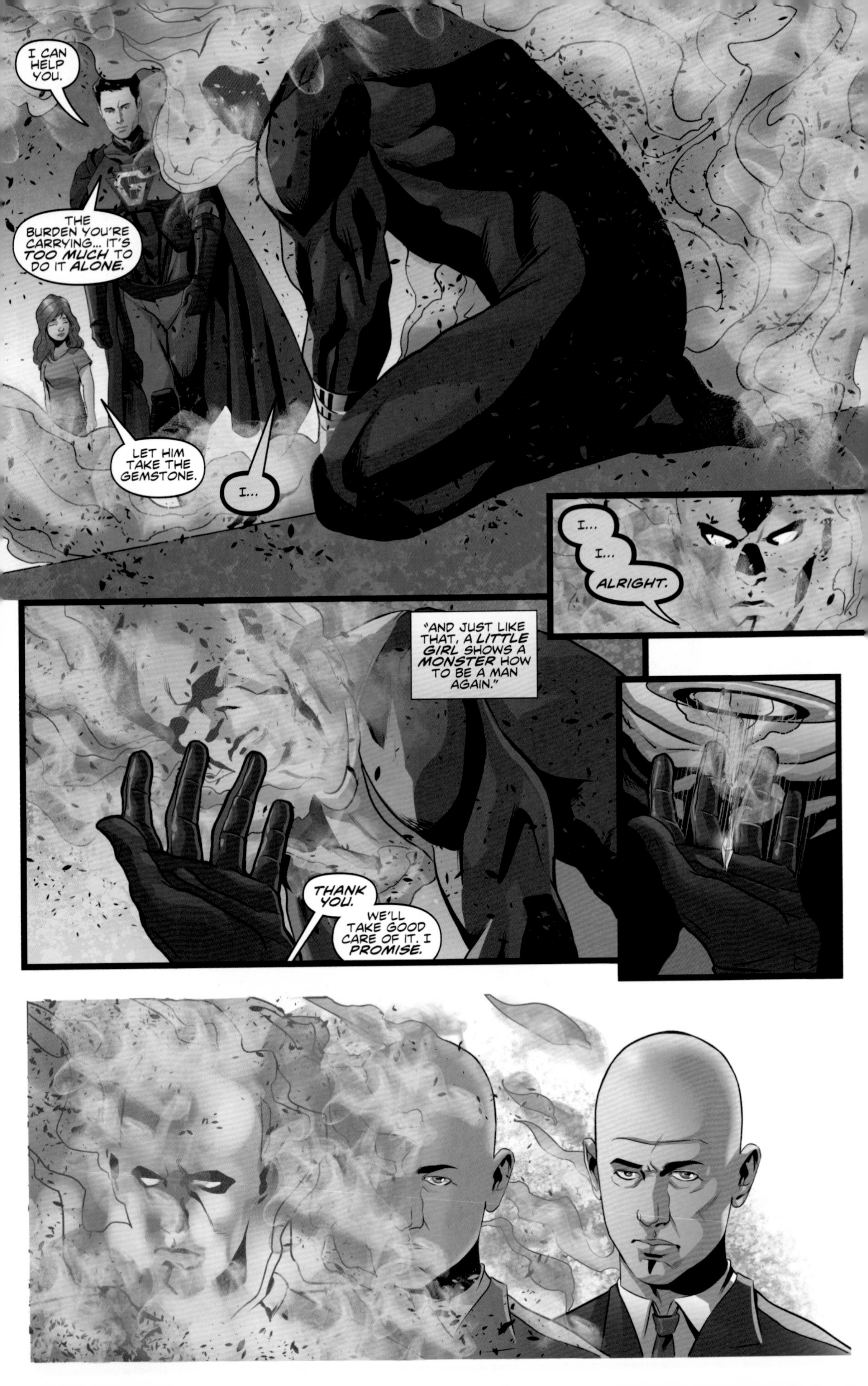
I CAN HELP YOU.
THE BURDEN YOU'RE CARRYING... IT'S TOO MUCH TO DO IT ALONE.
LET HIM TAKE THE GEMSTONE.
I...
I... I... ALRIGHT.
"AND JUST LIKE THAT, A LITTLE GIRL SHOWS A MONSTER HOW TO BE A MAN AGAIN."
THANK YOU.
WE'LL TAKE GOOD CARE OF IT. I PROMISE.

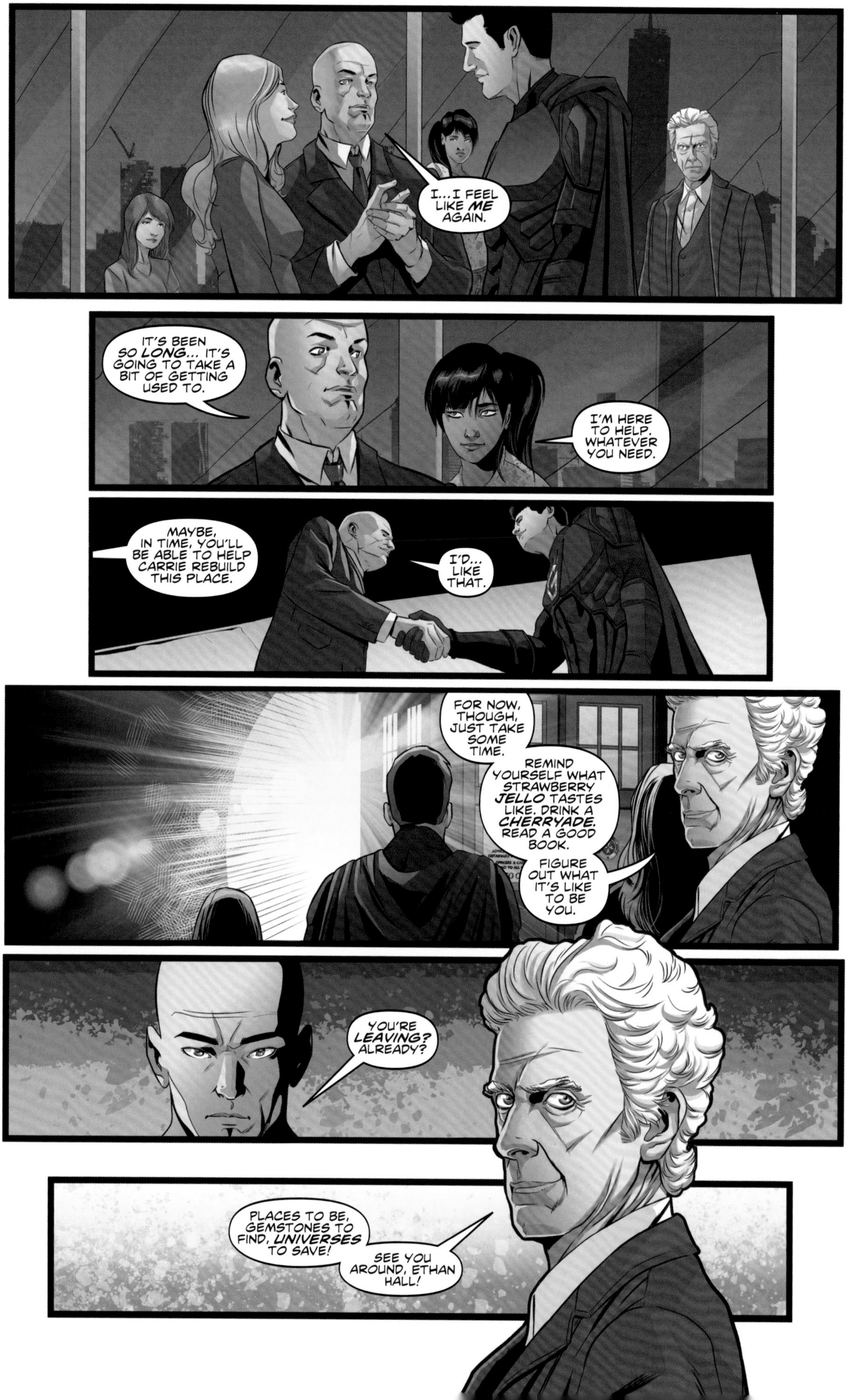

I... I FEEL LIKE *ME* AGAIN.
IT'S BEEN SO *LONG*... IT'S GOING TO TAKE A BIT OF GETTING USED TO.
I'M HERE TO HELP. WHATEVER YOU NEED.
MAYBE, IN TIME, YOU'LL BE ABLE TO HELP CARRIE REBUILD THIS PLACE.
I'D... LIKE THAT.
FOR NOW, THOUGH, JUST TAKE SOME TIME.
REMIND YOURSELF WHAT STRAWBERRY *JELLO* TASTES LIKE. DRINK A *CHERRYADE.* READ A GOOD BOOK.
FIGURE OUT WHAT IT'S LIKE TO BE YOU.
YOU'RE *LEAVING?* ALREADY?
PLACES TO BE, GEMSTONES TO FIND, *UNIVERSES* TO SAVE!
SEE YOU AROUND, ETHAN HALL!

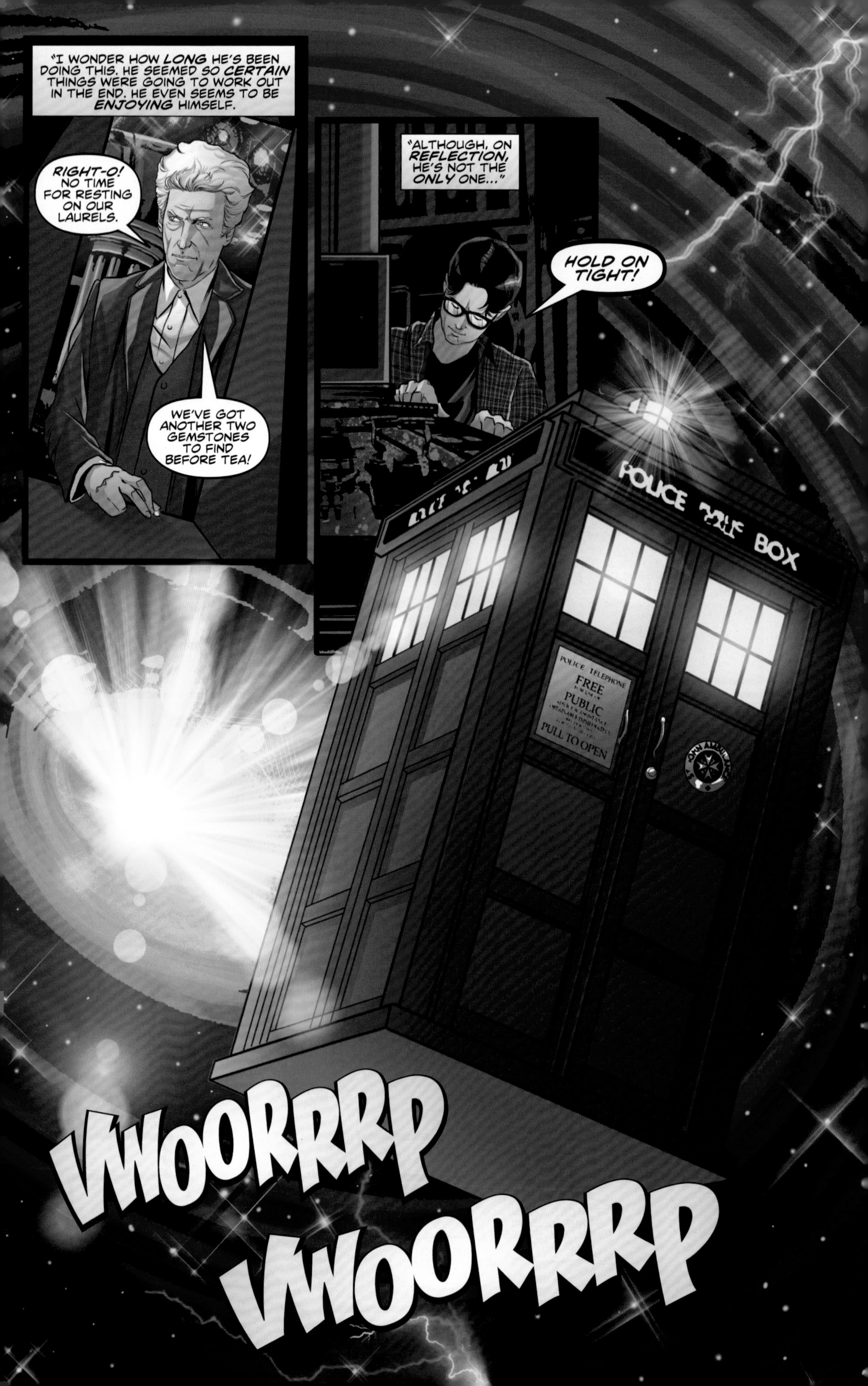
"I WONDER HOW LONG HE'S BEEN DOING THIS. HE SEEMED SO CERTAIN THINGS WERE GOING TO WORK OUT IN THE END. HE EVEN SEEMS TO BE ENJOYING HIMSELF.
RIGHT-O! NO TIME FOR RESTING ON OUR LAURELS.
WE'VE GOT ANOTHER TWO GEMSTONES TO FIND BEFORE TEA!
"ALTHOUGH, ON REFLECTION, HE'S NOT THE ONLY ONE..."
HOLD ON TIGHT!
POLICE BOX
POLICE TELEPHONE FREE PUBLIC
PULL TO OPEN
VWOORRRP
VWOORRRP

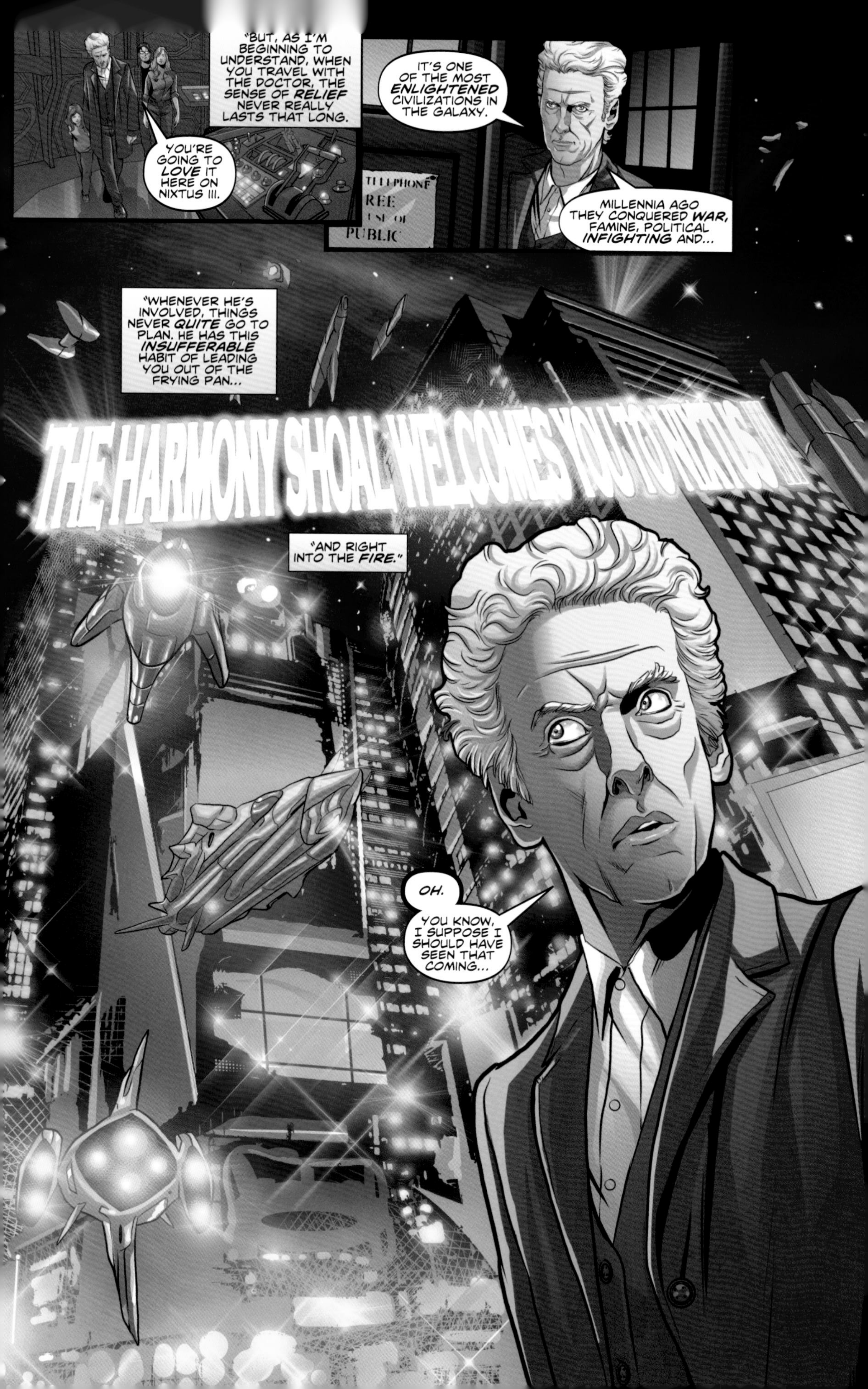
"BUT, AS I'M BEGINNING TO UNDERSTAND, WHEN YOU TRAVEL WITH THE DOCTOR, THE SENSE OF RELIEF NEVER REALLY LASTS THAT LONG.
YOU'RE GOING TO LOVE IT HERE ON NIXTUS III.
IT'S ONE OF THE MOST ENLIGHTENED CIVILIZATIONS IN THE GALAXY.
TELEPHONE
REE
PUBLIC
MILLENNIA AGO THEY CONQUERED WAR, FAMINE, POLITICAL INFIGHTING AND...
"WHENEVER HE'S INVOLVED, THINGS NEVER QUITE GO TO PLAN. HE HAS THIS INSUFFERABLE HABIT OF LEADING YOU OUT OF THE FRYING PAN...
THE HARMONY SHOAL WELCOMES YOU TO NIXTUS III
"AND RIGHT INTO THE FIRE."
OH.
YOU KNOW, I SUPPOSE I SHOULD HAVE SEEN THAT COMING...

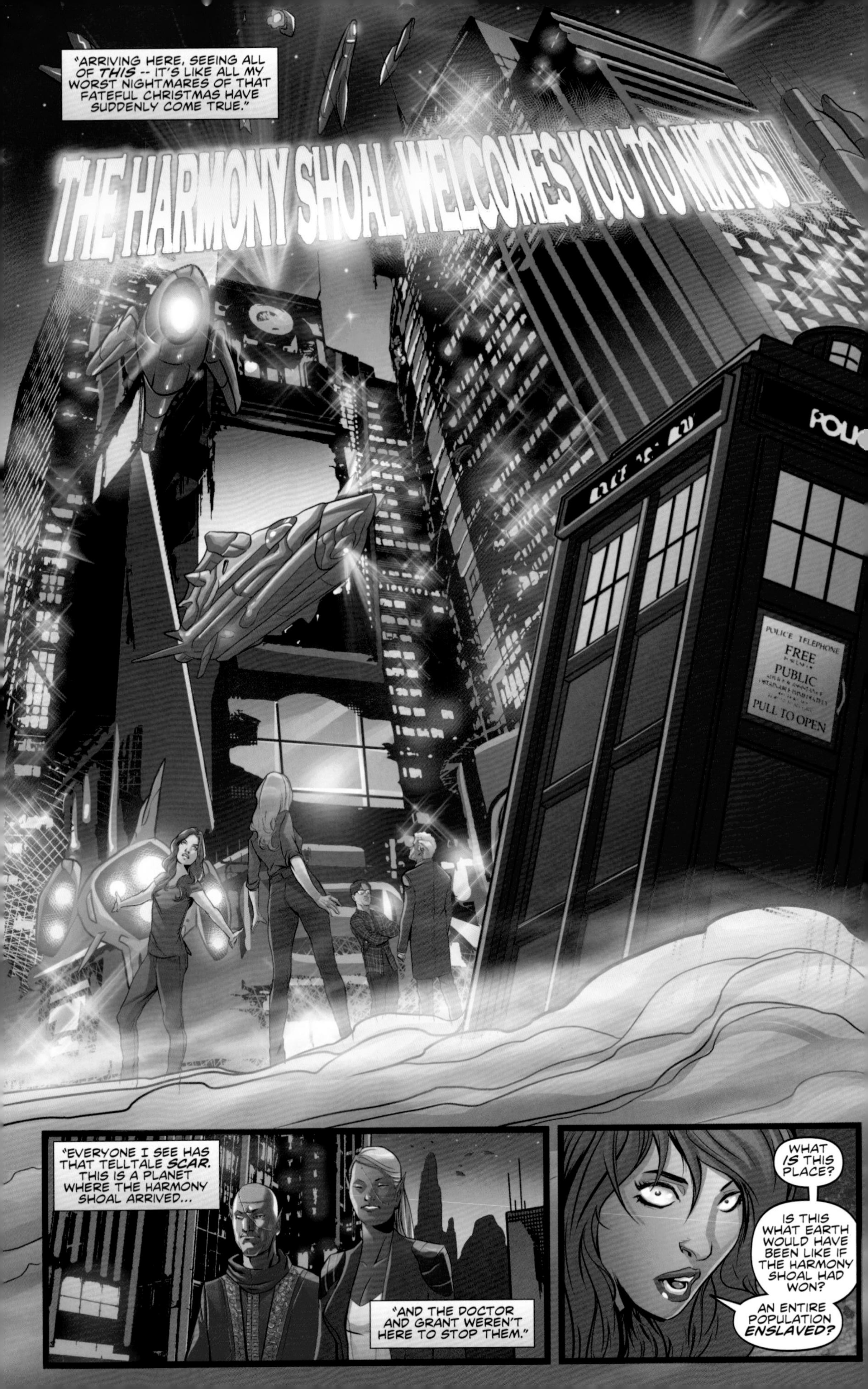
"ARRIVING HERE, SEEING ALL OF THIS -- IT'S LIKE ALL MY WORST NIGHTMARES OF THAT FATEFUL CHRISTMAS HAVE SUDDENLY COME TRUE."
THE HARMONY SHOAL WELCOMES YOU TO
POLICE TELEPHONE
FREE
PUBLIC
PULL TO OPEN
"EVERYONE I SEE HAS THAT TELLTALE SCAR. THIS IS A PLANET WHERE THE HARMONY SHOAL ARRIVED...
"AND THE DOCTOR AND GRANT WEREN'T HERE TO STOP THEM."
WHAT IS THIS PLACE?
IS THIS WHAT EARTH WOULD HAVE BEEN LIKE IF THE HARMONY SHOAL HAD WON?
AN ENTIRE POPULATION ENSLAVED?

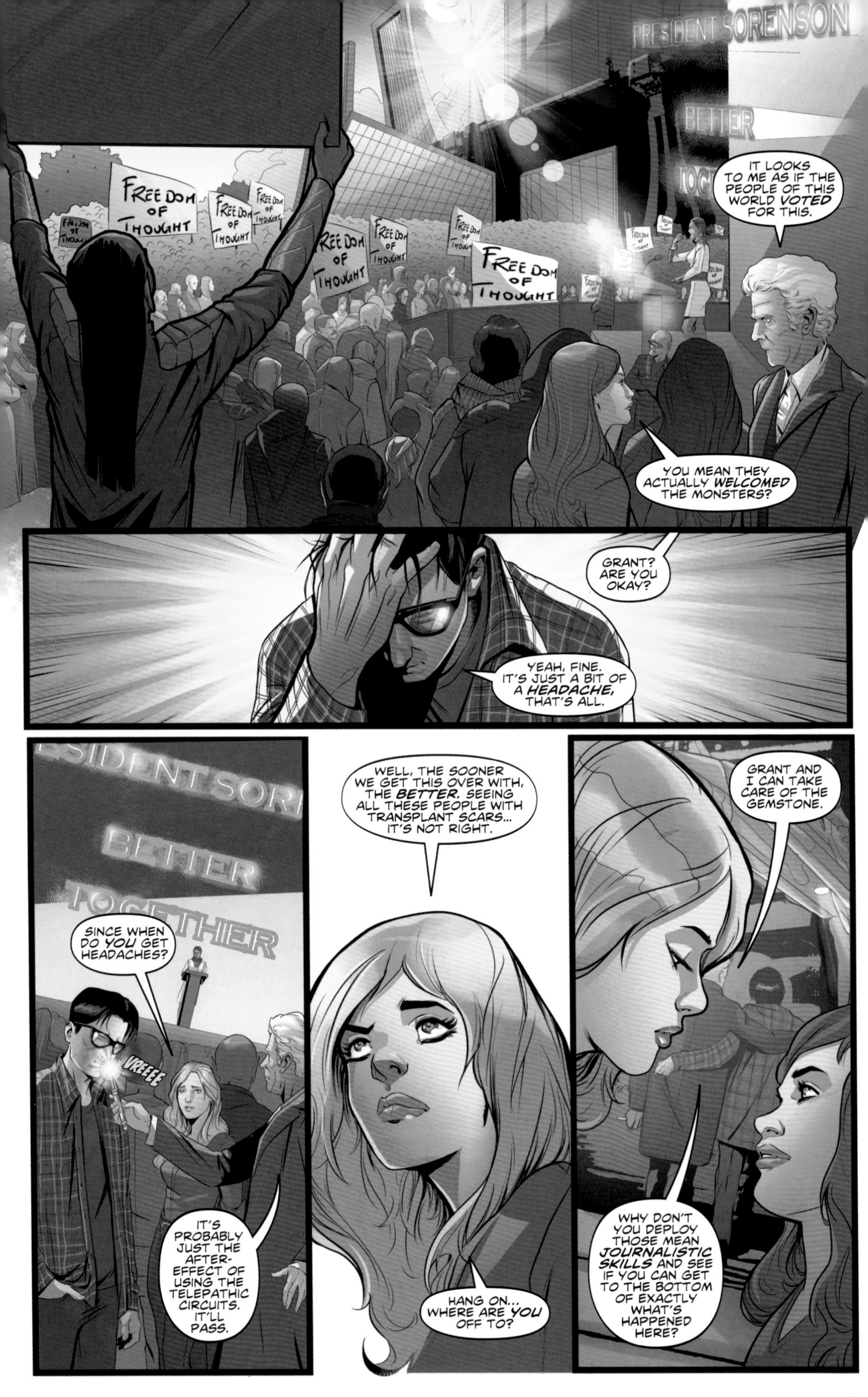

PRESIDENT SORENSON
BETTER
TOGETHER
FREEDOM OF THOUGHT
IT LOOKS TO ME AS IF THE PEOPLE OF THIS WORLD *VOTED* FOR THIS.
YOU MEAN THEY ACTUALLY *WELCOMED* THE MONSTERS?
GRANT? ARE YOU OKAY?
YEAH, FINE. IT'S JUST A BIT OF A *HEADACHE,* THAT'S ALL.
SINCE WHEN DO *YOU* GET HEADACHES?
VREEEE
IT'S PROBABLY JUST THE AFTER-EFFECT OF USING THE TELEPATHIC CIRCUITS. IT'LL PASS.
WELL, THE SOONER WE GET THIS OVER WITH, THE *BETTER.* SEEING ALL THESE PEOPLE WITH TRANSPLANT SCARS... IT'S NOT RIGHT.
HANG ON... WHERE ARE *YOU* OFF TO?
GRANT AND I CAN TAKE CARE OF THE GEMSTONE.
WHY DON'T YOU DEPLOY THOSE MEAN *JOURNALISTIC SKILLS* AND SEE IF YOU CAN GET TO THE BOTTOM OF EXACTLY WHAT'S HAPPENED HERE?

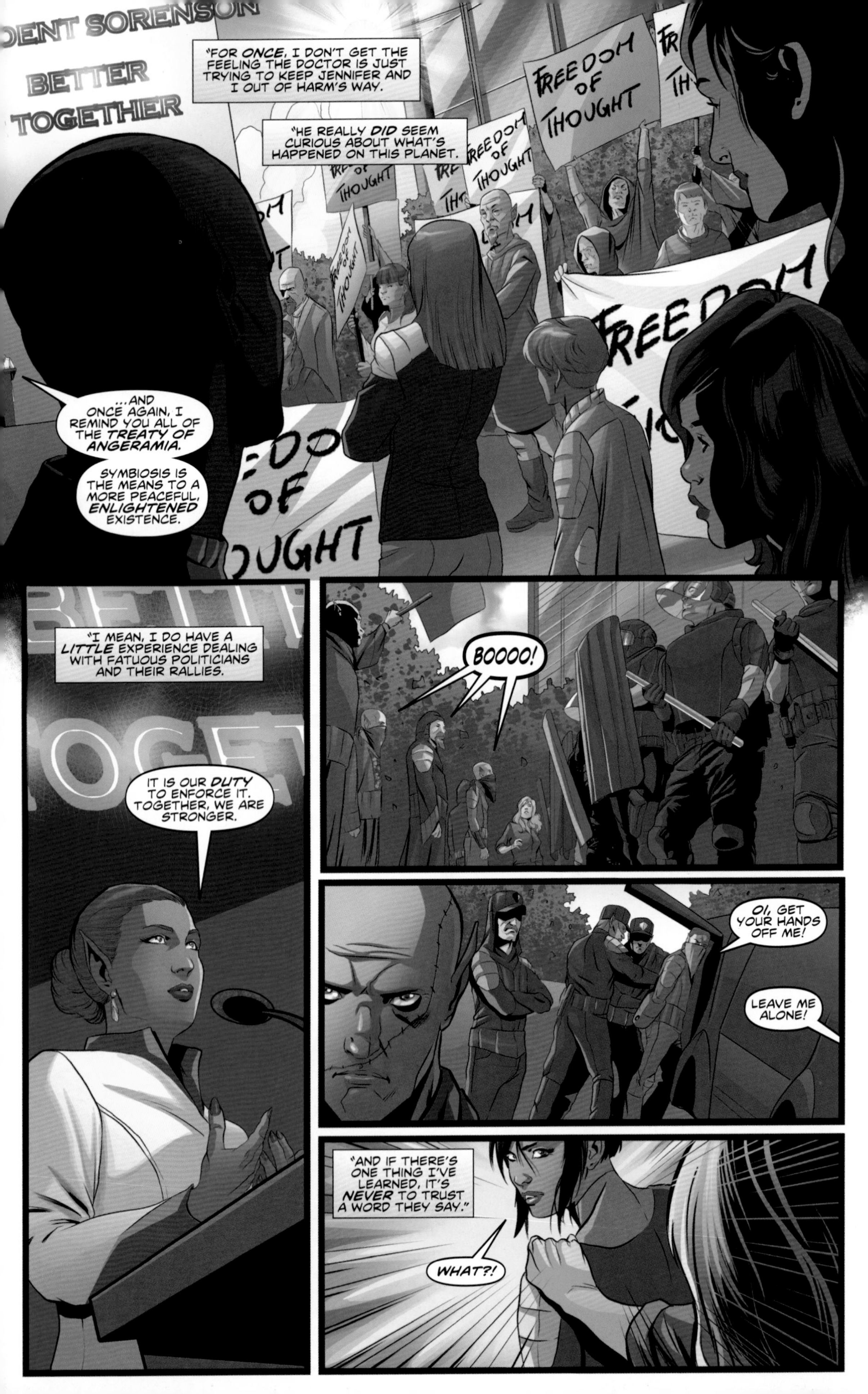
DENT SORENSON
BETTER TOGETHER
"FOR ONCE, I DON'T GET THE FEELING THE DOCTOR IS JUST TRYING TO KEEP JENNIFER AND I OUT OF HARM'S WAY.
"HE REALLY DID SEEM CURIOUS ABOUT WHAT'S HAPPENED ON THIS PLANET.
FREEDOM OF THOUGHT
...AND ONCE AGAIN, I REMIND YOU ALL OF THE TREATY OF ANGERAMIA.
SYMBIOSIS IS THE MEANS TO A MORE PEACEFUL, ENLIGHTENED EXISTENCE.
"I MEAN, I DO HAVE A LITTLE EXPERIENCE DEALING WITH FATUOUS POLITICIANS AND THEIR RALLIES.
IT IS OUR DUTY TO ENFORCE IT. TOGETHER, WE ARE STRONGER.
BOOOO!
OI, GET YOUR HANDS OFF ME!
LEAVE ME ALONE!
"AND IF THERE'S ONE THING I'VE LEARNED, IT'S NEVER TO TRUST A WORD THEY SAY."
WHAT?!

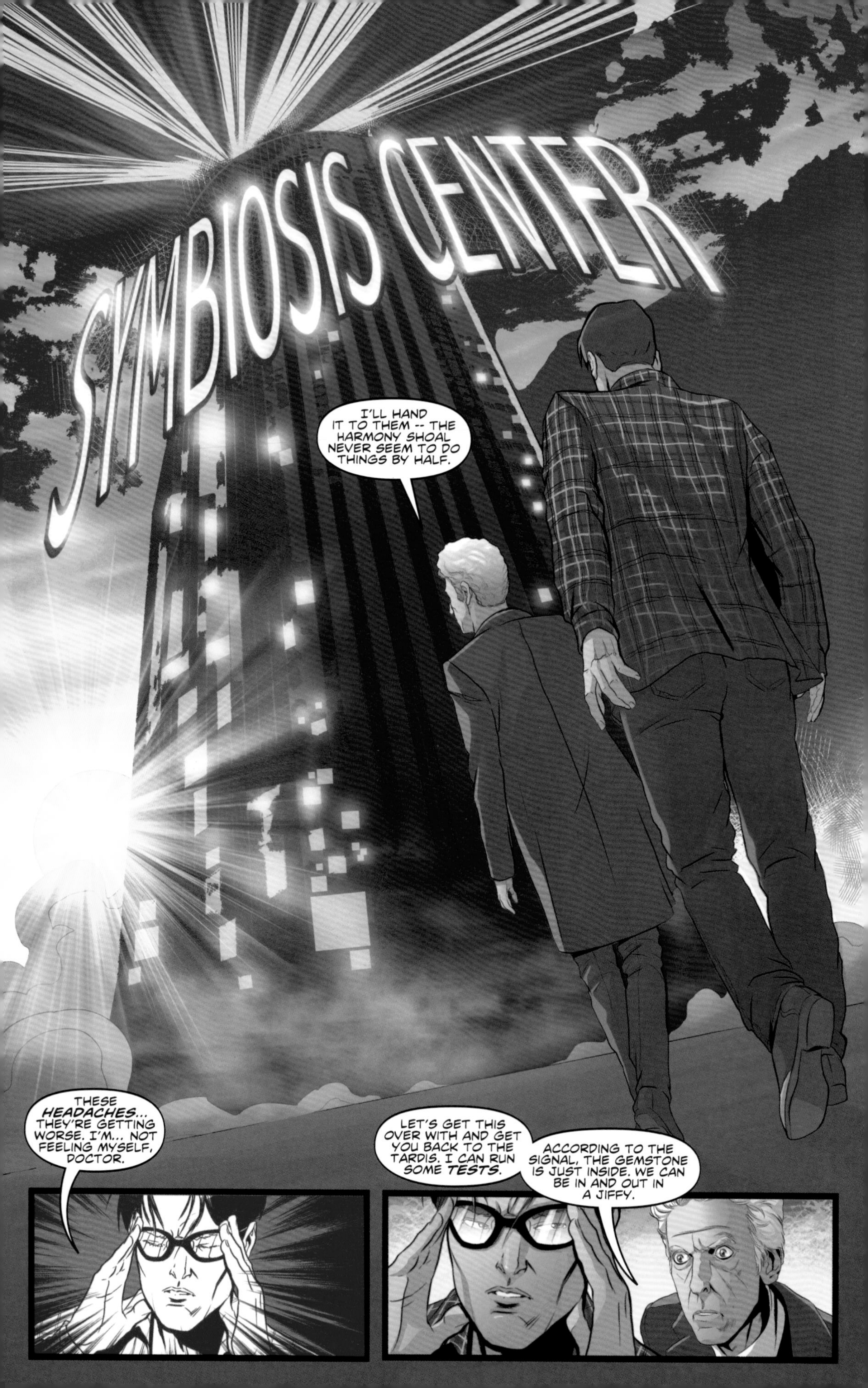
SYMBIOSIS CENTER
I'LL HAND IT TO THEM -- THE HARMONY SHOAL NEVER SEEM TO DO THINGS BY HALF.
THESE *HEADACHES*... THEY'RE GETTING WORSE. I'M... NOT FEELING MYSELF, DOCTOR.
LET'S GET THIS OVER WITH AND GET YOU BACK TO THE TARDIS. I CAN RUN SOME *TESTS*.
ACCORDING TO THE SIGNAL, THE GEMSTONE IS JUST INSIDE. WE CAN BE IN AND OUT IN A JIFFY.

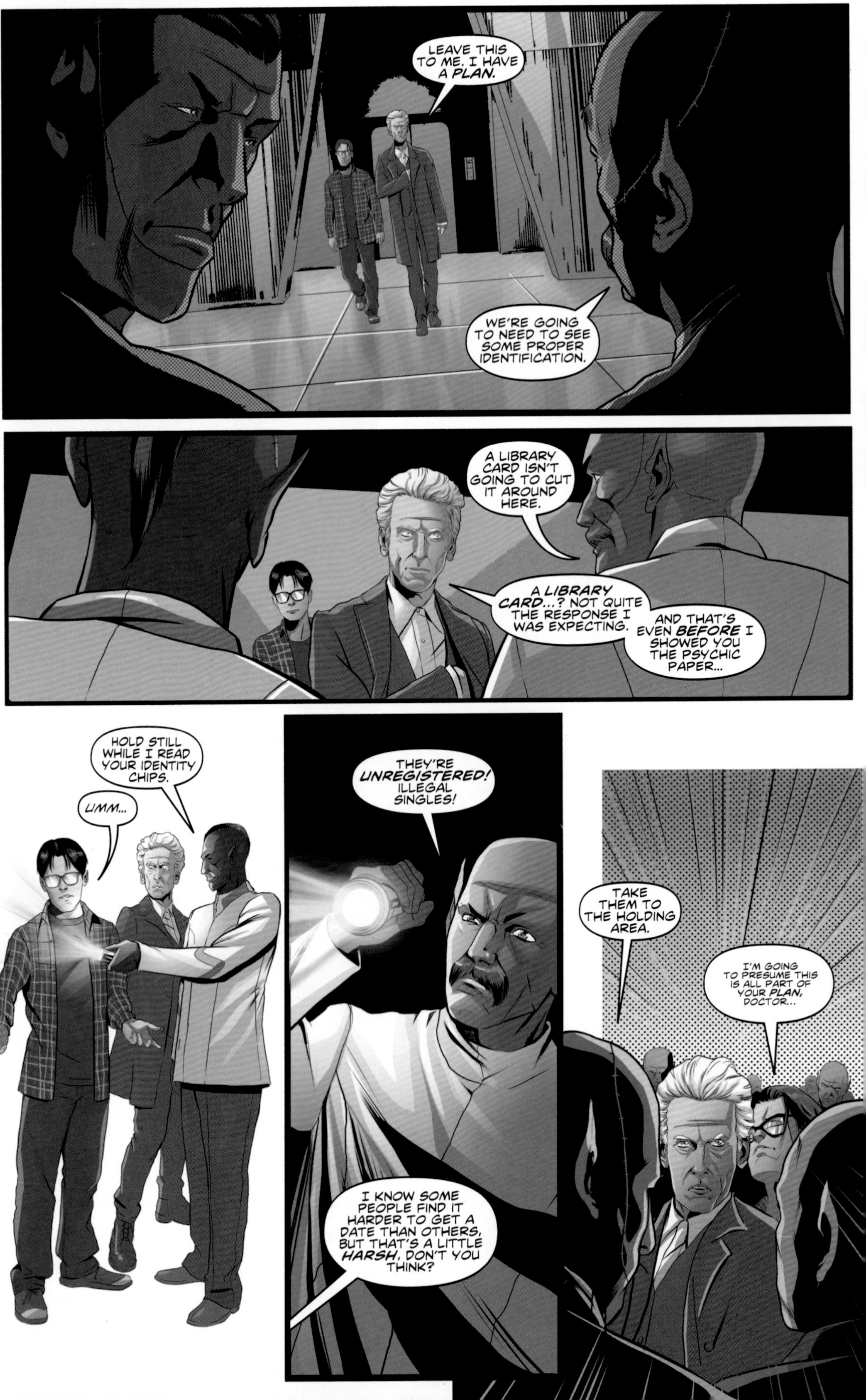
LEAVE THIS TO ME. I HAVE A *PLAN.*
WE'RE GOING TO NEED TO SEE SOME PROPER IDENTIFICATION.
A LIBRARY CARD ISN'T GOING TO CUT IT AROUND HERE.
A *LIBRARY CARD...?* NOT QUITE THE RESPONSE I WAS EXPECTING.
AND THAT'S EVEN *BEFORE* I SHOWED YOU THE PSYCHIC PAPER...
HOLD STILL WHILE I READ YOUR IDENTITY CHIPS.
UMM...
THEY'RE *UNREGISTERED!* ILLEGAL SINGLES!
I KNOW SOME PEOPLE FIND IT HARDER TO GET A DATE THAN OTHERS, BUT THAT'S A LITTLE *HARSH*, DON'T YOU THINK?
TAKE THEM TO THE HOLDING AREA.
I'M GOING TO PRESUME THIS IS ALL PART OF YOUR *PLAN,* DOCTOR...

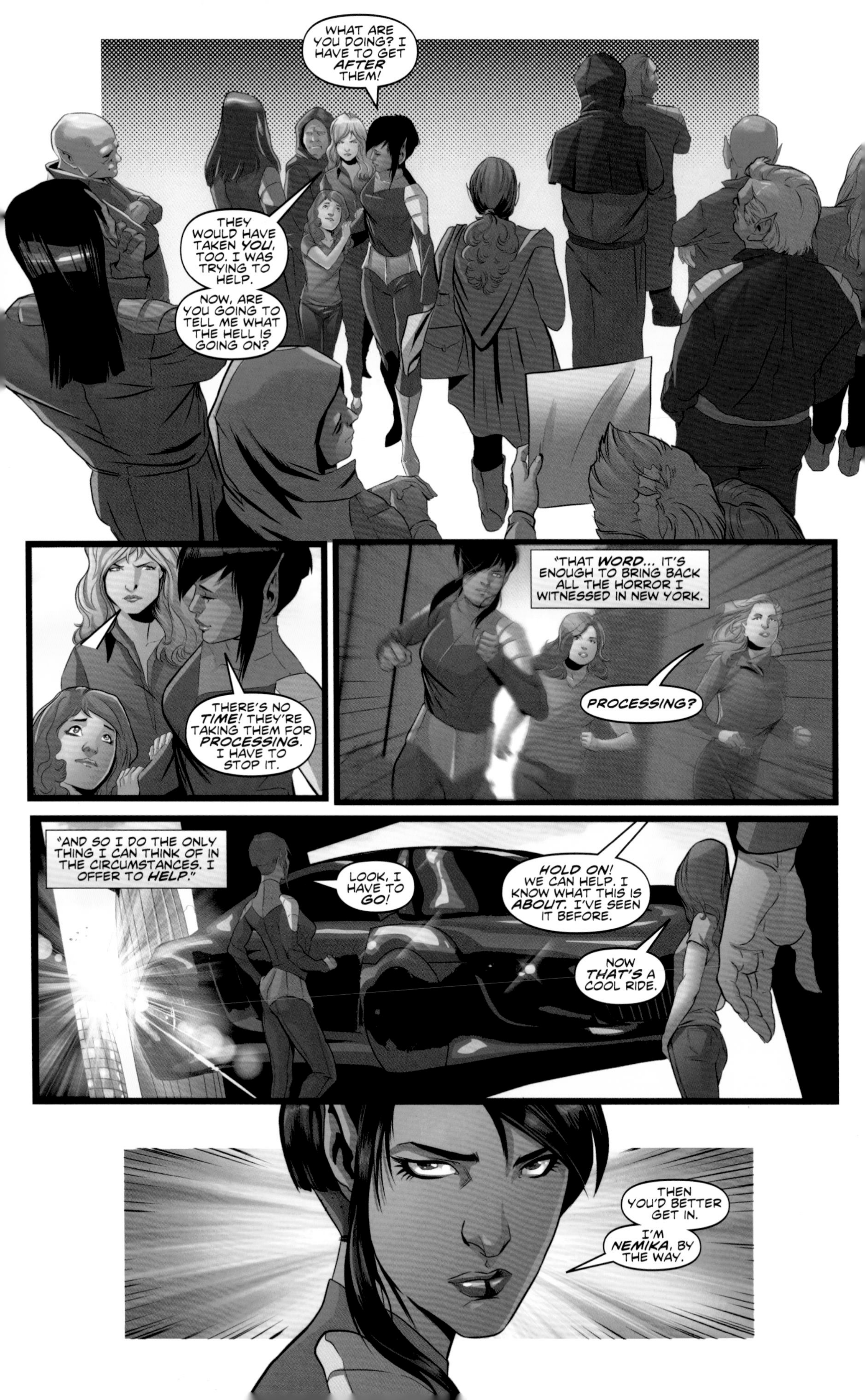

WHAT ARE YOU DOING? I HAVE TO GET AFTER THEM!
THEY WOULD HAVE TAKEN YOU, TOO. I WAS TRYING TO HELP.
NOW, ARE YOU GOING TO TELL ME WHAT THE HELL IS GOING ON?
THERE'S NO TIME! THEY'RE TAKING THEM FOR PROCESSING. I HAVE TO STOP IT.
"THAT WORD... IT'S ENOUGH TO BRING BACK ALL THE HORROR I WITNESSED IN NEW YORK.
PROCESSING?
"AND SO I DO THE ONLY THING I CAN THINK OF IN THE CIRCUMSTANCES. I OFFER TO HELP."
LOOK, I HAVE TO GO!
HOLD ON! WE CAN HELP. I KNOW WHAT THIS IS ABOUT. I'VE SEEN IT BEFORE.
NOW THAT'S A COOL RIDE.
THEN YOU'D BETTER GET IN.
I'M NEMIKA, BY THE WAY.

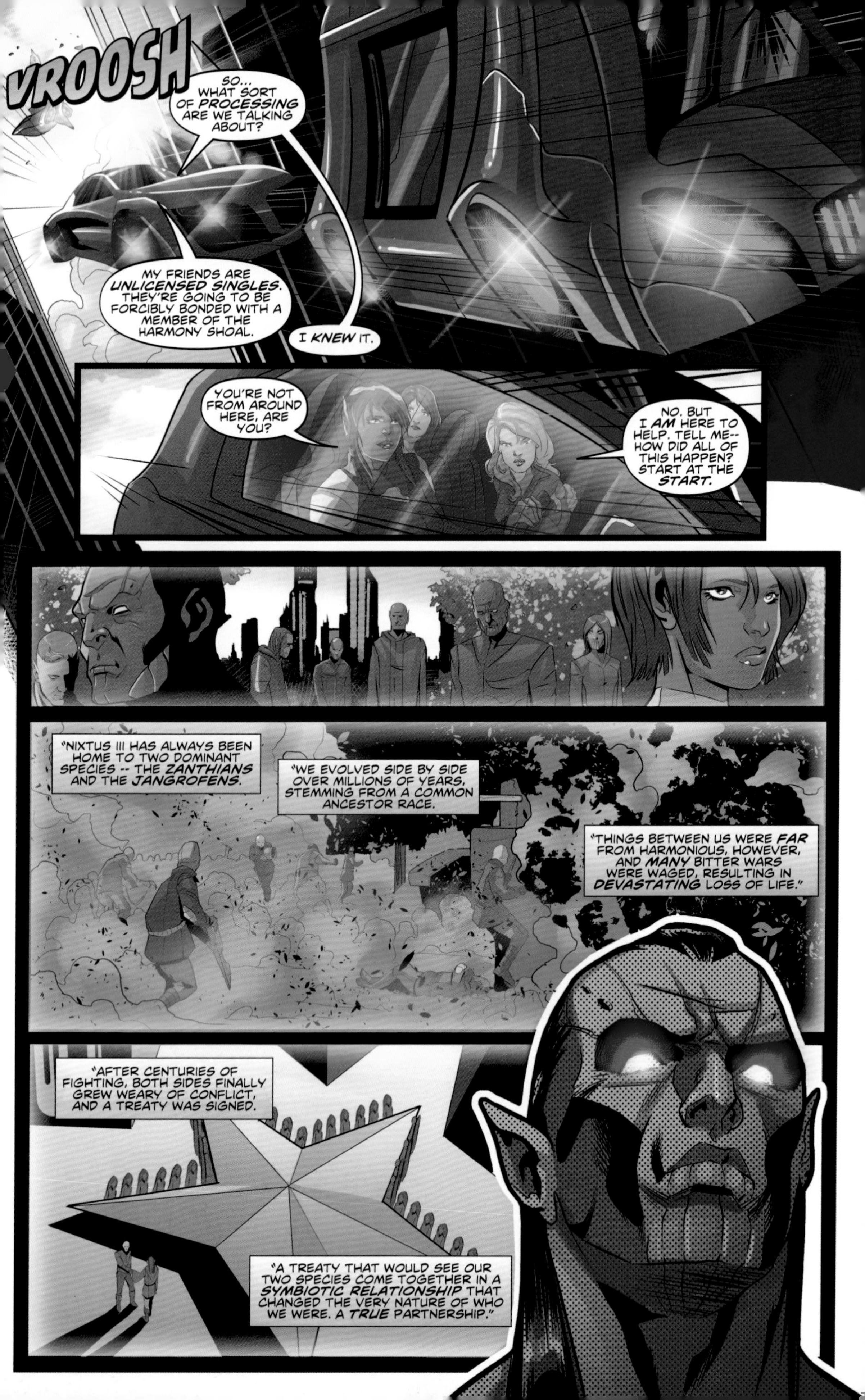
VROOSH
SO... WHAT SORT OF PROCESSING ARE WE TALKING ABOUT?
MY FRIENDS ARE UNLICENSED SINGLES. THEY'RE GOING TO BE FORCIBLY BONDED WITH A MEMBER OF THE HARMONY SHOAL.
I KNEW IT.
YOU'RE NOT FROM AROUND HERE, ARE YOU?
NO. BUT I AM HERE TO HELP. TELL ME-- HOW DID ALL OF THIS HAPPEN? START AT THE START.
"NIXTUS III HAS ALWAYS BEEN HOME TO TWO DOMINANT SPECIES -- THE ZANTHIANS AND THE JANGROFENS.
"WE EVOLVED SIDE BY SIDE OVER MILLIONS OF YEARS, STEMMING FROM A COMMON ANCESTOR RACE.
"THINGS BETWEEN US WERE FAR FROM HARMONIOUS, HOWEVER, AND MANY BITTER WARS WERE WAGED, RESULTING IN DEVASTATING LOSS OF LIFE."
"AFTER CENTURIES OF FIGHTING, BOTH SIDES FINALLY GREW WEARY OF CONFLICT, AND A TREATY WAS SIGNED.
"A TREATY THAT WOULD SEE OUR TWO SPECIES COME TOGETHER IN A SYMBIOTIC RELATIONSHIP THAT CHANGED THE VERY NATURE OF WHO WE WERE. A TRUE PARTNERSHIP."

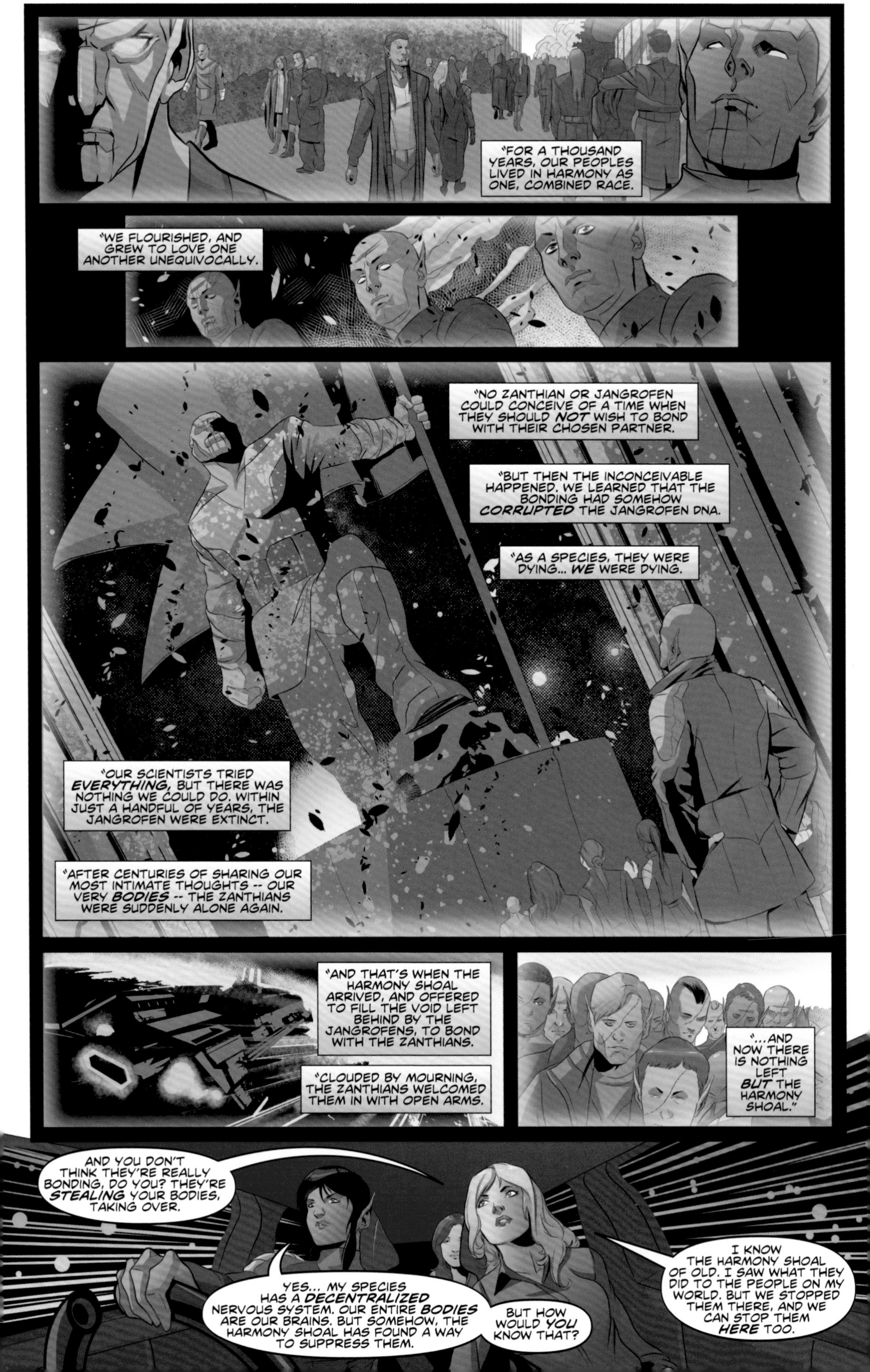
"FOR A THOUSAND YEARS, OUR PEOPLES LIVED IN HARMONY AS ONE, COMBINED RACE.
"WE FLOURISHED, AND GREW TO LOVE ONE ANOTHER UNEQUIVOCALLY.
"NO ZANTHIAN OR JANGROFEN COULD CONCEIVE OF A TIME WHEN THEY SHOULD NOT WISH TO BOND WITH THEIR CHOSEN PARTNER.
"BUT THEN THE INCONCEIVABLE HAPPENED. WE LEARNED THAT THE BONDING HAD SOMEHOW CORRUPTED THE JANGROFEN DNA.
"AS A SPECIES, THEY WERE DYING... WE WERE DYING.
"OUR SCIENTISTS TRIED EVERYTHING, BUT THERE WAS NOTHING WE COULD DO. WITHIN JUST A HANDFUL OF YEARS, THE JANGROFEN WERE EXTINCT.
"AFTER CENTURIES OF SHARING OUR MOST INTIMATE THOUGHTS -- OUR VERY BODIES -- THE ZANTHIANS WERE SUDDENLY ALONE AGAIN.
"AND THAT'S WHEN THE HARMONY SHOAL ARRIVED, AND OFFERED TO FILL THE VOID LEFT BEHIND BY THE JANGROFENS, TO BOND WITH THE ZANTHIANS.
"CLOUDED BY MOURNING, THE ZANTHIANS WELCOMED THEM IN WITH OPEN ARMS.
"...AND NOW THERE IS NOTHING LEFT BUT THE HARMONY SHOAL."
AND YOU DON'T THINK THEY'RE REALLY BONDING, DO YOU? THEY'RE STEALING YOUR BODIES, TAKING OVER.
YES... MY SPECIES HAS A DECENTRALIZED NERVOUS SYSTEM. OUR ENTIRE BODIES ARE OUR BRAINS. BUT SOMEHOW, THE HARMONY SHOAL HAS FOUND A WAY TO SUPPRESS THEM.
BUT HOW WOULD YOU KNOW THAT?
I KNOW THE HARMONY SHOAL OF OLD. I SAW WHAT THEY DID TO THE PEOPLE ON MY WORLD. BUT WE STOPPED THEM THERE, AND WE CAN STOP THEM HERE TOO.

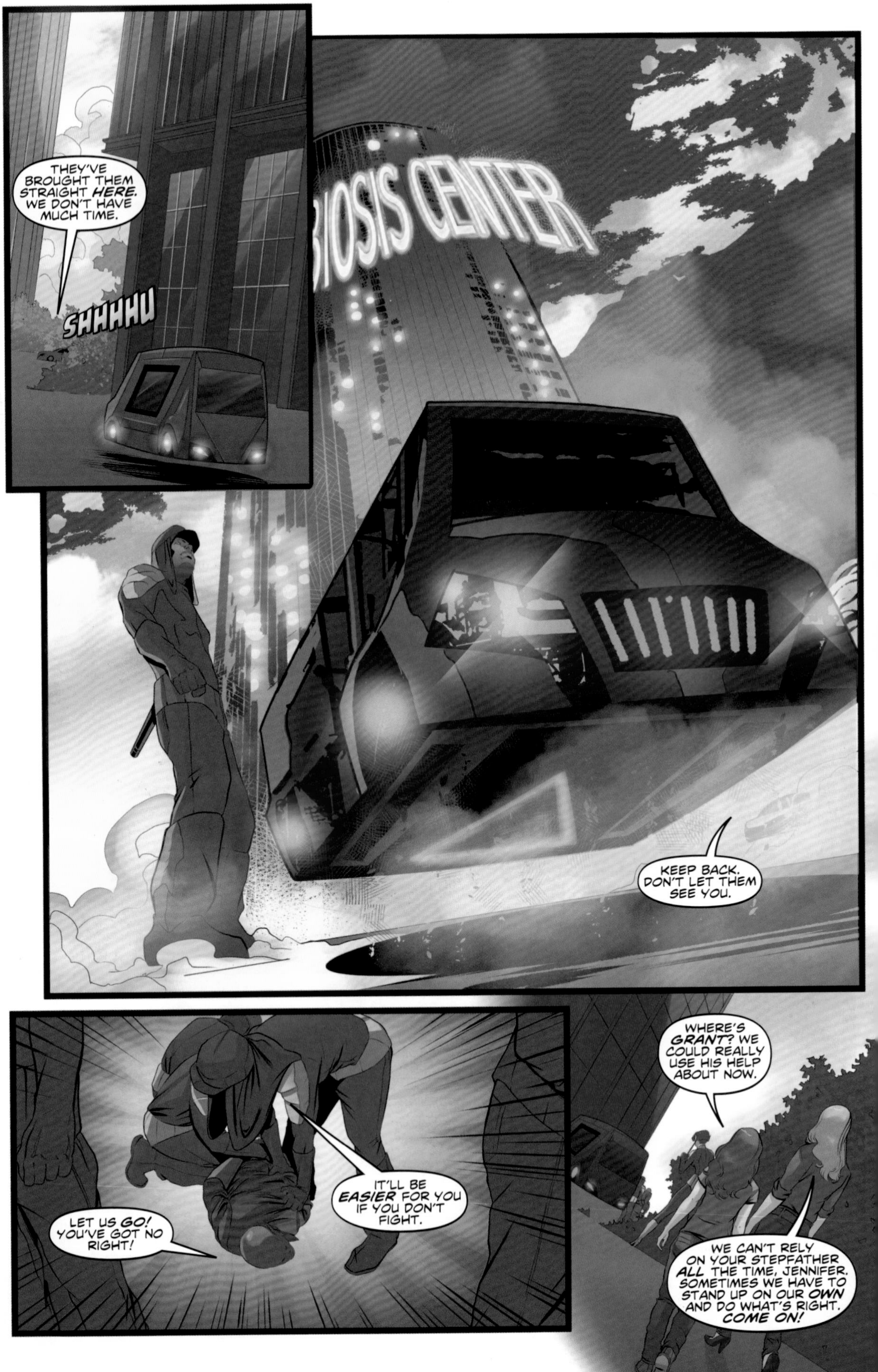
THEY'VE BROUGHT THEM STRAIGHT HERE. WE DON'T HAVE MUCH TIME.
SHHHHU
BIOSIS CENTER
KEEP BACK. DON'T LET THEM SEE YOU.
WHERE'S GRANT? WE COULD REALLY USE HIS HELP ABOUT NOW.
WE CAN'T RELY ON YOUR STEPFATHER ALL THE TIME, JENNIFER. SOMETIMES WE HAVE TO STAND UP ON OUR OWN AND DO WHAT'S RIGHT. COME ON!
LET US GO! YOU'VE GOT NO RIGHT!
IT'LL BE EASIER FOR YOU IF YOU DON'T FIGHT.

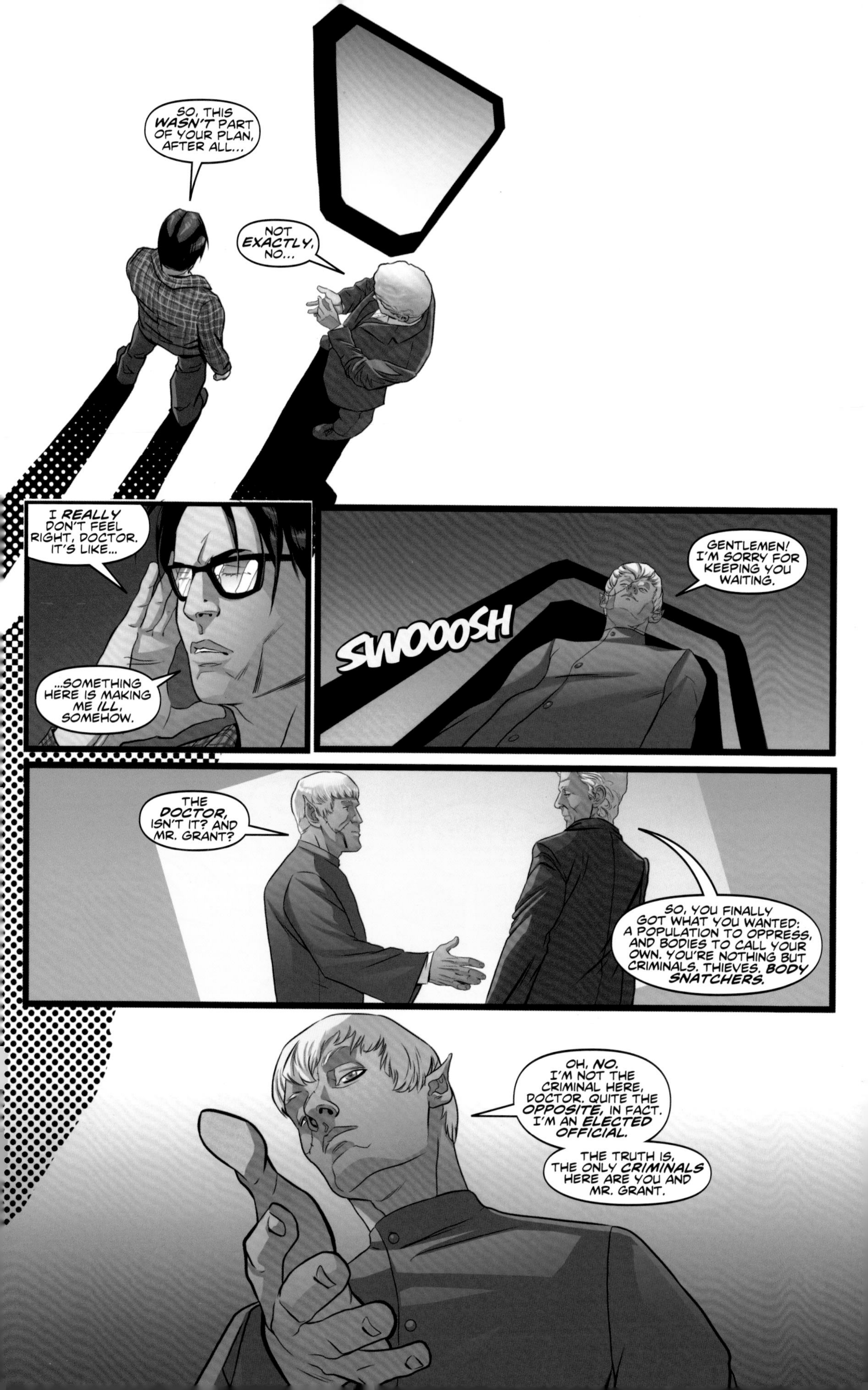
SO, THIS WASN'T PART OF YOUR PLAN, AFTER ALL...
NOT EXACTLY, NO...
I REALLY DON'T FEEL RIGHT, DOCTOR. IT'S LIKE...
...SOMETHING HERE IS MAKING ME ILL, SOMEHOW.
SWOOOSH
GENTLEMEN! I'M SORRY FOR KEEPING YOU WAITING.
THE DOCTOR, ISN'T IT? AND MR. GRANT?
SO, YOU FINALLY GOT WHAT YOU WANTED: A POPULATION TO OPPRESS, AND BODIES TO CALL YOUR OWN. YOU'RE NOTHING BUT CRIMINALS. THIEVES. BODY SNATCHERS.
OH, NO. I'M NOT THE CRIMINAL HERE, DOCTOR. QUITE THE OPPOSITE, IN FACT. I'M AN ELECTED OFFICIAL.
THE TRUTH IS, THE ONLY CRIMINALS HERE ARE YOU AND MR. GRANT.

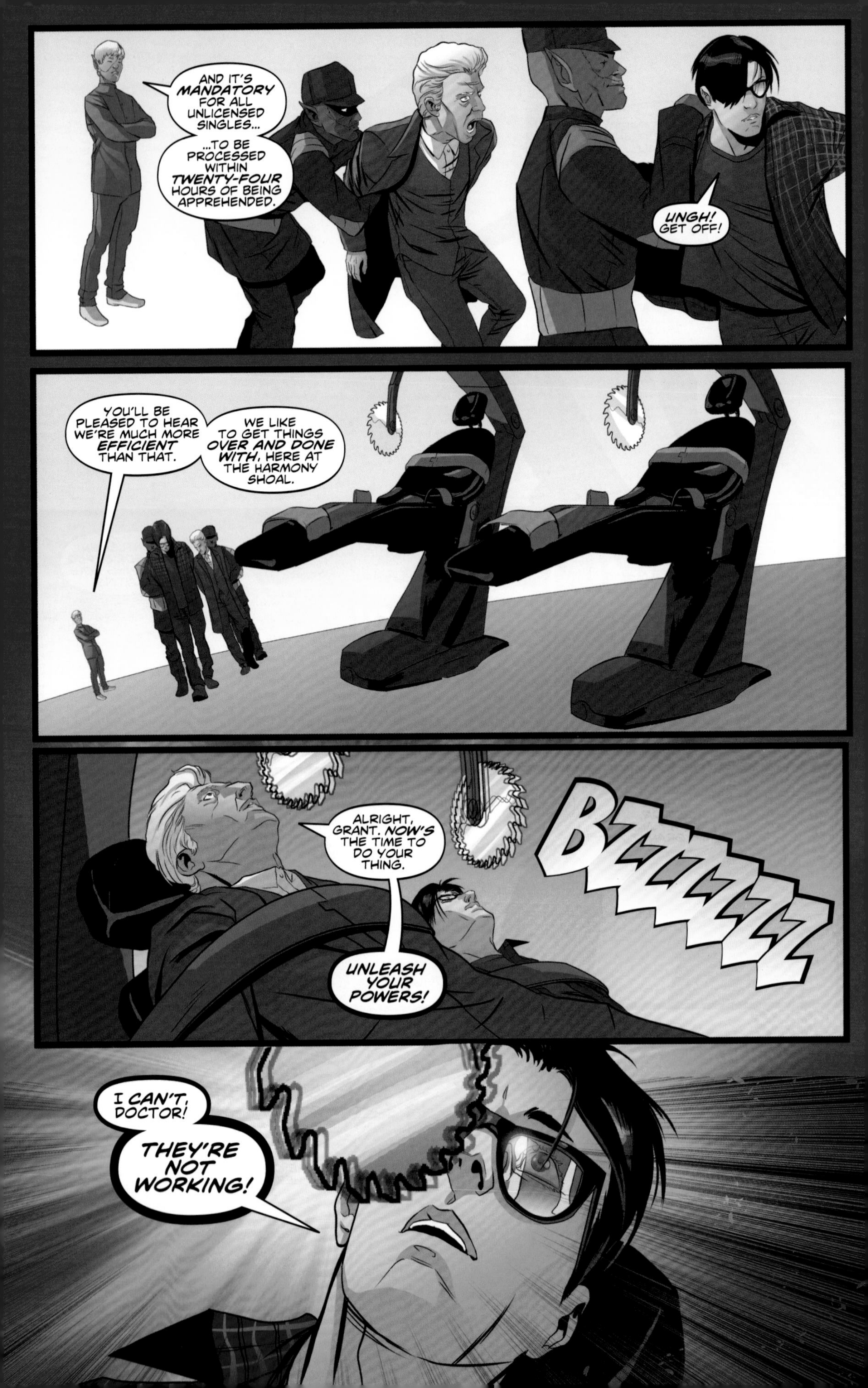
AND IT'S MANDATORY FOR ALL UNLICENSED SINGLES...
...TO BE PROCESSED WITHIN TWENTY-FOUR HOURS OF BEING APPREHENDED.
UNGH! GET OFF!
YOU'LL BE PLEASED TO HEAR WE'RE MUCH MORE EFFICIENT THAN THAT.
WE LIKE TO GET THINGS OVER AND DONE WITH, HERE AT THE HARMONY SHOAL.
BZZZZZ
ALRIGHT, GRANT. NOW'S THE TIME TO DO YOUR THING.
UNLEASH YOUR POWERS!
I CAN'T, DOCTOR!
THEY'RE NOT WORKING!

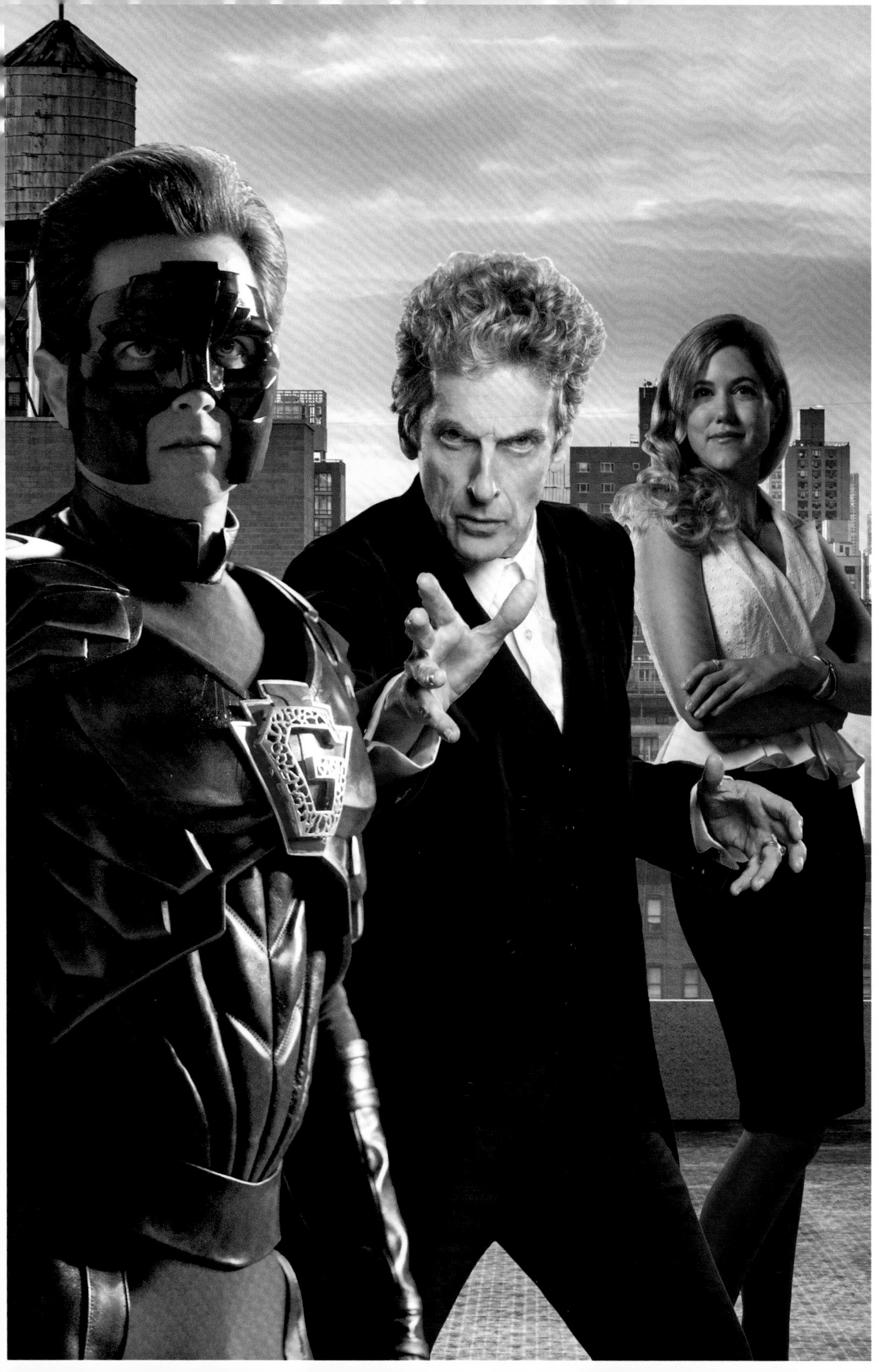

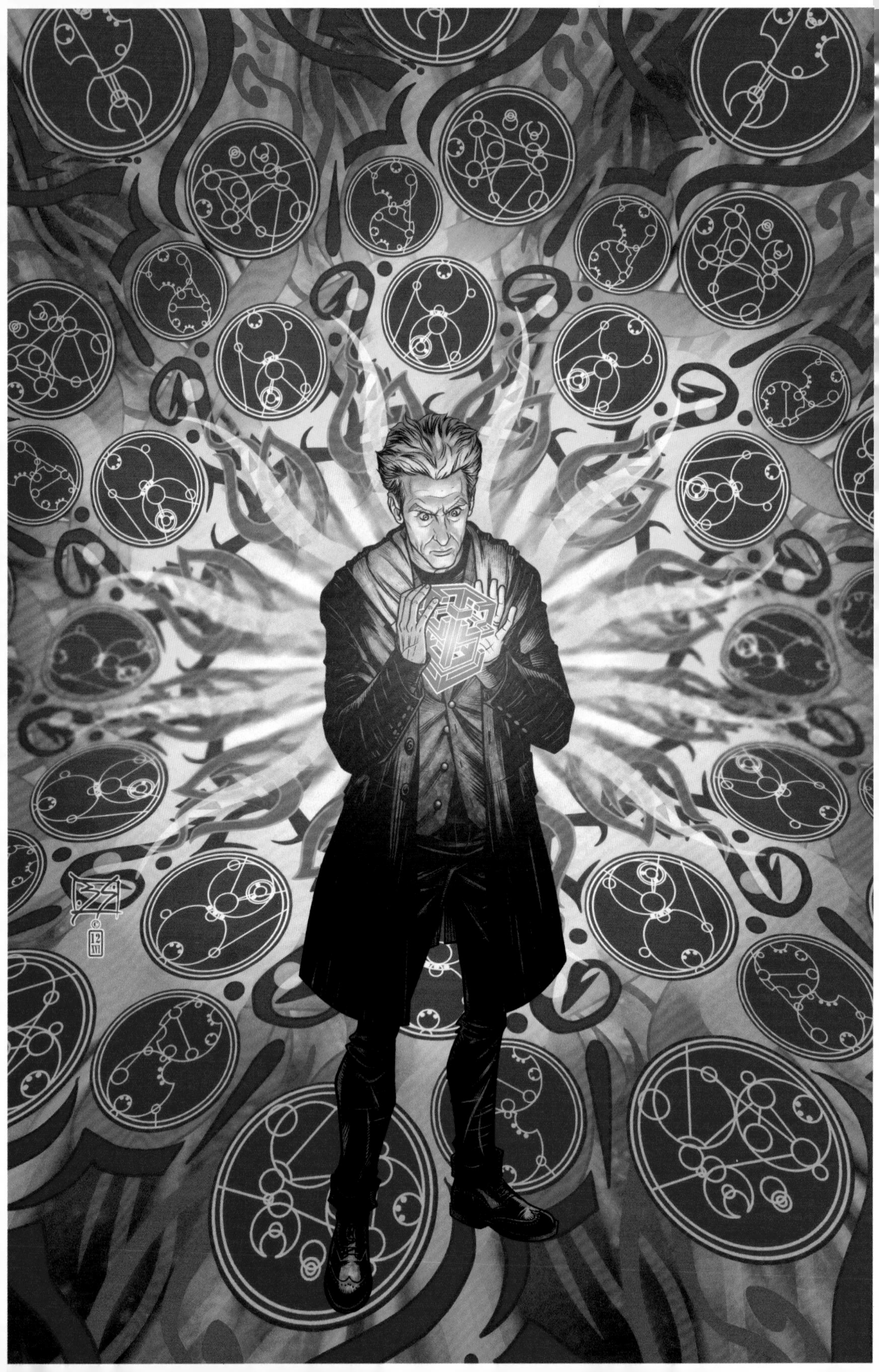

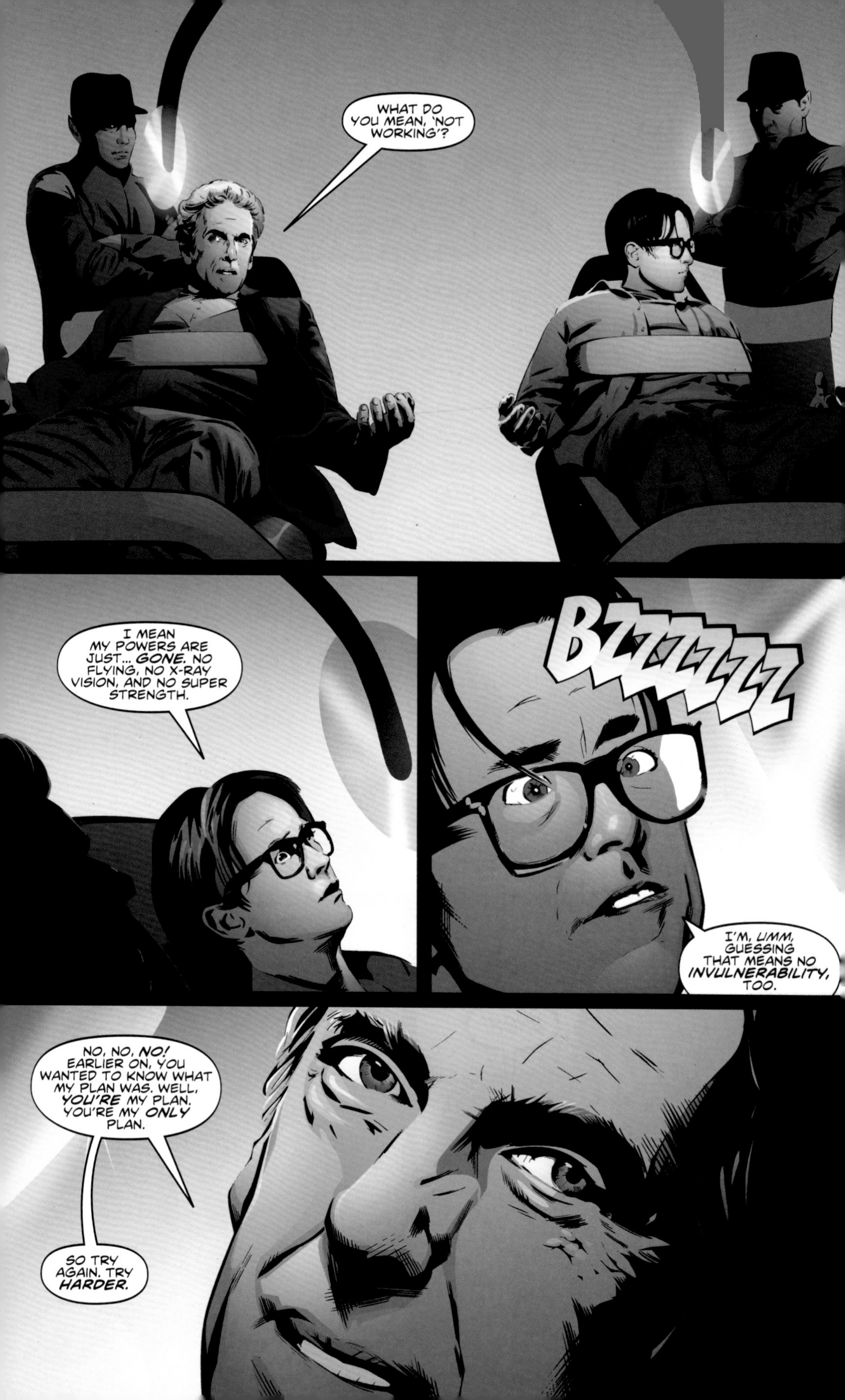
WHAT DO YOU MEAN, 'NOT WORKING'?
I MEAN MY POWERS ARE JUST... **GONE.** NO FLYING, NO X-RAY VISION, AND NO SUPER STRENGTH.
BZZZZZZ
I'M, *UMM*, GUESSING THAT MEANS NO ***INVULNERABILITY***, TOO.
NO, NO, ***NO!*** EARLIER ON, YOU WANTED TO KNOW WHAT MY PLAN WAS. WELL, ***YOU'RE*** MY PLAN. YOU'RE MY ***ONLY*** PLAN.
SO TRY AGAIN. TRY **HARDER.**

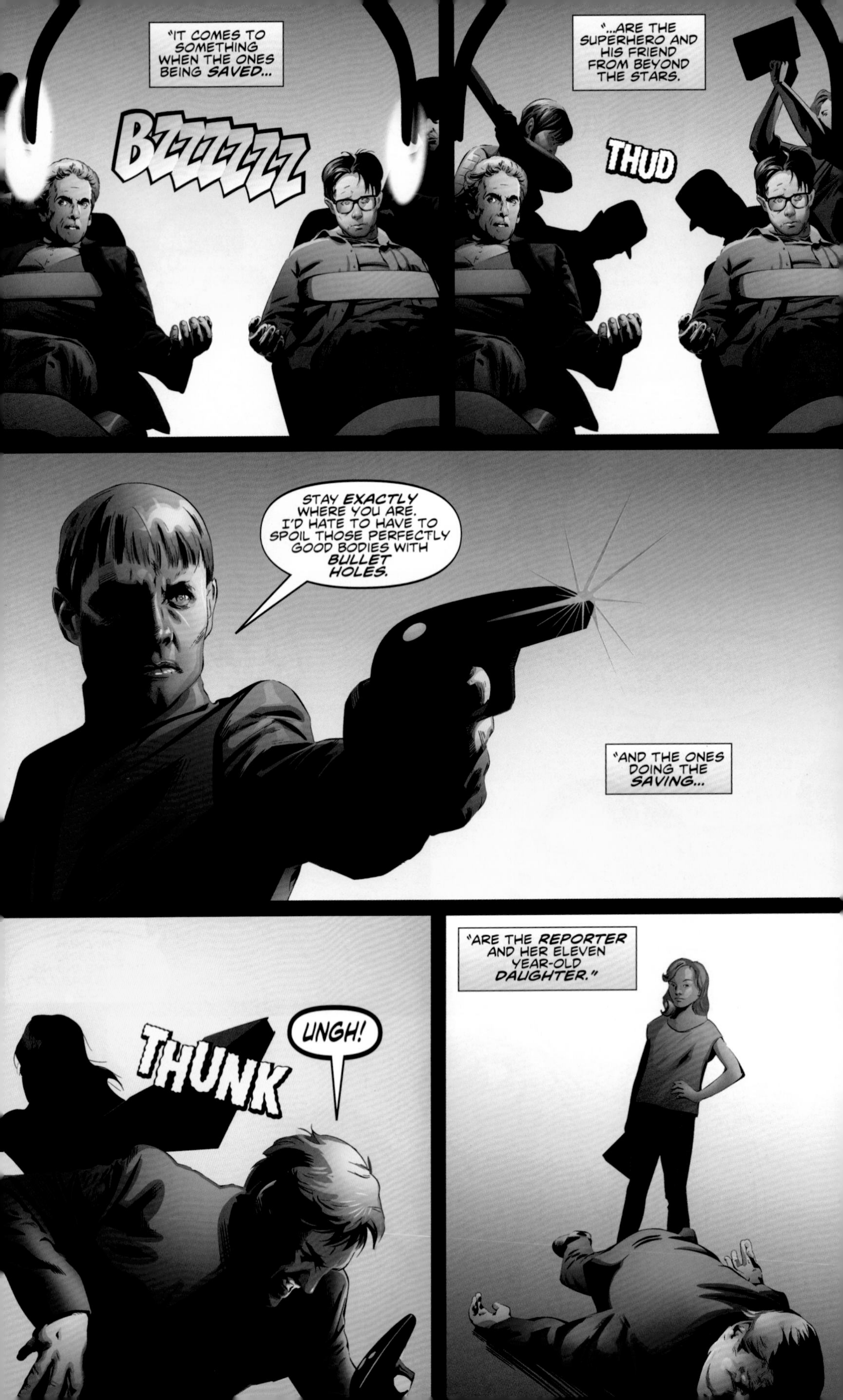
"IT COMES TO SOMETHING WHEN THE ONES BEING SAVED...
BZZZZZZ
"...ARE THE SUPERHERO AND HIS FRIEND FROM BEYOND THE STARS.
THUD
STAY EXACTLY WHERE YOU ARE. I'D HATE TO HAVE TO SPOIL THOSE PERFECTLY GOOD BODIES WITH BULLET HOLES.
"AND THE ONES DOING THE SAVING...
THUNK
UNGH!
"ARE THE REPORTER AND HER ELEVEN YEAR-OLD DAUGHTER."

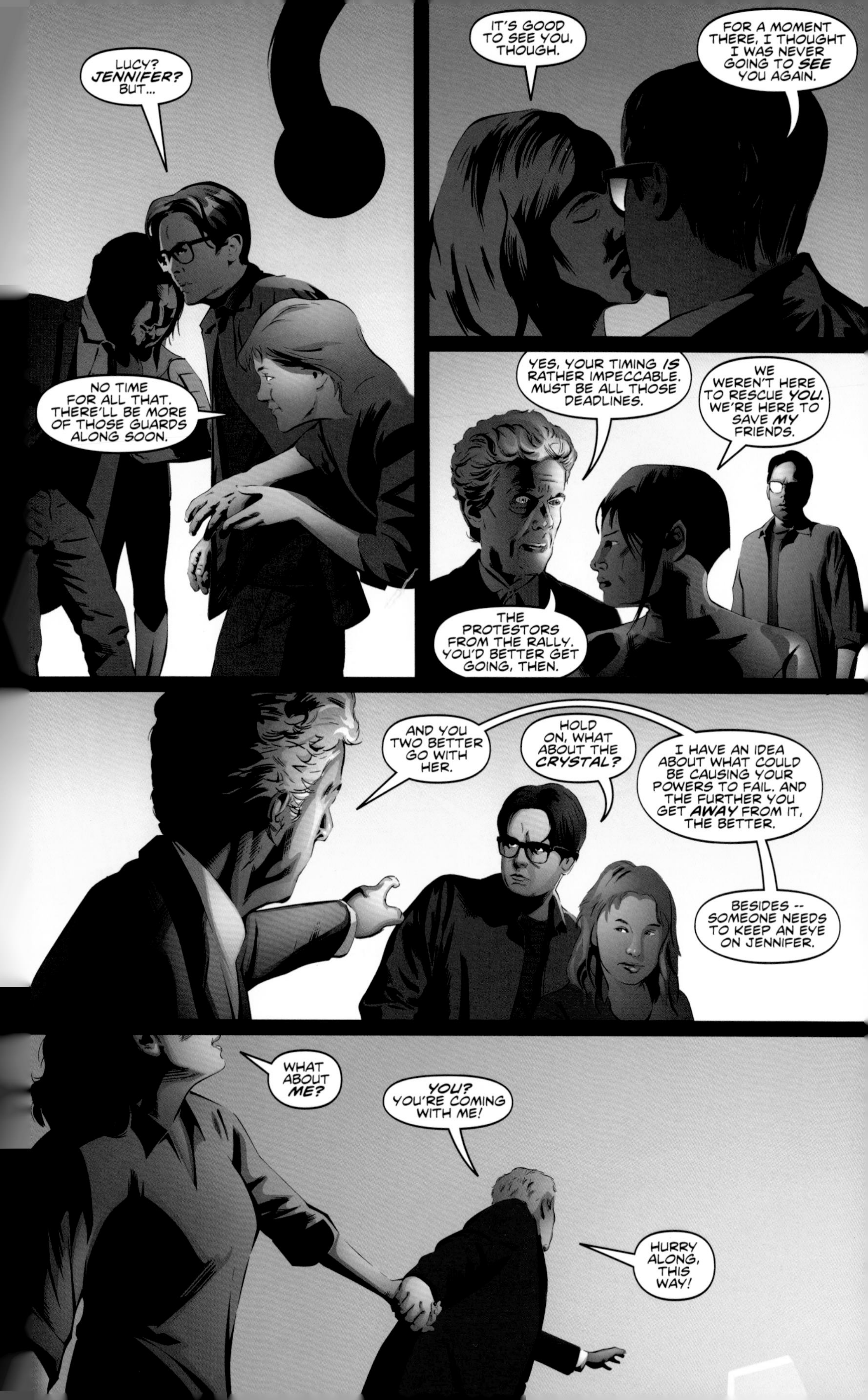
LUCY? JENNIFER? BUT...
NO TIME FOR ALL THAT. THERE'LL BE MORE OF THOSE GUARDS ALONG SOON.
IT'S GOOD TO SEE YOU, THOUGH.
FOR A MOMENT THERE, I THOUGHT I WAS NEVER GOING TO SEE YOU AGAIN.
YES, YOUR TIMING IS RATHER IMPECCABLE. MUST BE ALL THOSE DEADLINES.
WE WEREN'T HERE TO RESCUE YOU. WE'RE HERE TO SAVE MY FRIENDS.
THE PROTESTORS FROM THE RALLY. YOU'D BETTER GET GOING, THEN.
AND YOU TWO BETTER GO WITH HER.
HOLD ON, WHAT ABOUT THE CRYSTAL?
I HAVE AN IDEA ABOUT WHAT COULD BE CAUSING YOUR POWERS TO FAIL. AND THE FURTHER YOU GET AWAY FROM IT, THE BETTER.
BESIDES -- SOMEONE NEEDS TO KEEP AN EYE ON JENNIFER.
WHAT ABOUT ME?
YOU? YOU'RE COMING WITH ME!
HURRY ALONG, THIS WAY!

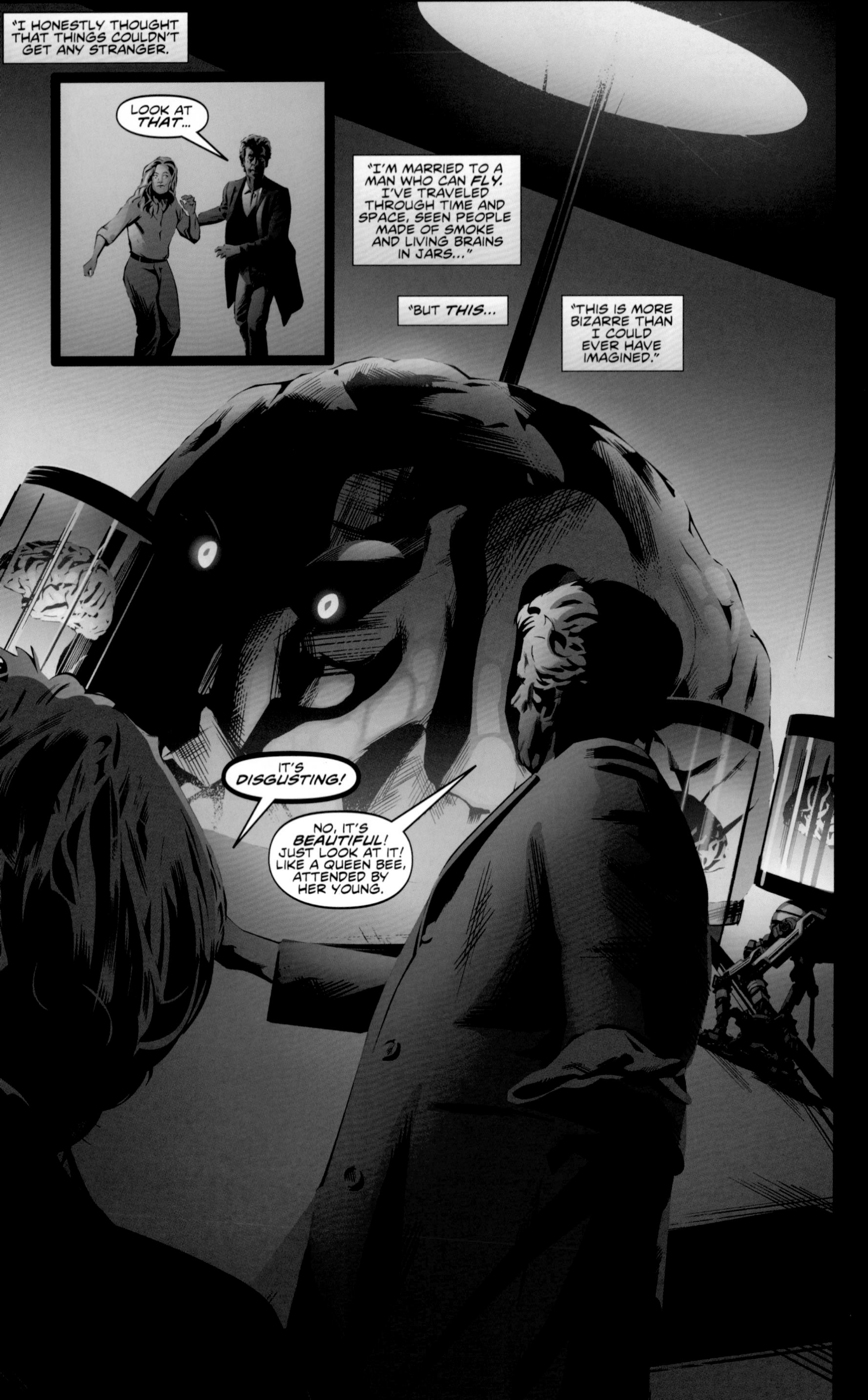
"I HONESTLY THOUGHT THAT THINGS COULDN'T GET ANY STRANGER.
LOOK AT *THAT*...
"I'M MARRIED TO A MAN WHO CAN *FLY*. I'VE TRAVELED THROUGH TIME AND SPACE, SEEN PEOPLE MADE OF SMOKE AND LIVING BRAINS IN JARS..."
"BUT *THIS*...
"THIS IS MORE BIZARRE THAN I COULD EVER HAVE IMAGINED."
IT'S *DISGUSTING!*
NO, IT'S *BEAUTIFUL!* JUST LOOK AT IT! LIKE A QUEEN BEE, ATTENDED BY HER YOUNG.

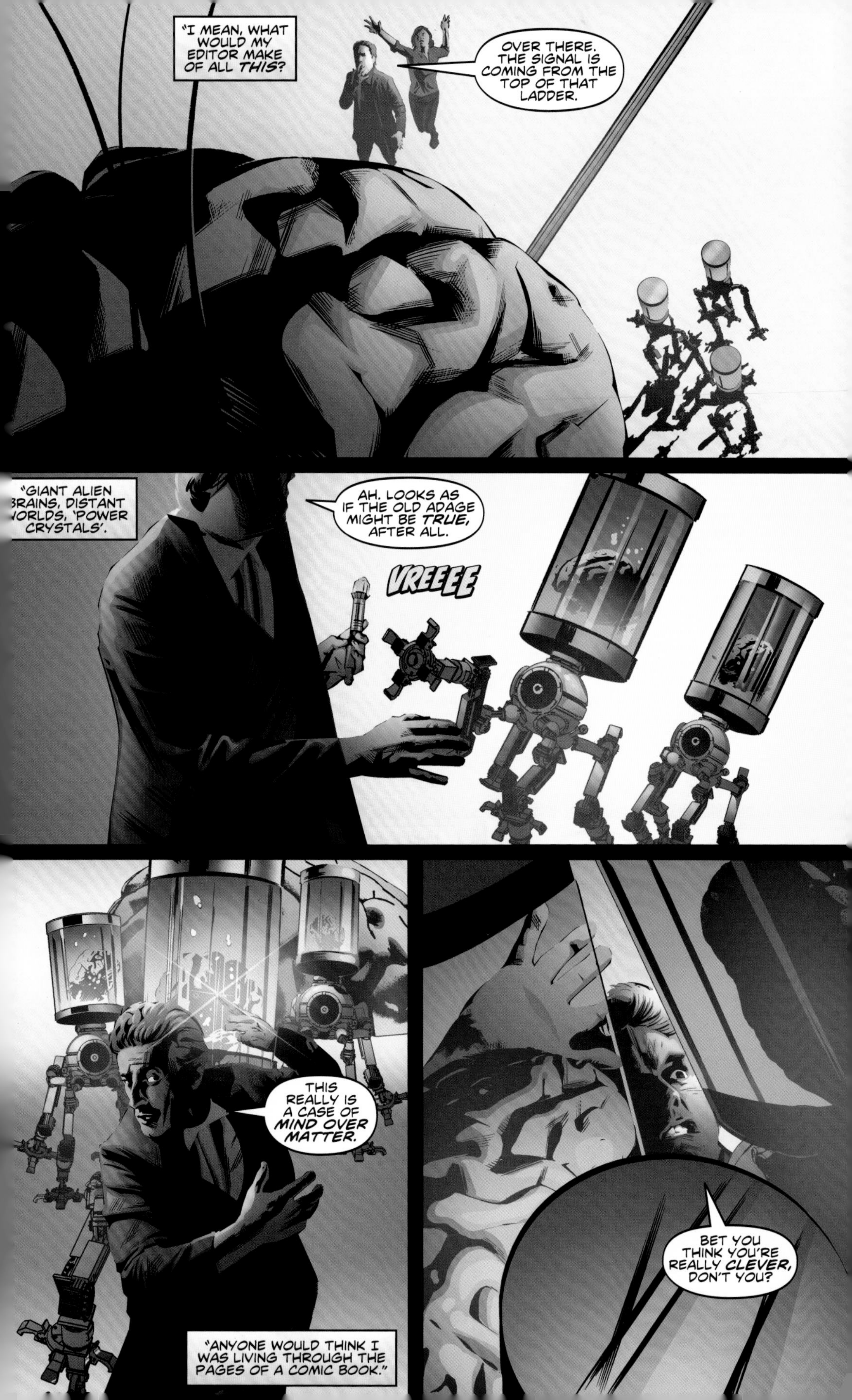
"I MEAN, WHAT WOULD MY EDITOR MAKE OF ALL *THIS*?
OVER THERE. THE SIGNAL IS COMING FROM THE TOP OF THAT LADDER.
"GIANT ALIEN BRAINS, DISTANT WORLDS, 'POWER CRYSTALS'.
AH. LOOKS AS IF THE OLD ADAGE MIGHT BE *TRUE*, AFTER ALL.
VREEEE
THIS REALLY IS A CASE OF *MIND OVER MATTER*.
"ANYONE WOULD THINK I WAS LIVING THROUGH THE PAGES OF A COMIC BOOK."
BET YOU THINK YOU'RE REALLY *CLEVER*, DON'T YOU?

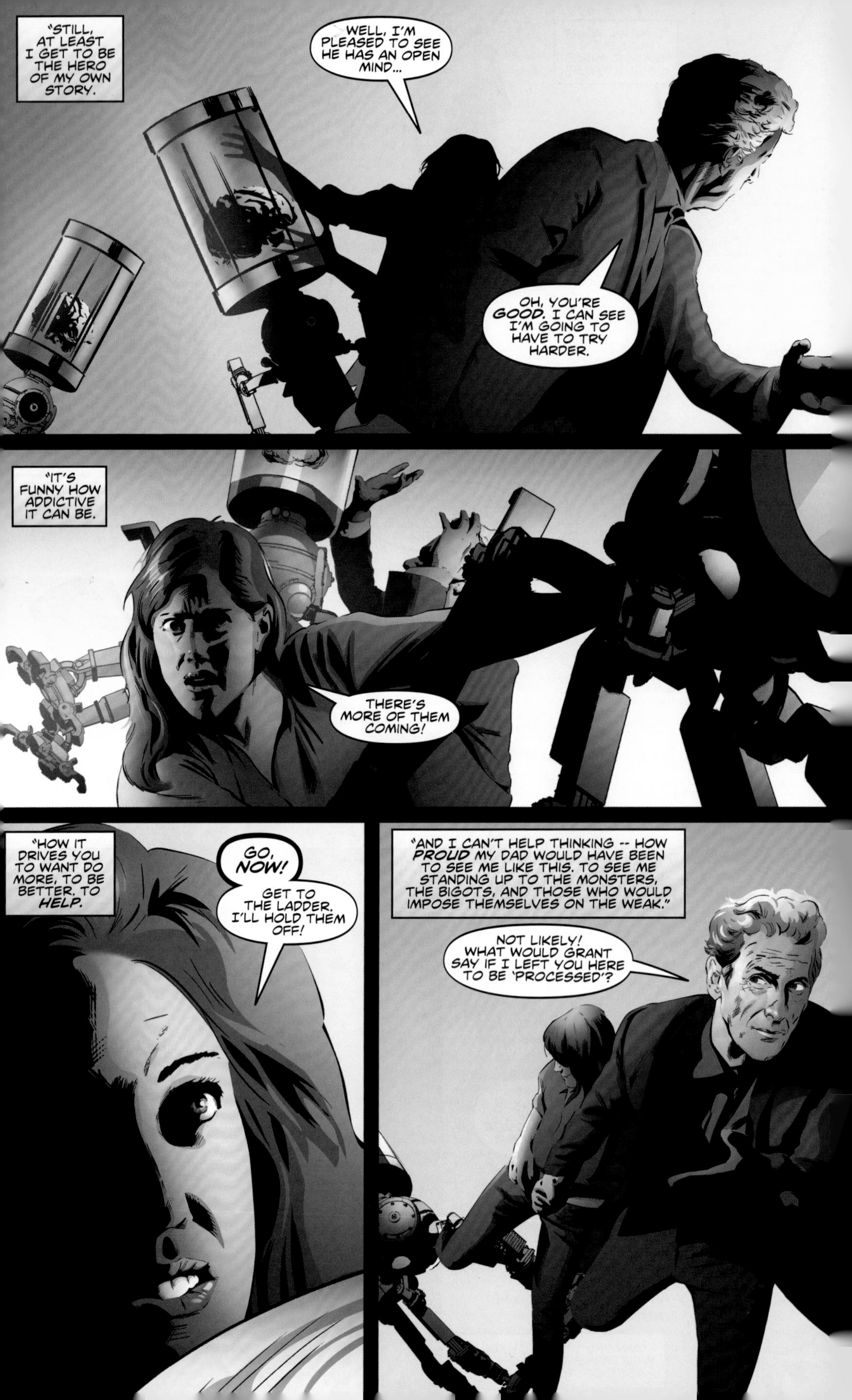
"STILL, AT LEAST I GET TO BE THE HERO OF MY OWN STORY.
WELL, I'M PLEASED TO SEE HE HAS AN OPEN MIND...
OH, YOU'RE GOOD. I CAN SEE I'M GOING TO HAVE TO TRY HARDER.
"IT'S FUNNY HOW ADDICTIVE IT CAN BE.
THERE'S MORE OF THEM COMING!
"HOW IT DRIVES YOU TO WANT DO MORE, TO BE BETTER. TO HELP.
GO, NOW!
GET TO THE LADDER. I'LL HOLD THEM OFF!
"AND I CAN'T HELP THINKING -- HOW PROUD MY DAD WOULD HAVE BEEN TO SEE ME LIKE THIS. TO SEE ME STANDING UP TO THE MONSTERS, THE BIGOTS, AND THOSE WHO WOULD IMPOSE THEMSELVES ON THE WEAK."
NOT LIKELY! WHAT WOULD GRANT SAY IF I LEFT YOU HERE TO BE 'PROCESSED'?

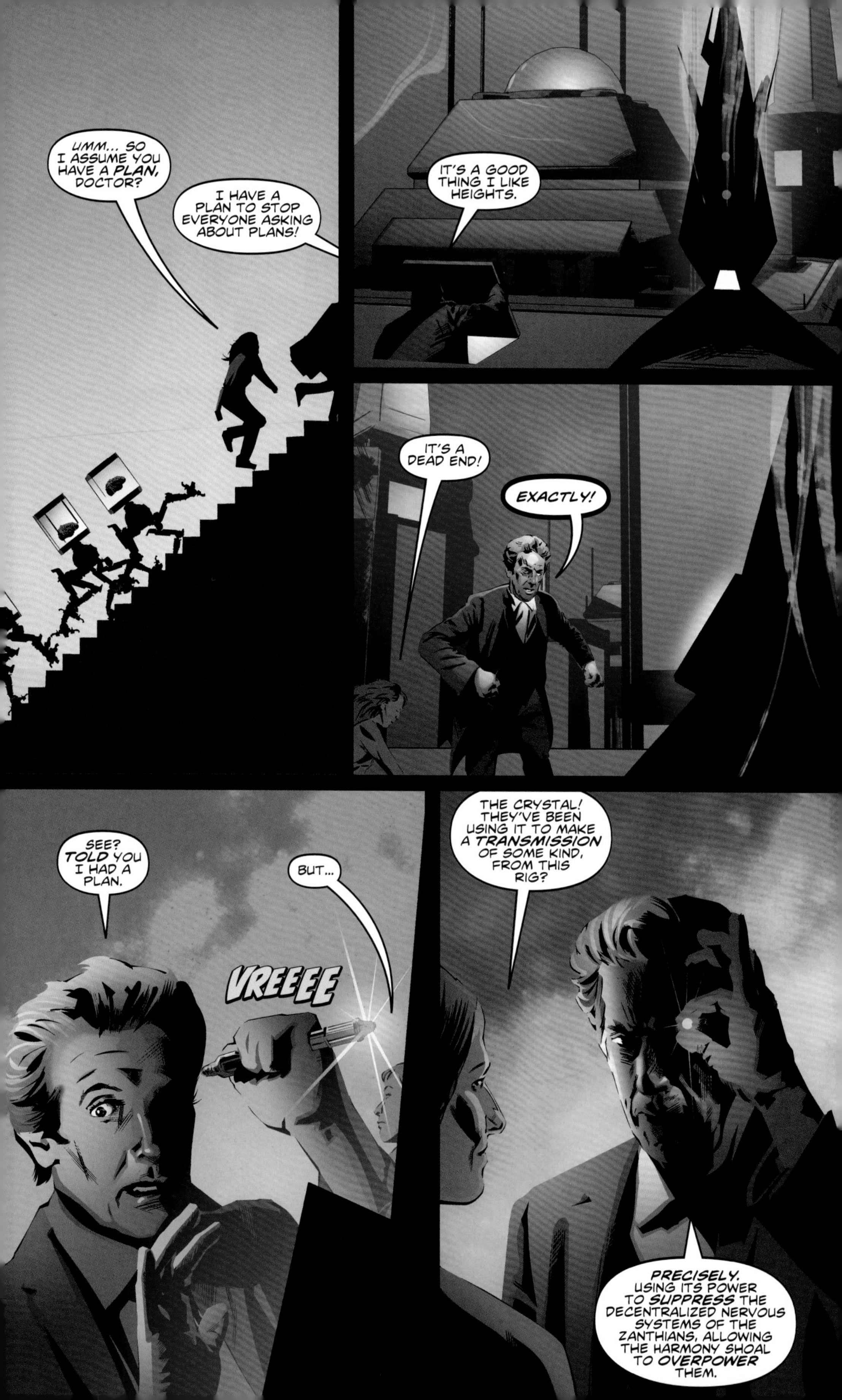
UMM... SO I ASSUME YOU HAVE A PLAN, DOCTOR?
I HAVE A PLAN TO STOP EVERYONE ASKING ABOUT PLANS!
IT'S A GOOD THING I LIKE HEIGHTS.
IT'S A DEAD END!
EXACTLY!
SEE? TOLD YOU I HAD A PLAN.
BUT...
VREEEE
THE CRYSTAL! THEY'VE BEEN USING IT TO MAKE A TRANSMISSION OF SOME KIND, FROM THIS RIG?
PRECISELY. USING ITS POWER TO SUPPRESS THE DECENTRALIZED NERVOUS SYSTEMS OF THE ZANTHIANS, ALLOWING THE HARMONY SHOAL TO OVERPOWER THEM.

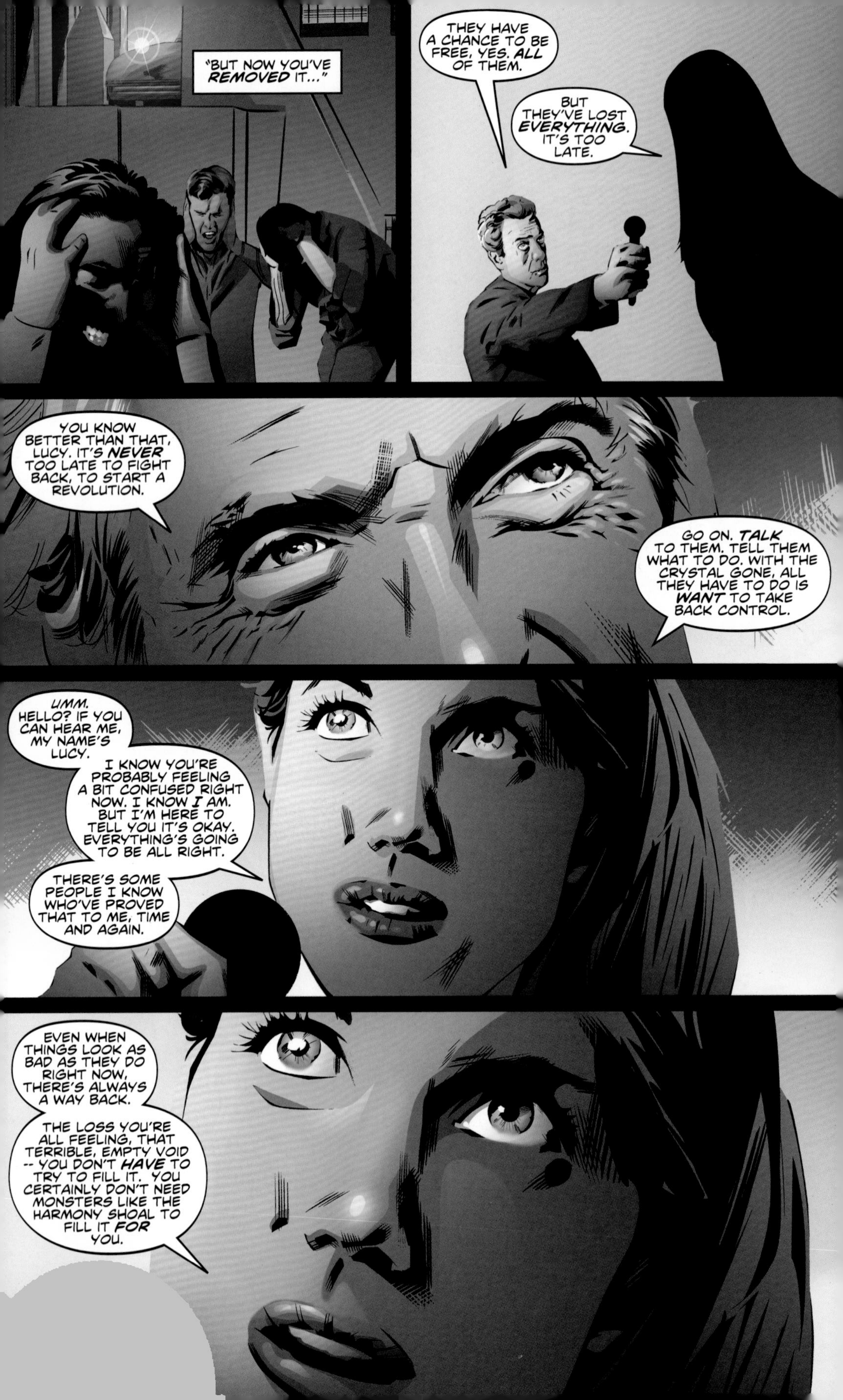

"BUT NOW YOU'VE REMOVED IT..."
THEY HAVE A CHANCE TO BE FREE, YES. ALL OF THEM.
BUT THEY'VE LOST EVERYTHING. IT'S TOO LATE.
YOU KNOW BETTER THAN THAT, LUCY. IT'S NEVER TOO LATE TO FIGHT BACK, TO START A REVOLUTION.
GO ON. TALK TO THEM. TELL THEM WHAT TO DO. WITH THE CRYSTAL GONE, ALL THEY HAVE TO DO IS WANT TO TAKE BACK CONTROL.
UMM. HELLO? IF YOU CAN HEAR ME, MY NAME'S LUCY.
I KNOW YOU'RE PROBABLY FEELING A BIT CONFUSED RIGHT NOW. I KNOW I AM. BUT I'M HERE TO TELL YOU IT'S OKAY. EVERYTHING'S GOING TO BE ALL RIGHT.
THERE'S SOME PEOPLE I KNOW WHO'VE PROVED THAT TO ME, TIME AND AGAIN.
EVEN WHEN THINGS LOOK AS BAD AS THEY DO RIGHT NOW, THERE'S ALWAYS A WAY BACK.
THE LOSS YOU'RE ALL FEELING, THAT TERRIBLE, EMPTY VOID -- YOU DON'T HAVE TO TRY TO FILL IT. YOU CERTAINLY DON'T NEED MONSTERS LIKE THE HARMONY SHOAL TO FILL IT FOR YOU.

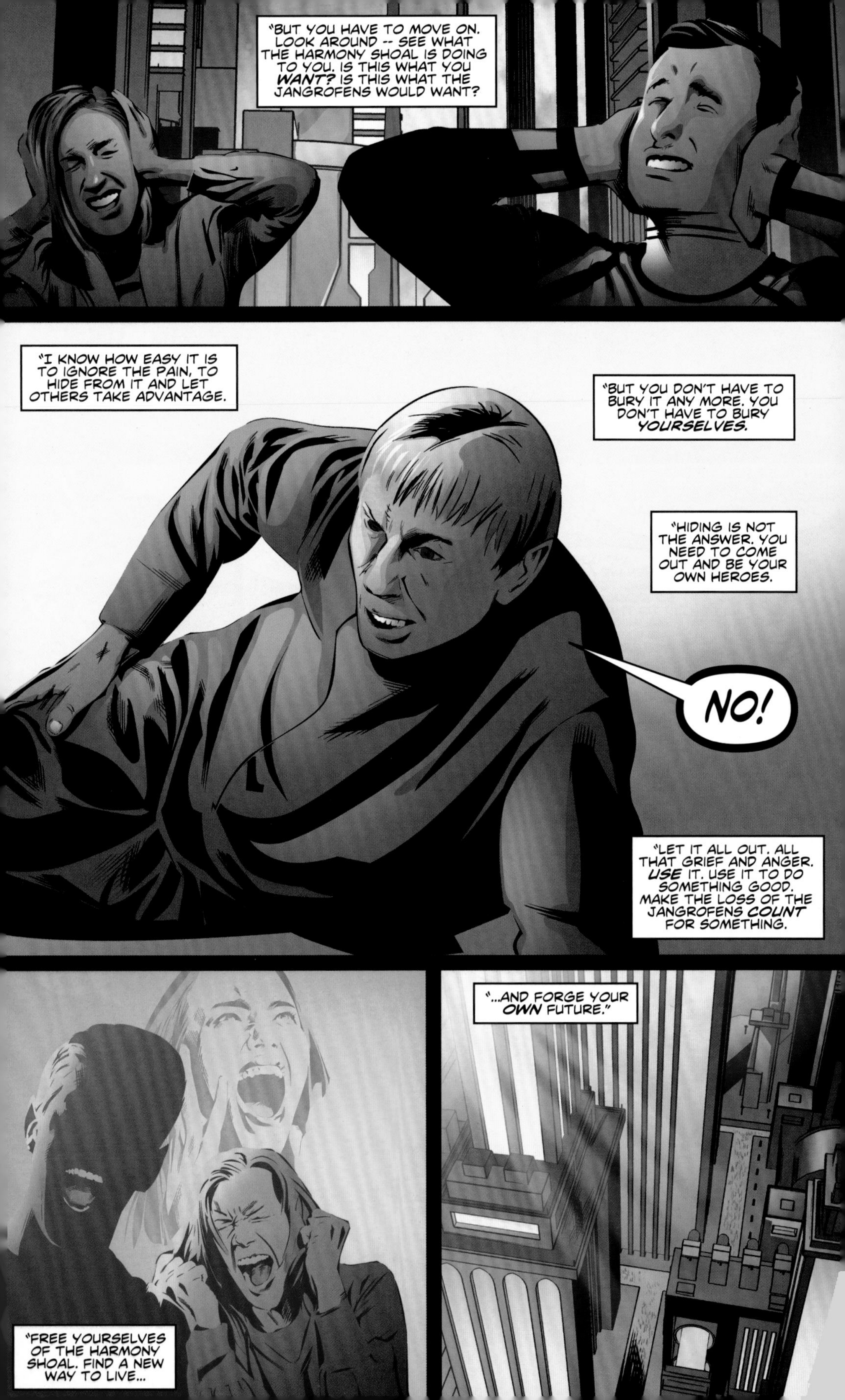
"BUT YOU HAVE TO MOVE ON. LOOK AROUND -- SEE WHAT THE HARMONY SHOAL IS DOING TO YOU. IS THIS WHAT YOU WANT? IS THIS WHAT THE JANGROFENS WOULD WANT?
"I KNOW HOW EASY IT IS TO IGNORE THE PAIN, TO HIDE FROM IT AND LET OTHERS TAKE ADVANTAGE.
"BUT YOU DON'T HAVE TO BURY IT ANY MORE. YOU DON'T HAVE TO BURY YOURSELVES.
"HIDING IS NOT THE ANSWER. YOU NEED TO COME OUT AND BE YOUR OWN HEROES.
NO!
"LET IT ALL OUT. ALL THAT GRIEF AND ANGER. USE IT. USE IT TO DO SOMETHING GOOD. MAKE THE LOSS OF THE JANGROFENS COUNT FOR SOMETHING.
"FREE YOURSELVES OF THE HARMONY SHOAL. FIND A NEW WAY TO LIVE...
"...AND FORGE YOUR OWN FUTURE."

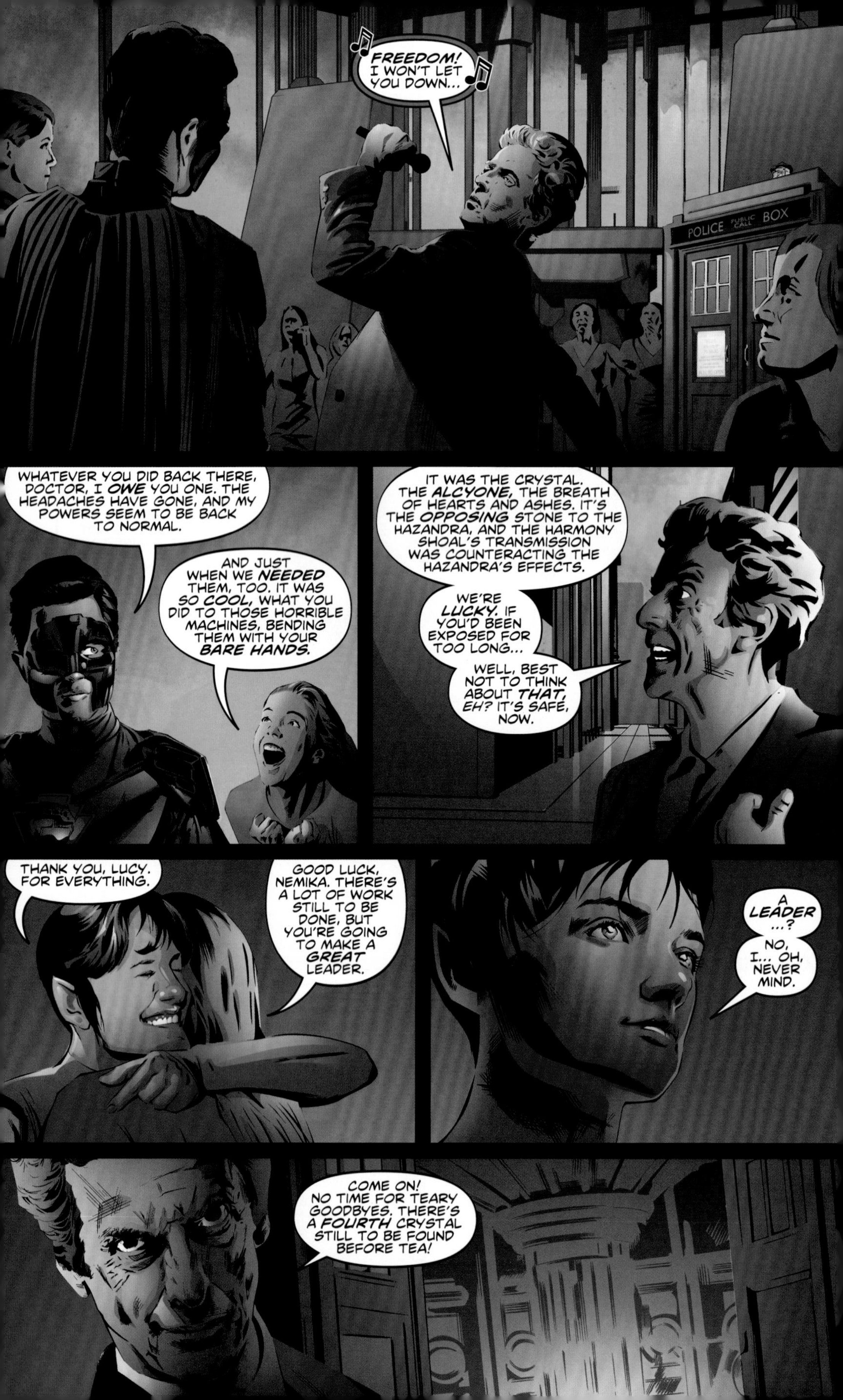

FREEDOM! I WON'T LET YOU DOWN...
BOX
WHATEVER YOU DID BACK THERE, DOCTOR, I OWE YOU ONE. THE HEADACHES HAVE GONE, AND MY POWERS SEEM TO BE BACK TO NORMAL.
AND JUST WHEN WE NEEDED THEM, TOO. IT WAS SO COOL, WHAT YOU DID TO THOSE HORRIBLE MACHINES, BENDING THEM WITH YOUR BARE HANDS.
IT WAS THE CRYSTAL. THE ALCYONE, THE BREATH OF HEARTS AND ASHES. IT'S THE OPPOSING STONE TO THE HAZANDRA, AND THE HARMONY SHOAL'S TRANSMISSION WAS COUNTERACTING THE HAZANDRA'S EFFECTS.
WE'RE LUCKY. IF YOU'D BEEN EXPOSED FOR TOO LONG...
WELL, BEST NOT TO THINK ABOUT THAT, EH? IT'S SAFE, NOW.
THANK YOU, LUCY. FOR EVERYTHING.
GOOD LUCK, NEMIKA. THERE'S A LOT OF WORK STILL TO BE DONE, BUT YOU'RE GOING TO MAKE A GREAT LEADER.
A LEADER ...?
NO, I... OH, NEVER MIND.
COME ON! NO TIME FOR TEARY GOODBYES. THERE'S A FOURTH CRYSTAL STILL TO BE FOUND BEFORE TEA!

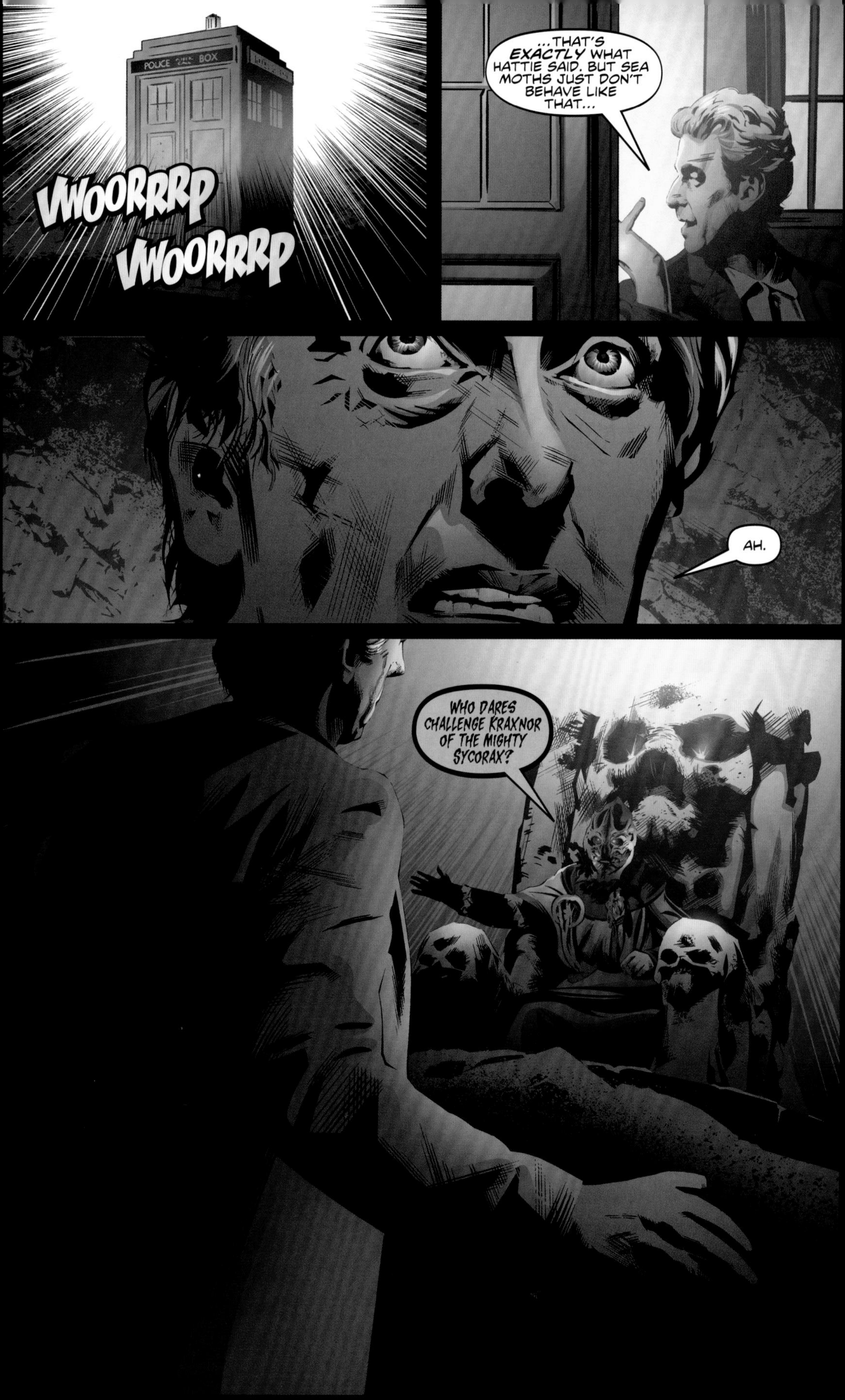

VWOORRRP
VWOORRRP
...THAT'S EXACTLY WHAT HATTIE SAID. BUT SEA MOTHS JUST DON'T BEHAVE LIKE THAT...
AH.
WHO DARES CHALLENGE KRAXNOR OF THE MIGHTY SYCORAX?

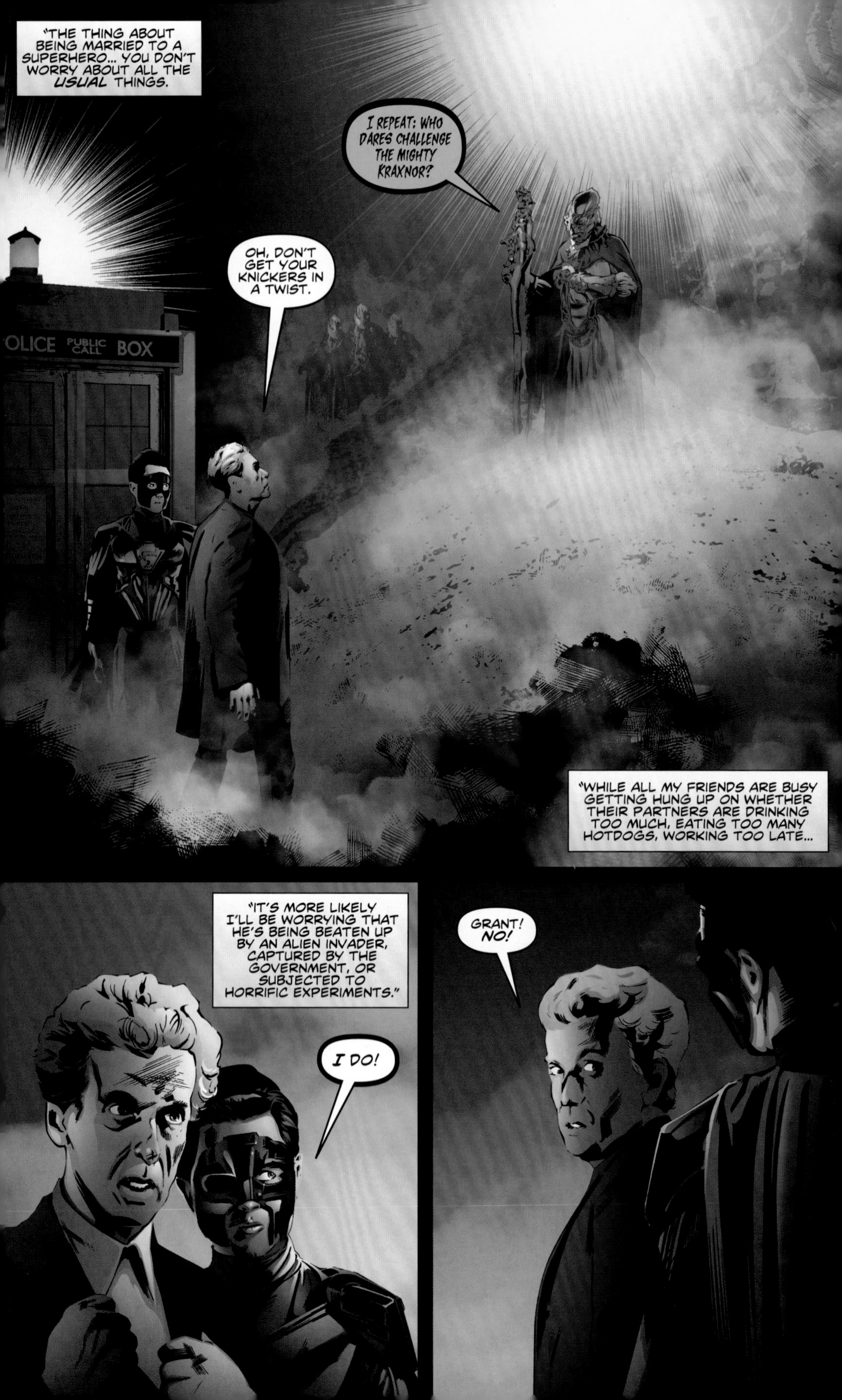
"THE THING ABOUT BEING MARRIED TO A SUPERHERO... YOU DON'T WORRY ABOUT ALL THE USUAL THINGS.
I REPEAT: WHO DARES CHALLENGE THE MIGHTY KRAXNOR?
OH, DON'T GET YOUR KNICKERS IN A TWIST.
POLICE PUBLIC CALL BOX
"WHILE ALL MY FRIENDS ARE BUSY GETTING HUNG UP ON WHETHER THEIR PARTNERS ARE DRINKING TOO MUCH, EATING TOO MANY HOTDOGS, WORKING TOO LATE...
"IT'S MORE LIKELY I'LL BE WORRYING THAT HE'S BEING BEATEN UP BY AN ALIEN INVADER, CAPTURED BY THE GOVERNMENT, OR SUBJECTED TO HORRIFIC EXPERIMENTS."
I DO!
GRANT! NO!

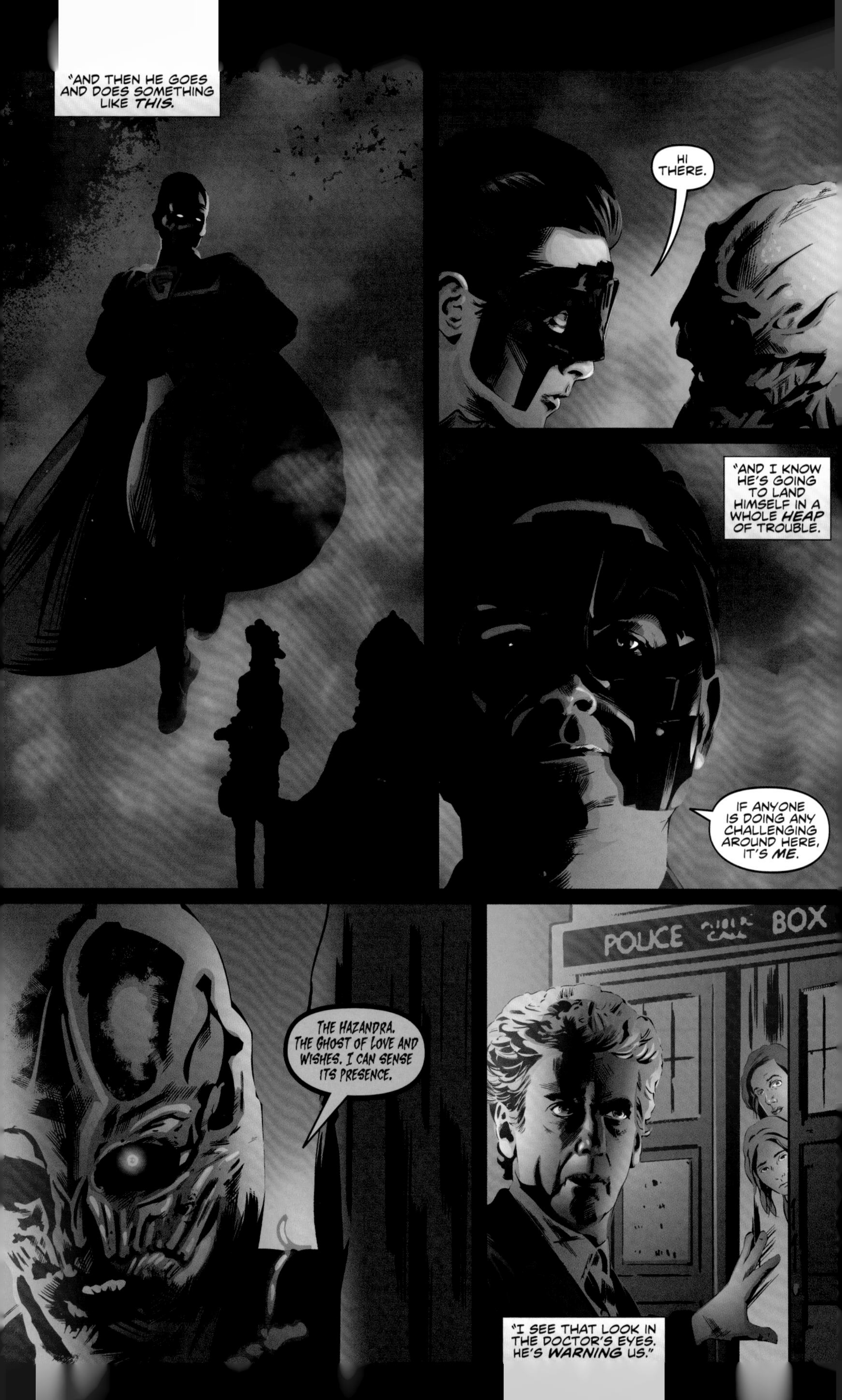
"AND THEN HE GOES AND DOES SOMETHING LIKE THIS.
HI THERE.
"AND I KNOW HE'S GOING TO LAND HIMSELF IN A WHOLE HEAP OF TROUBLE.
IF ANYONE IS DOING ANY CHALLENGING AROUND HERE, IT'S ME.
THE HAZANDRA. THE GHOST OF LOVE AND WISHES. I CAN SENSE ITS PRESENCE.
POLICE BOX
"I SEE THAT LOOK IN THE DOCTOR'S EYES. HE'S WARNING US."

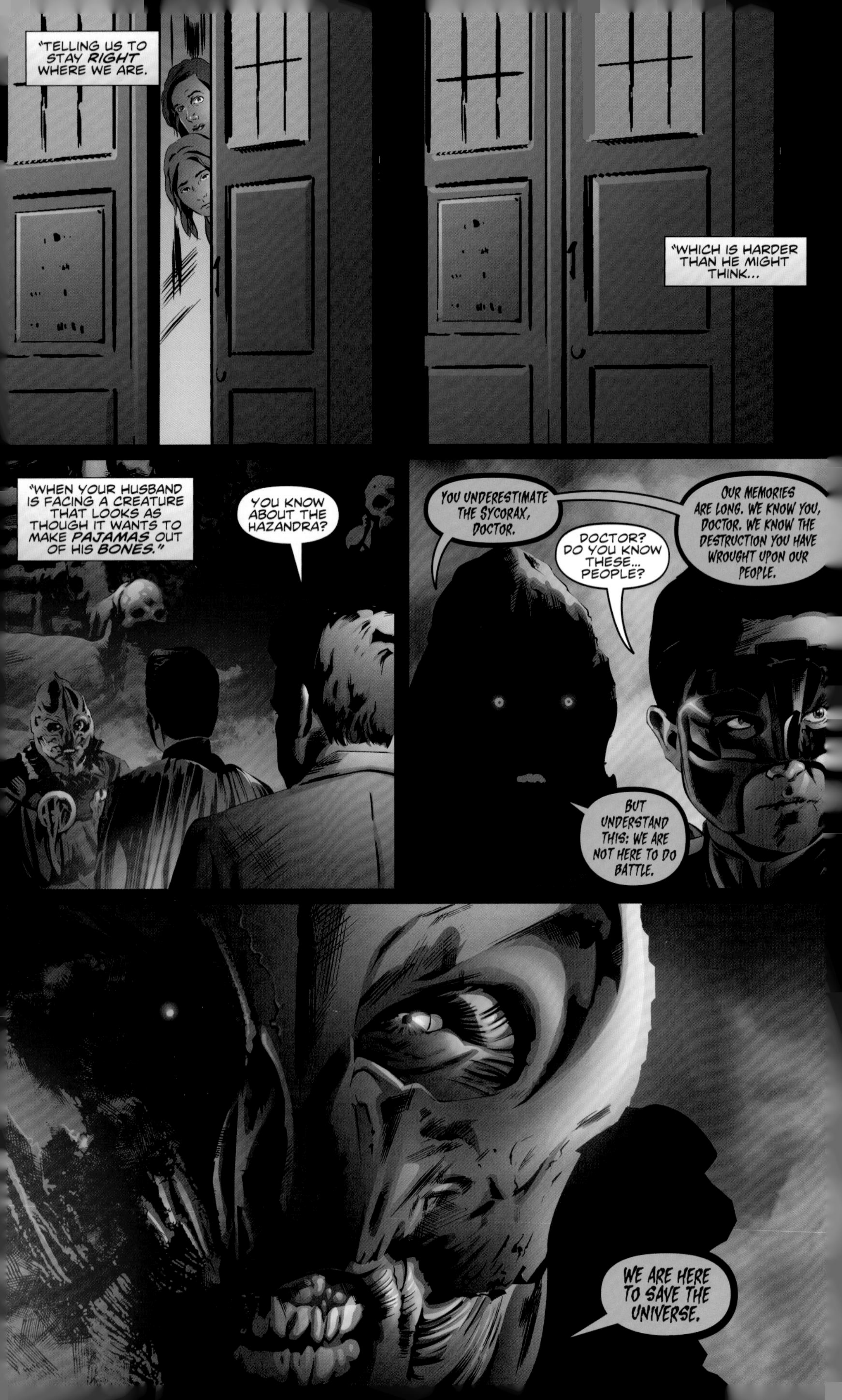
"TELLING US TO STAY RIGHT WHERE WE ARE.
"WHICH IS HARDER THAN HE MIGHT THINK...
"WHEN YOUR HUSBAND IS FACING A CREATURE THAT LOOKS AS THOUGH IT WANTS TO MAKE PAJAMAS OUT OF HIS BONES."
YOU KNOW ABOUT THE HAZANDRA?
YOU UNDERESTIMATE THE SYCORAX, DOCTOR.
OUR MEMORIES ARE LONG. WE KNOW YOU, DOCTOR. WE KNOW THE DESTRUCTION YOU HAVE WROUGHT UPON OUR PEOPLE.
DOCTOR? DO YOU KNOW THESE... PEOPLE?
BUT UNDERSTAND THIS: WE ARE NOT HERE TO DO BATTLE.
WE ARE HERE TO SAVE THE UNIVERSE.

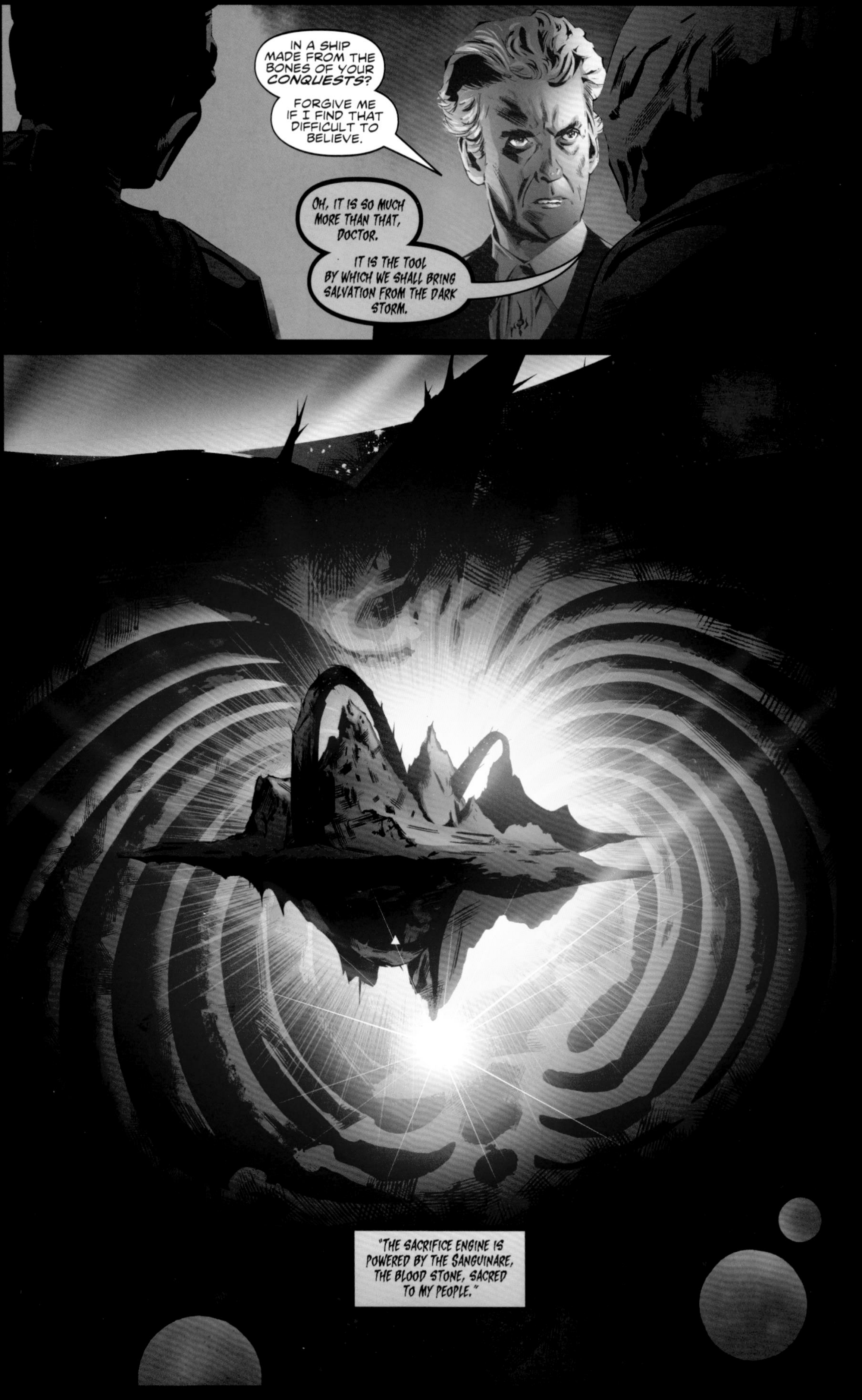
IN A SHIP MADE FROM THE BONES OF YOUR CONQUESTS?
FORGIVE ME IF I FIND THAT DIFFICULT TO BELIEVE.
OH, IT IS SO MUCH MORE THAN THAT, DOCTOR.
IT IS THE TOOL BY WHICH WE SHALL BRING SALVATION FROM THE DARK STORM.
"THE SACRIFICE ENGINE IS POWERED BY THE SANGUINARE, THE BLOOD STONE, SACRED TO MY PEOPLE."

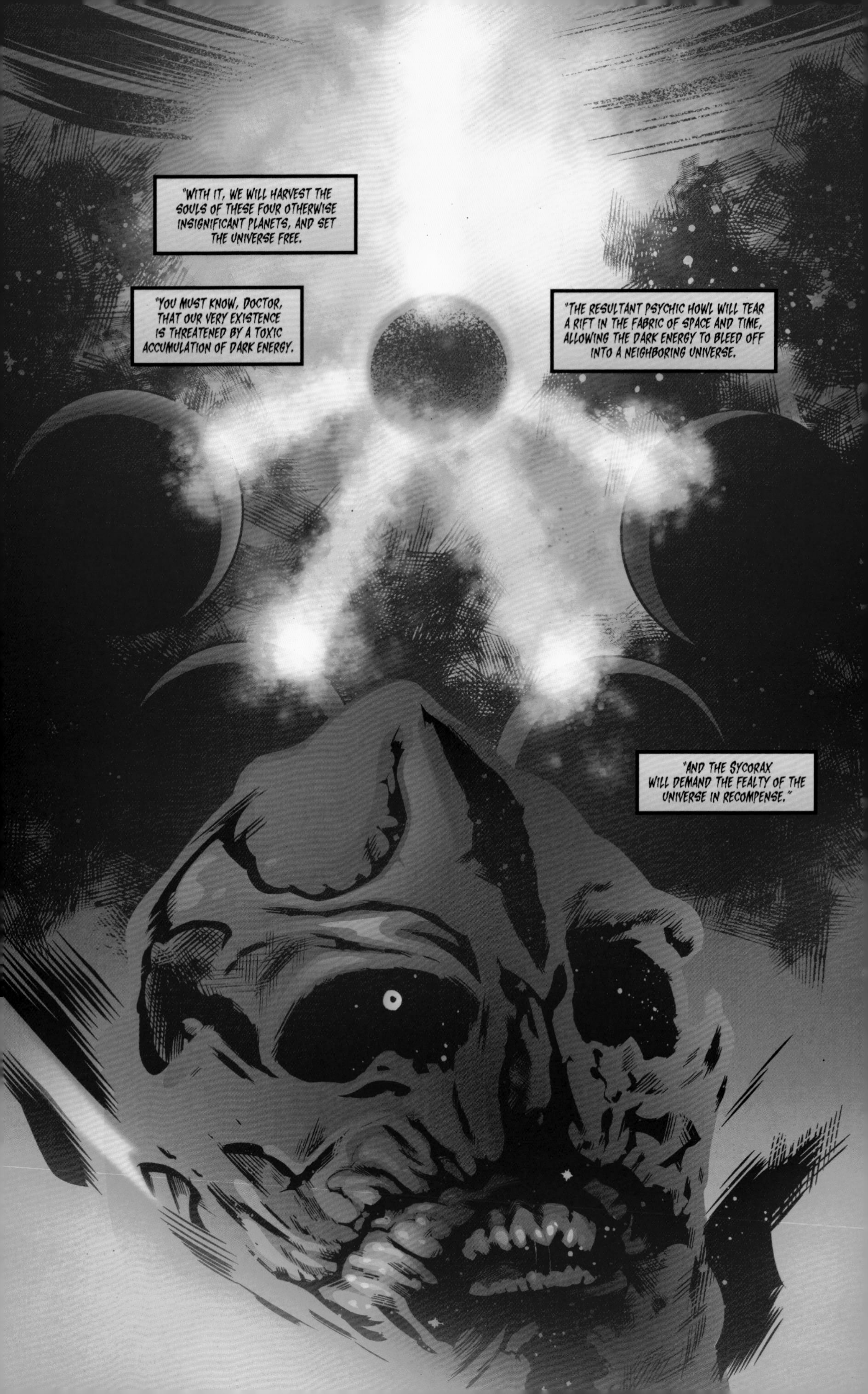
"WITH IT, WE WILL HARVEST THE SOULS OF THESE FOUR OTHERWISE INSIGNIFICANT PLANETS, AND SET THE UNIVERSE FREE.
"YOU MUST KNOW, DOCTOR, THAT OUR VERY EXISTENCE IS THREATENED BY A TOXIC ACCUMULATION OF DARK ENERGY.
"THE RESULTANT PSYCHIC HOWL WILL TEAR A RIFT IN THE FABRIC OF SPACE AND TIME, ALLOWING THE DARK ENERGY TO BLEED OFF INTO A NEIGHBORING UNIVERSE.
"AND THE SYCORAX WILL DEMAND THE FEALTY OF THE UNIVERSE IN RECOMPENSE."

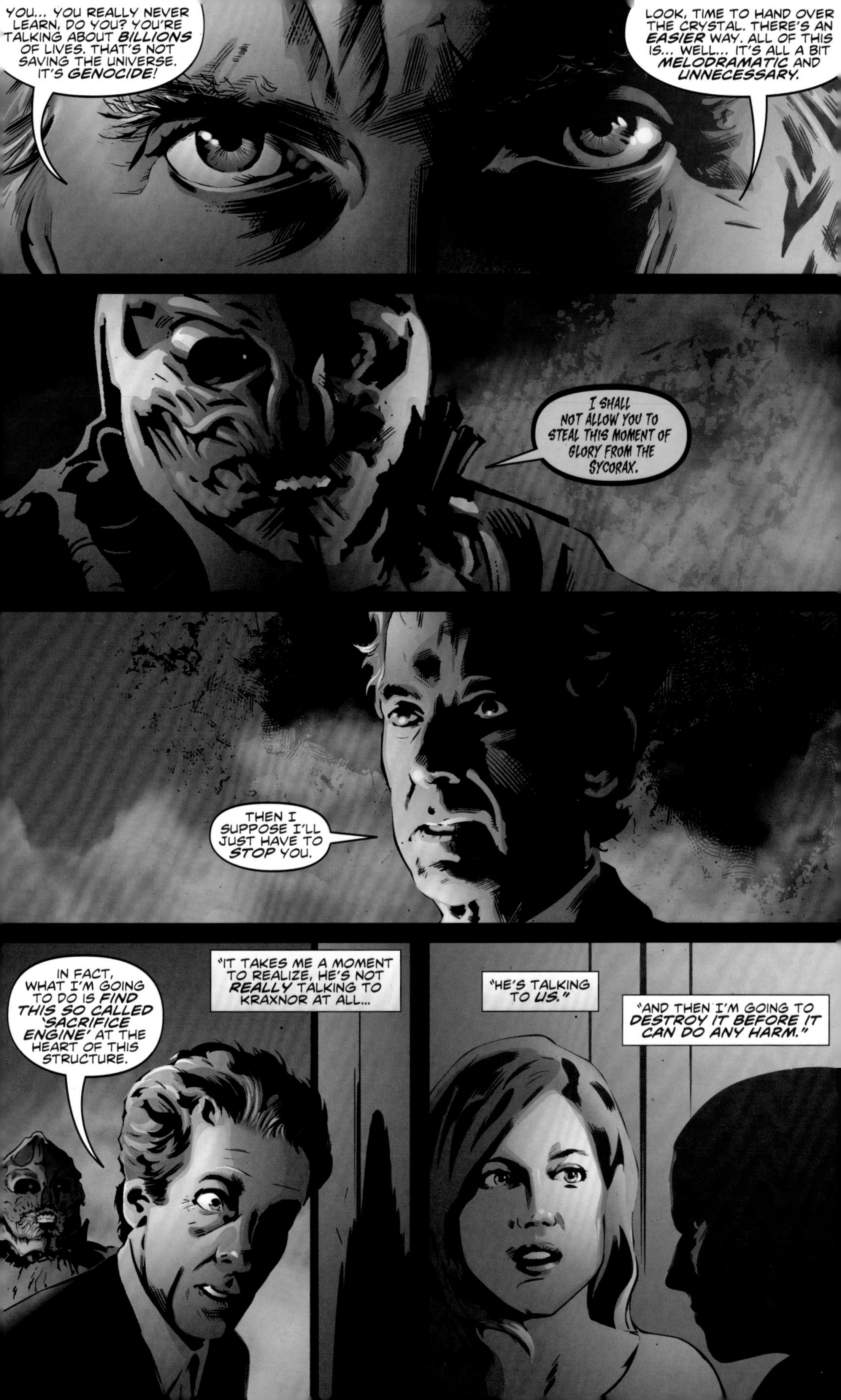

YOU... YOU REALLY NEVER LEARN, DO YOU? YOU'RE TALKING ABOUT BILLIONS OF LIVES. THAT'S NOT SAVING THE UNIVERSE. IT'S GENOCIDE!
LOOK, TIME TO HAND OVER THE CRYSTAL. THERE'S AN EASIER WAY. ALL OF THIS IS... WELL... IT'S ALL A BIT MELODRAMATIC AND UNNECESSARY.
I SHALL NOT ALLOW YOU TO STEAL THIS MOMENT OF GLORY FROM THE SYCORAX.
THEN I SUPPOSE I'LL JUST HAVE TO STOP YOU.
IN FACT, WHAT I'M GOING TO DO IS FIND THIS SO CALLED 'SACRIFICE ENGINE' AT THE HEART OF THIS STRUCTURE.
"IT TAKES ME A MOMENT TO REALIZE, HE'S NOT REALLY TALKING TO KRAXNOR AT ALL...
"HE'S TALKING TO US."
"AND THEN I'M GOING TO DESTROY IT BEFORE IT CAN DO ANY HARM."

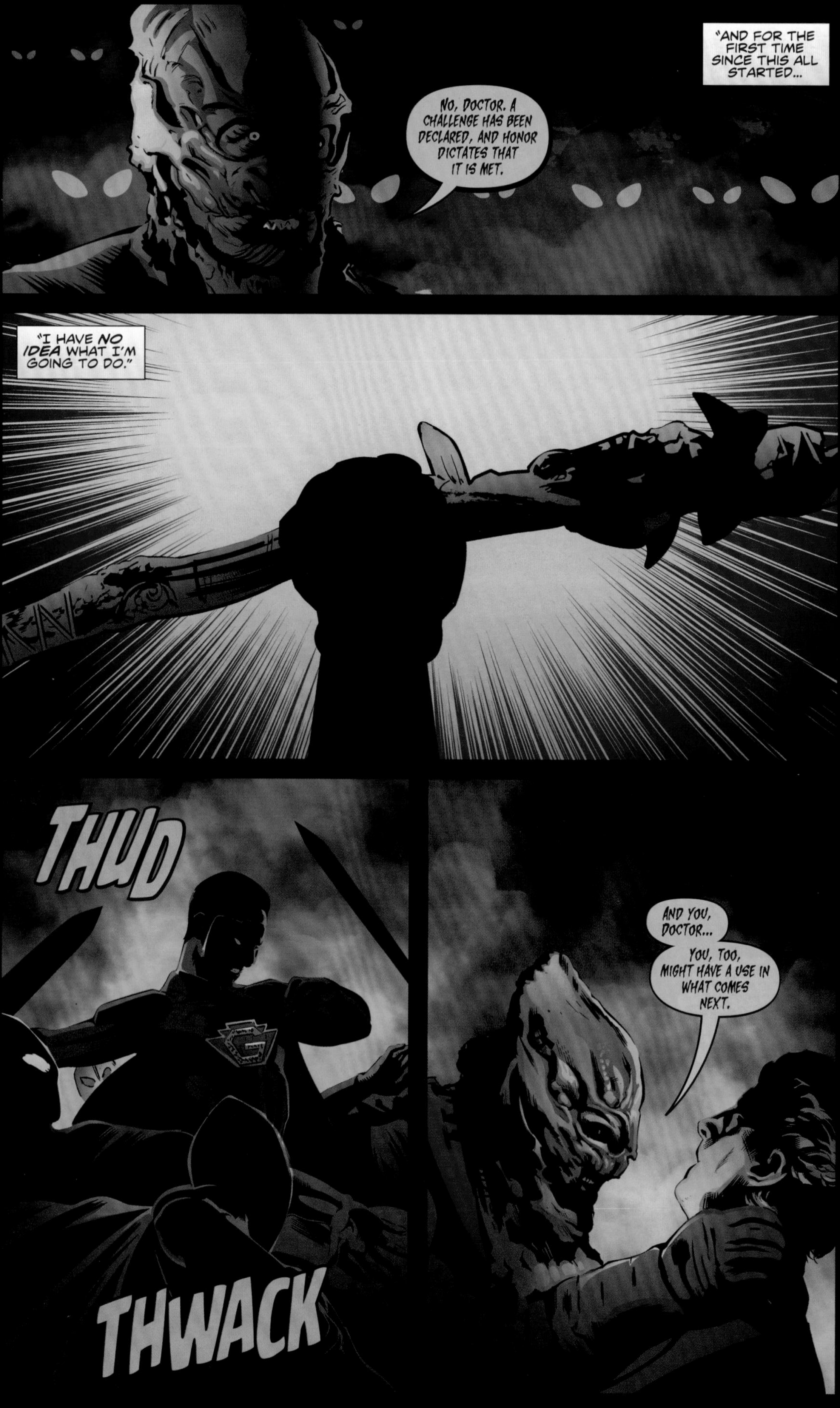
"AND FOR THE FIRST TIME SINCE THIS ALL STARTED...
NO, DOCTOR. A CHALLENGE HAS BEEN DECLARED, AND HONOR DICTATES THAT IT IS MET.
"I HAVE NO IDEA WHAT I'M GOING TO DO."
THUD
THWACK
AND YOU, DOCTOR...
YOU, TOO, MIGHT HAVE A USE IN WHAT COMES NEXT.

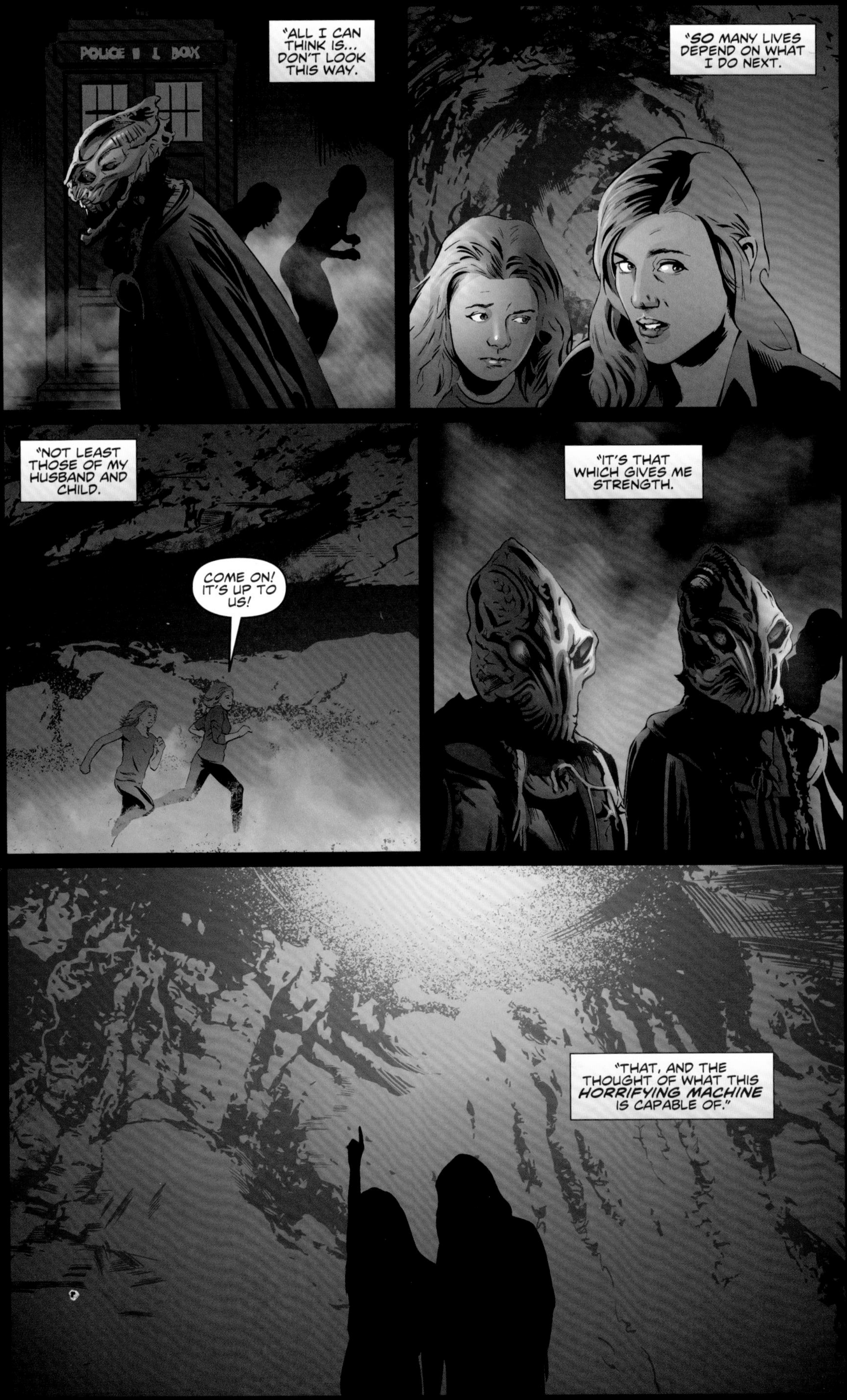
POLICE BOX
"ALL I CAN THINK IS... DON'T LOOK THIS WAY.
"SO MANY LIVES DEPEND ON WHAT I DO NEXT.
"NOT LEAST THOSE OF MY HUSBAND AND CHILD.
COME ON! IT'S UP TO US!
"IT'S THAT WHICH GIVES ME STRENGTH.
"THAT, AND THE THOUGHT OF WHAT THIS HORRIFYING MACHINE IS CAPABLE OF."

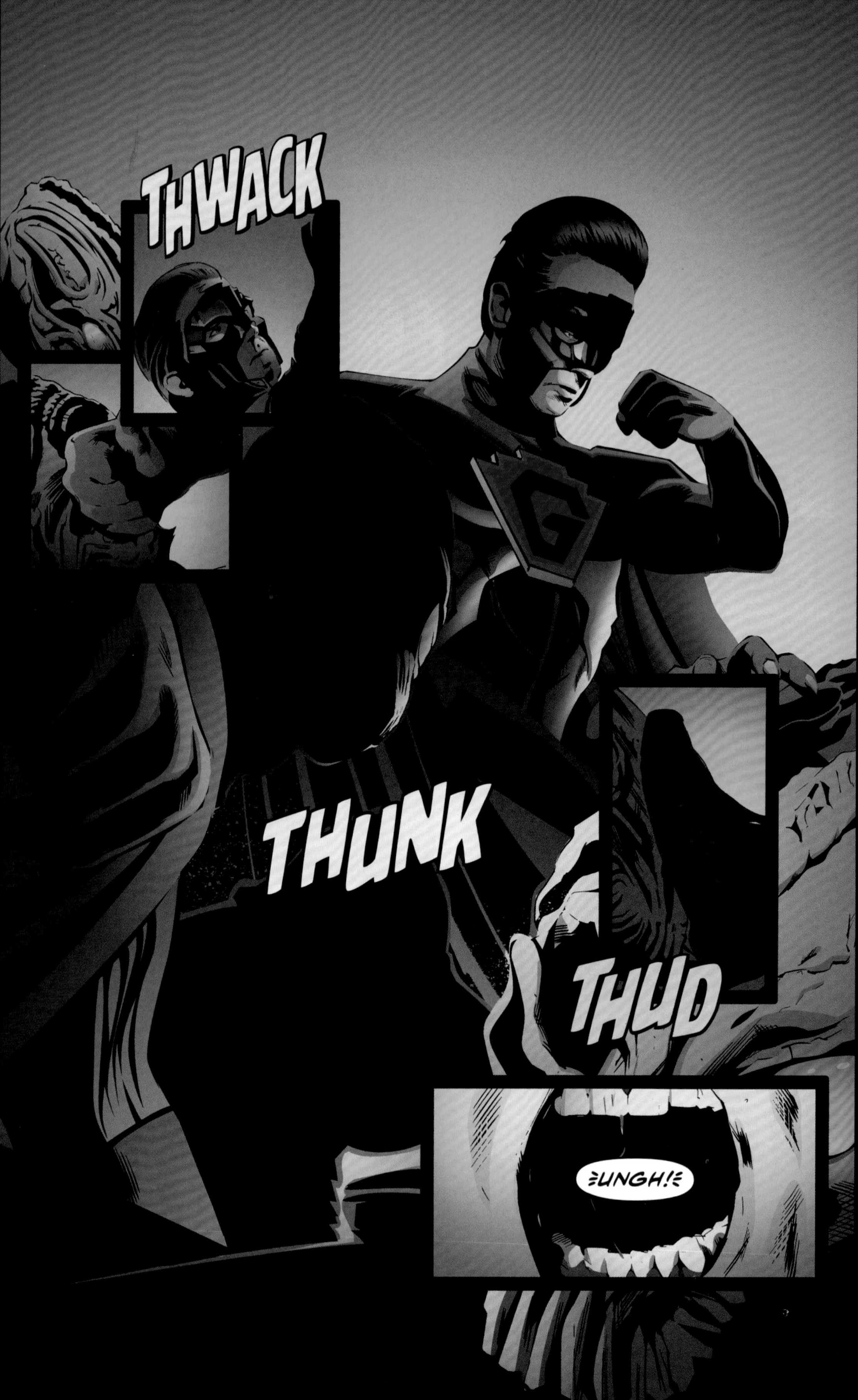
THWACK
THUNK
THUD
UNGH!

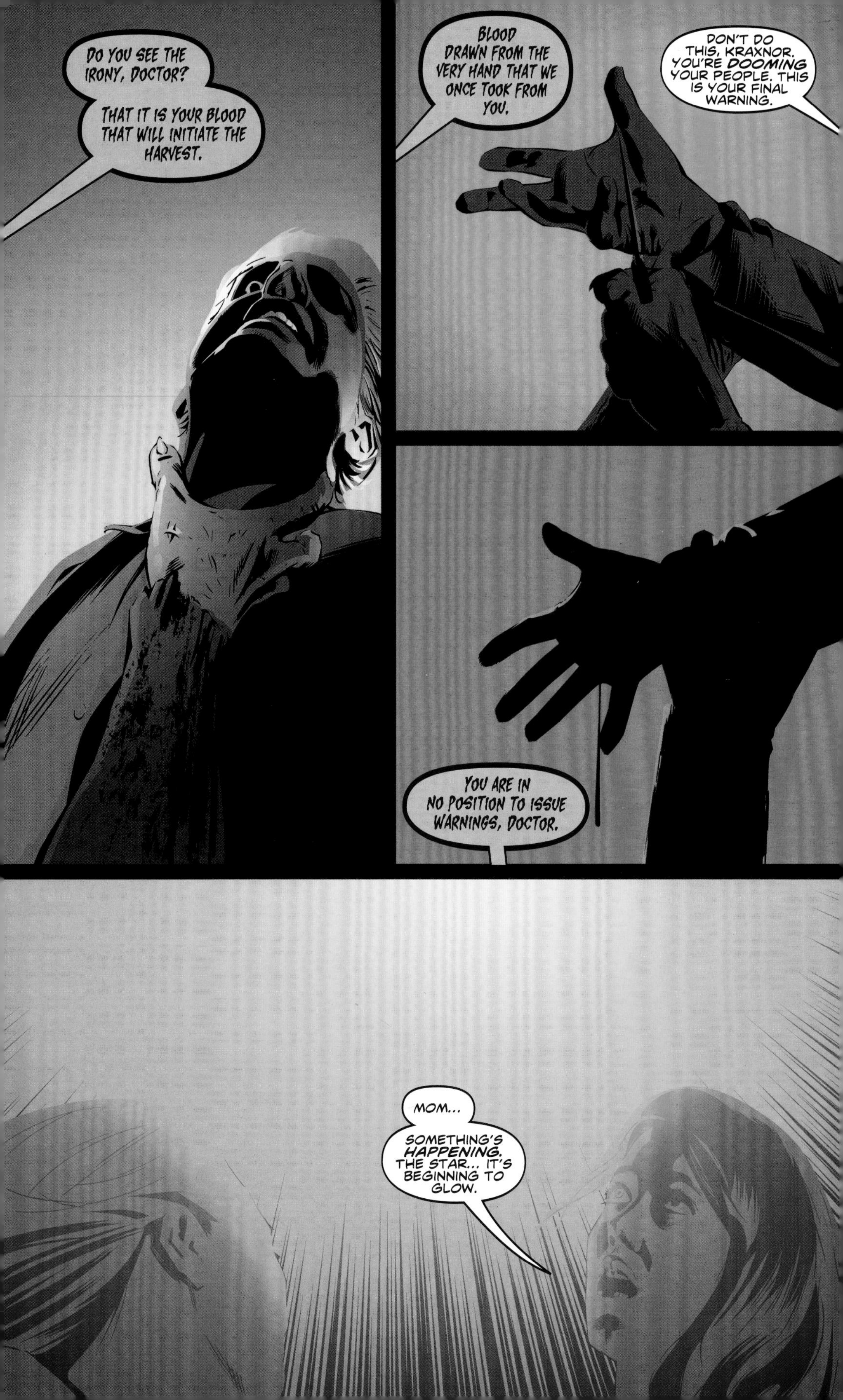

DO YOU SEE THE IRONY, DOCTOR?
THAT IT IS YOUR BLOOD THAT WILL INITIATE THE HARVEST.
BLOOD DRAWN FROM THE VERY HAND THAT WE ONCE TOOK FROM YOU.
DON'T DO THIS, KRAXNOR. YOU'RE *DOOMING* YOUR PEOPLE. THIS IS YOUR FINAL WARNING.
YOU ARE IN NO POSITION TO ISSUE WARNINGS, DOCTOR.
MOM...
SOMETHING'S *HAPPENING*. THE STAR... IT'S BEGINNING TO GLOW.

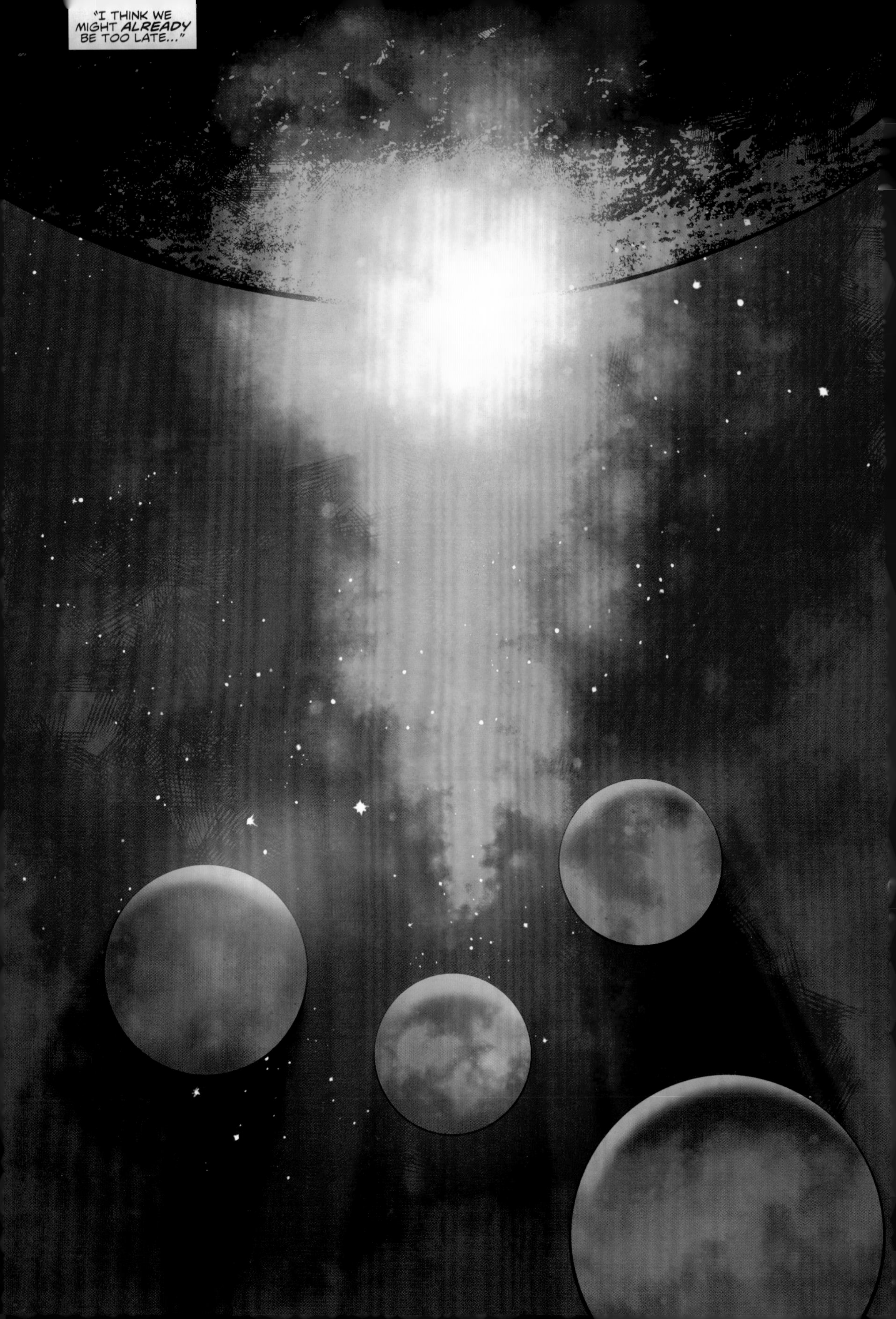
"I THINK WE MIGHT *ALREADY* BE TOO LATE..."

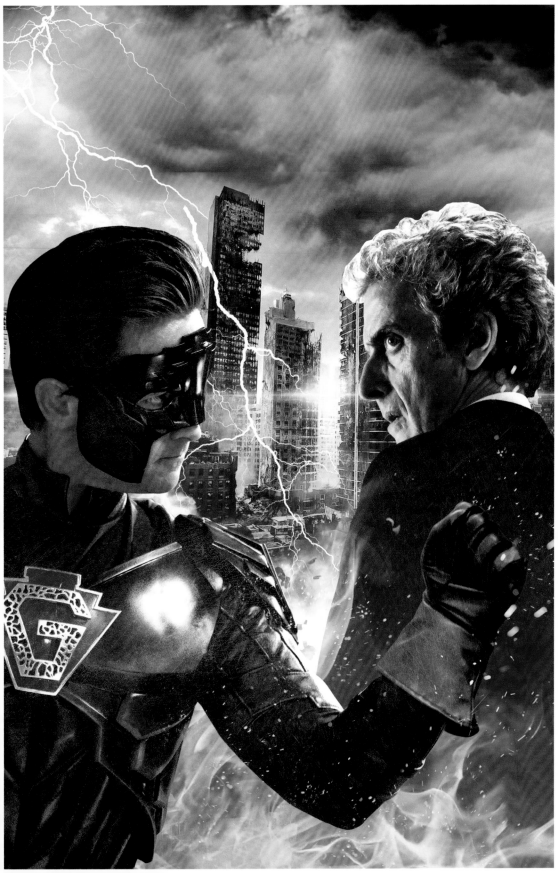

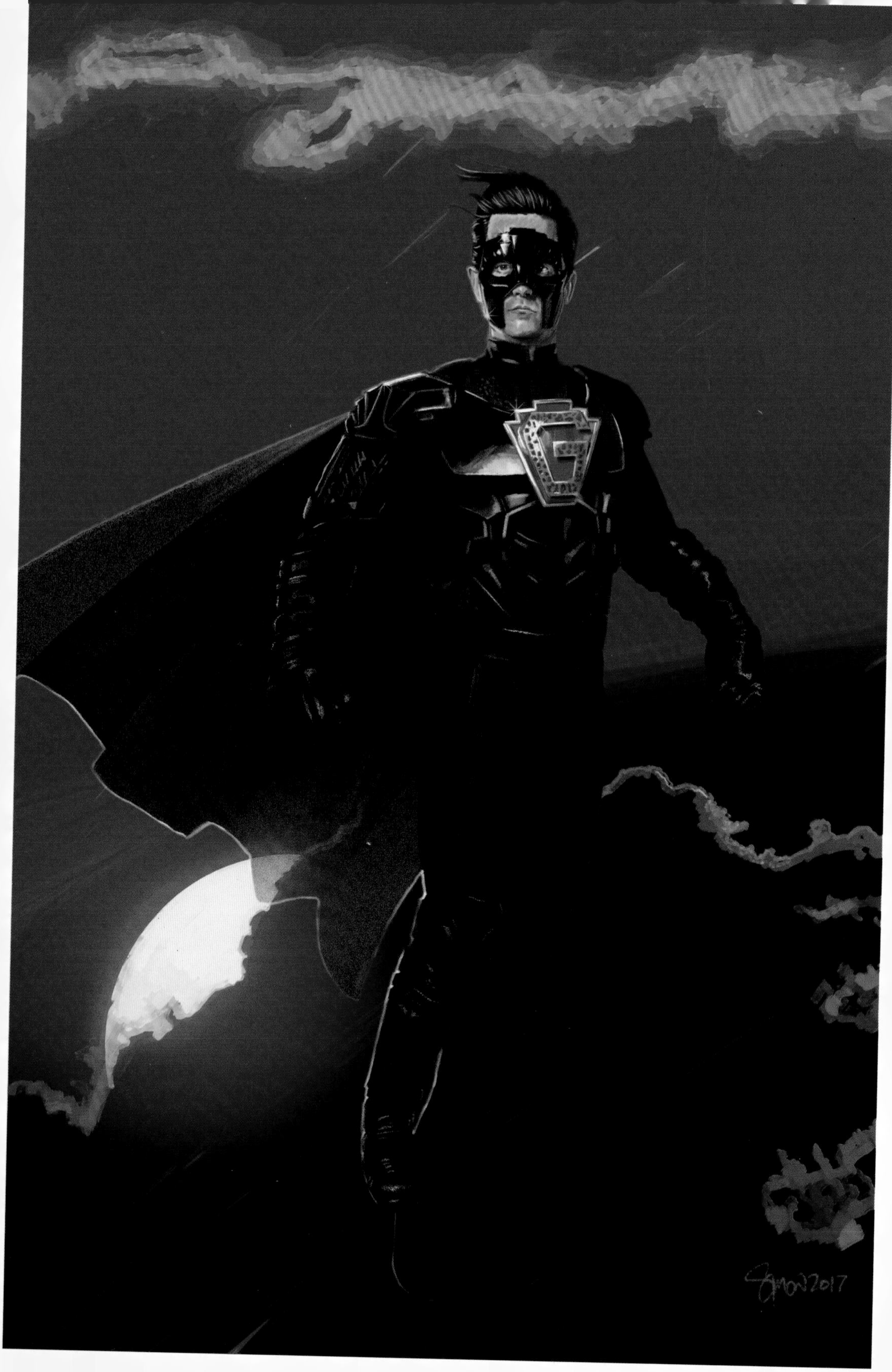

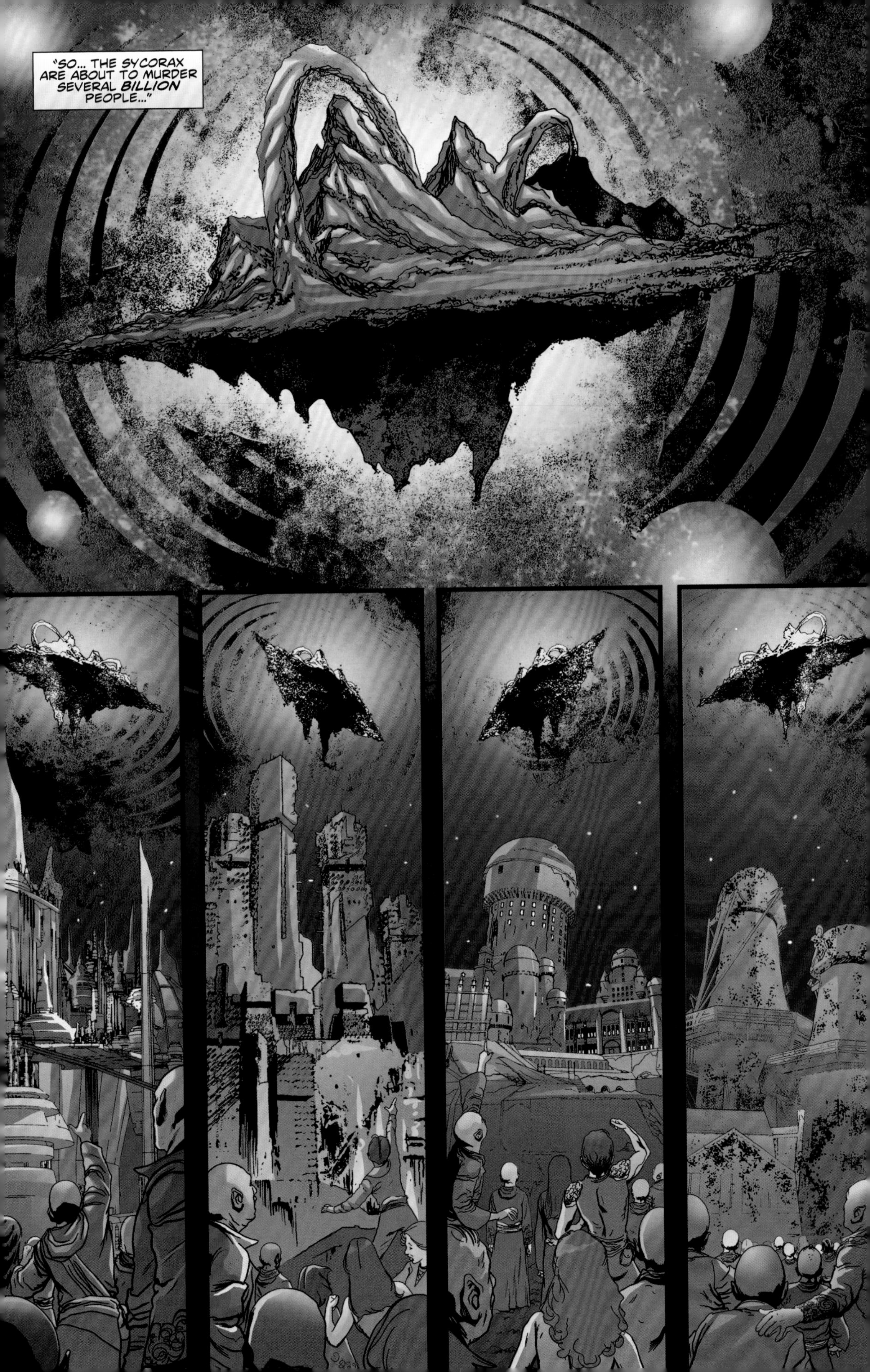
"SO... THE SYCORAX ARE ABOUT TO MURDER SEVERAL BILLION PEOPLE..."

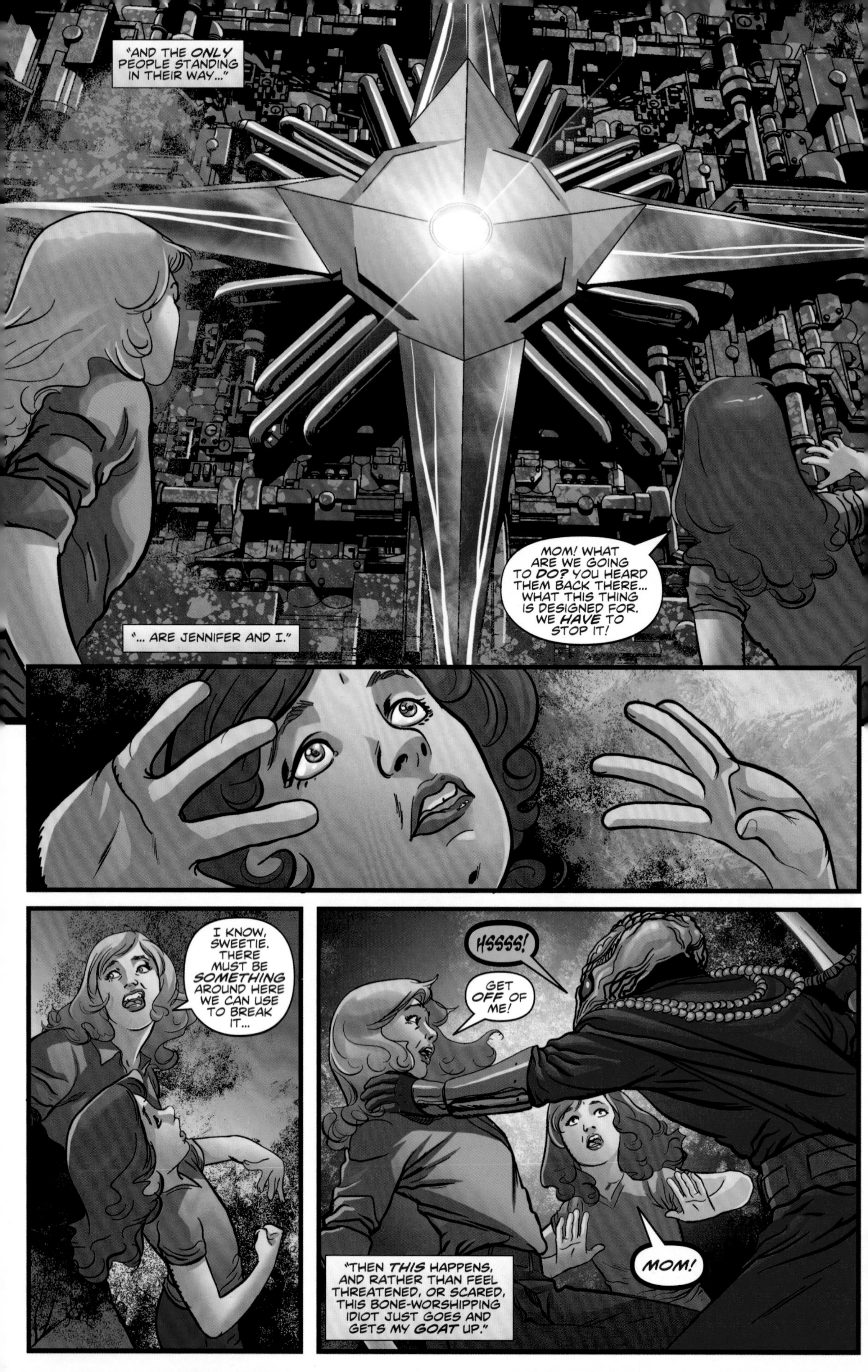
"AND THE ONLY PEOPLE STANDING IN THEIR WAY..."
MOM! WHAT ARE WE GOING TO DO? YOU HEARD THEM BACK THERE... WHAT THIS THING IS DESIGNED FOR. WE HAVE TO STOP IT!
"... ARE JENNIFER AND I."
I KNOW, SWEETIE. THERE MUST BE SOMETHING AROUND HERE WE CAN USE TO BREAK IT...
HSSSS!
GET OFF OF ME!
MOM!
"THEN THIS HAPPENS, AND RATHER THAN FEEL THREATENED, OR SCARED, THIS BONE-WORSHIPPING IDIOT JUST GOES AND GETS MY GOAT UP."

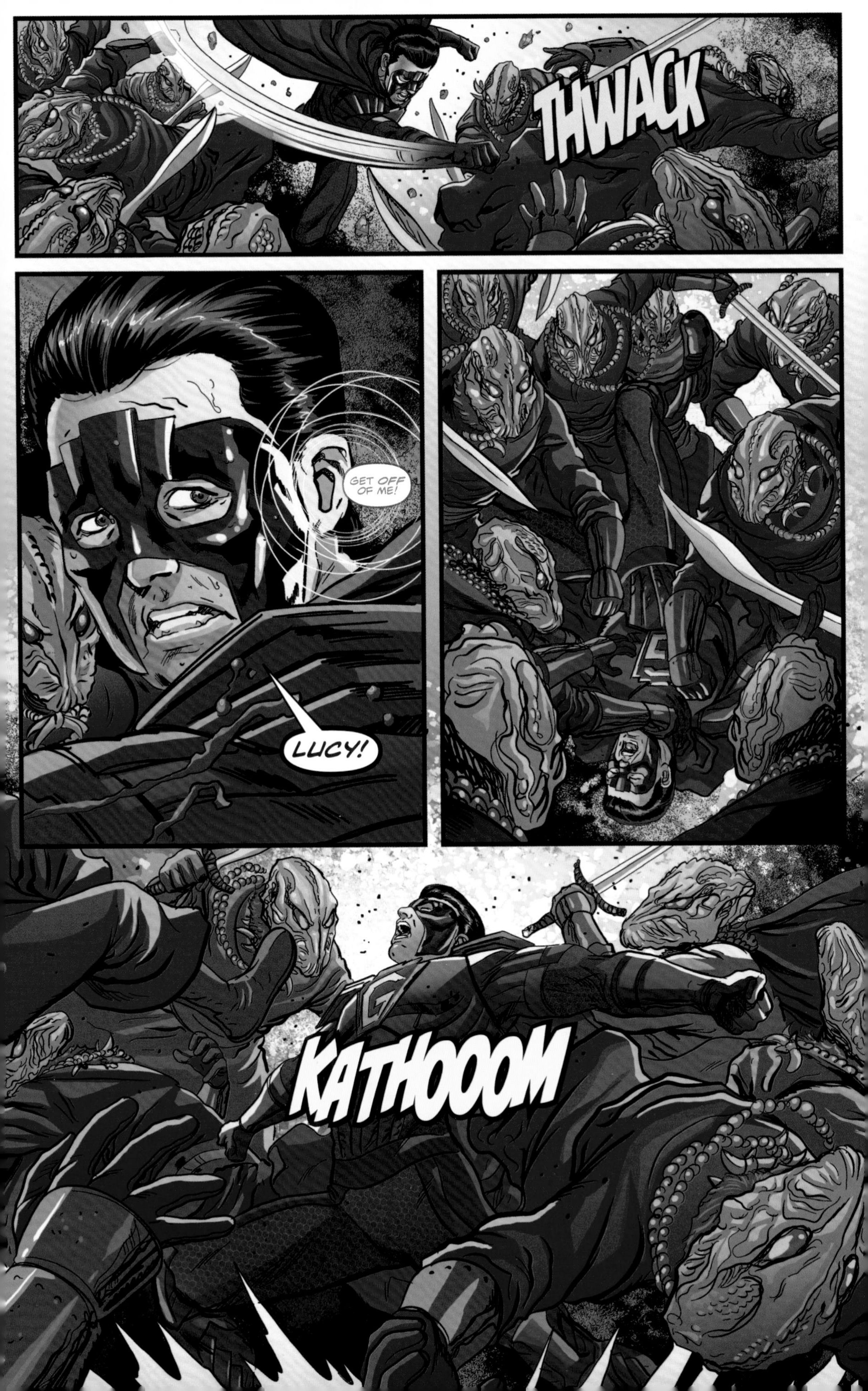
THWACK
GET OFF OF ME!
LUCY!
KATHOOOM

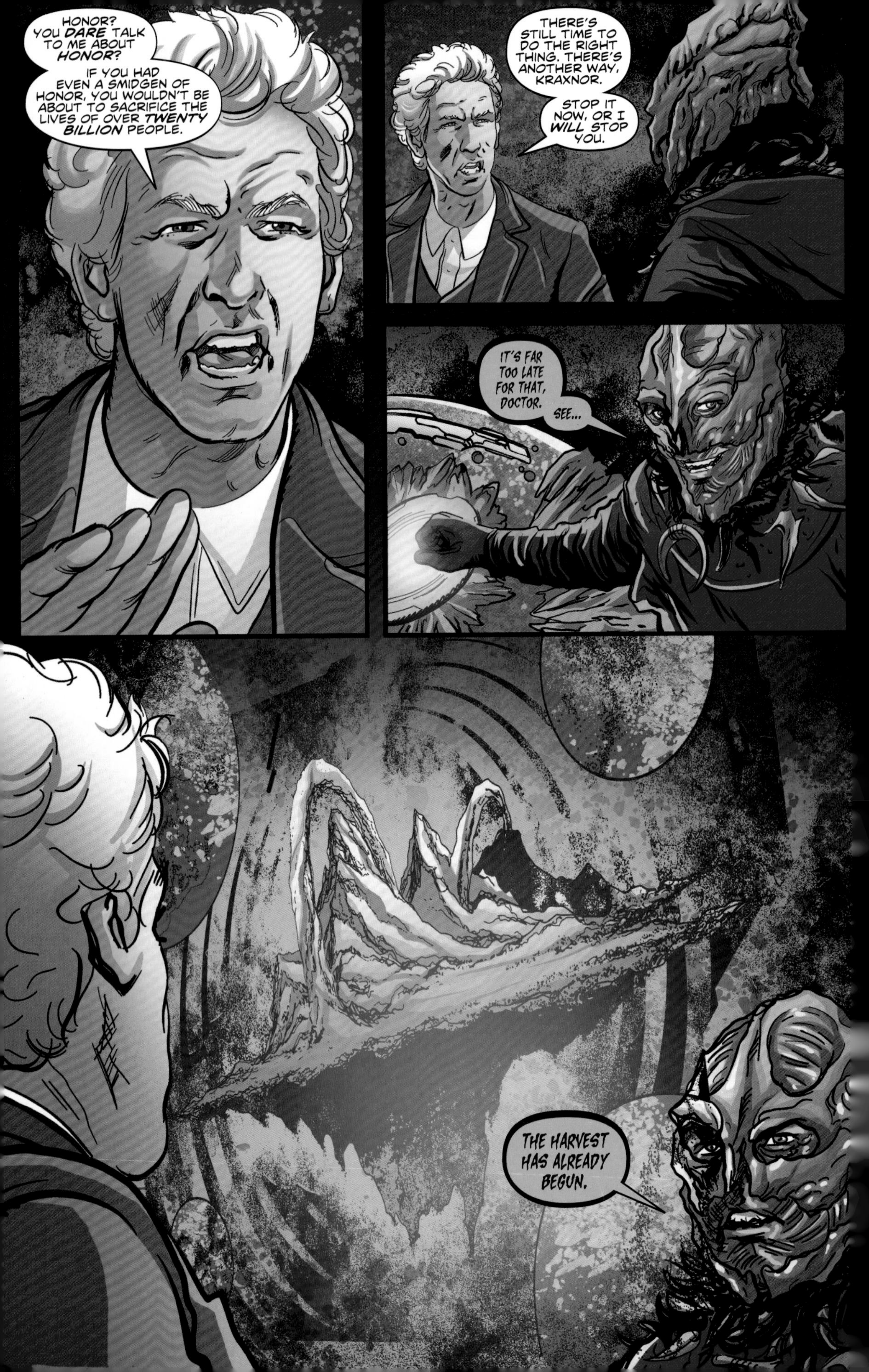
HONOR? YOU DARE TALK TO ME ABOUT HONOR?
IF YOU HAD EVEN A SMIDGEN OF HONOR, YOU WOULDN'T BE ABOUT TO SACRIFICE THE LIVES OF OVER TWENTY BILLION PEOPLE.
THERE'S STILL TIME TO DO THE RIGHT THING. THERE'S ANOTHER WAY, KRAXNOR.
STOP IT NOW, OR I WILL STOP YOU.
IT'S FAR TOO LATE FOR THAT, DOCTOR.
SEE...
THE HARVEST HAS ALREADY BEGUN.

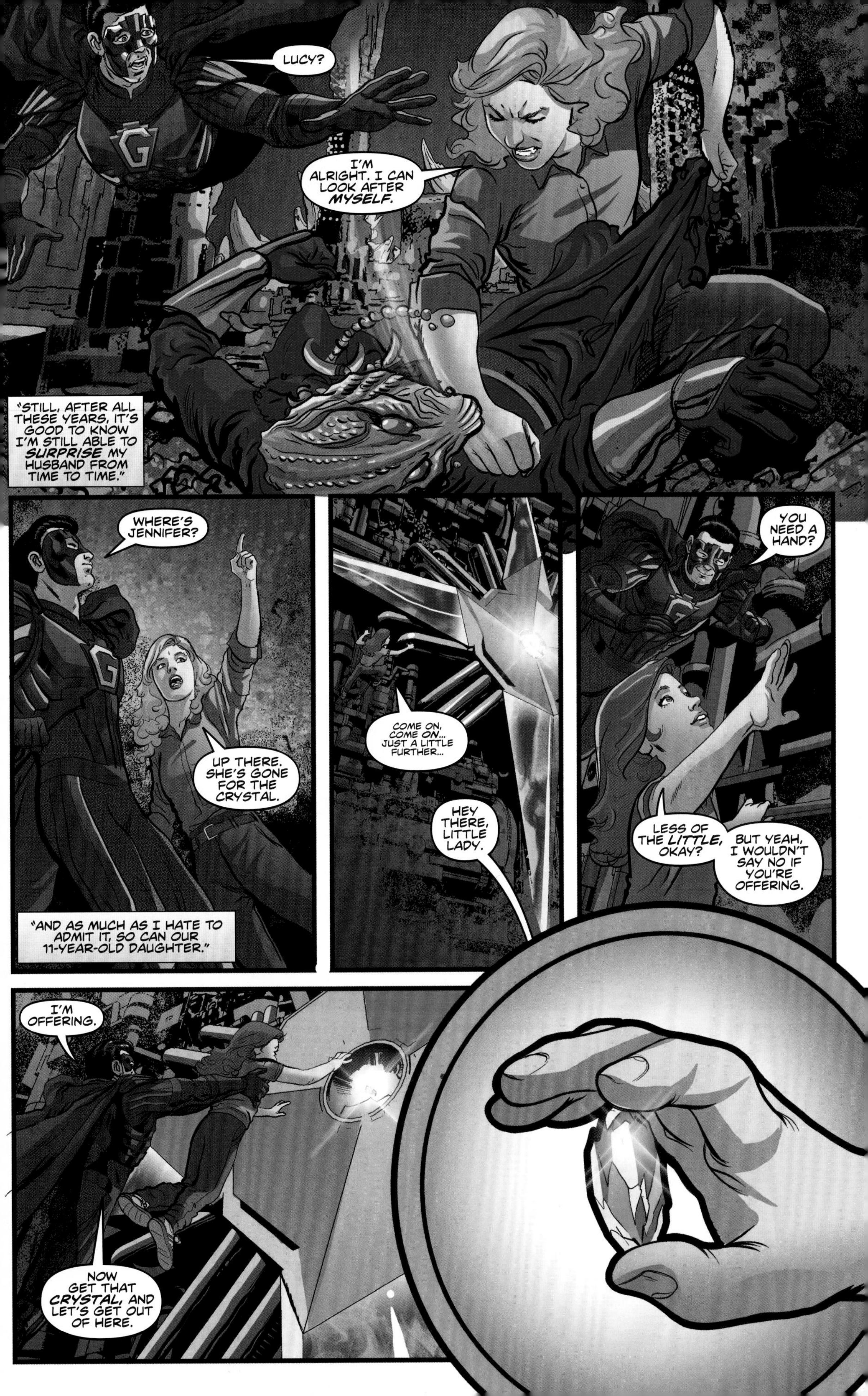
LUCY?
I'M ALRIGHT. I CAN LOOK AFTER MYSELF.
"STILL, AFTER ALL THESE YEARS, IT'S GOOD TO KNOW I'M STILL ABLE TO SURPRISE MY HUSBAND FROM TIME TO TIME."
WHERE'S JENNIFER?
UP THERE. SHE'S GONE FOR THE CRYSTAL.
"AND AS MUCH AS I HATE TO ADMIT IT, SO CAN OUR 11-YEAR-OLD DAUGHTER."
COME ON, COME ON... JUST A LITTLE FURTHER...
HEY THERE, LITTLE LADY.
YOU NEED A HAND?
LESS OF THE LITTLE, OKAY?
BUT YEAH, I WOULDN'T SAY NO IF YOU'RE OFFERING.
I'M OFFERING.
NOW GET THAT CRYSTAL, AND LET'S GET OUT OF HERE.

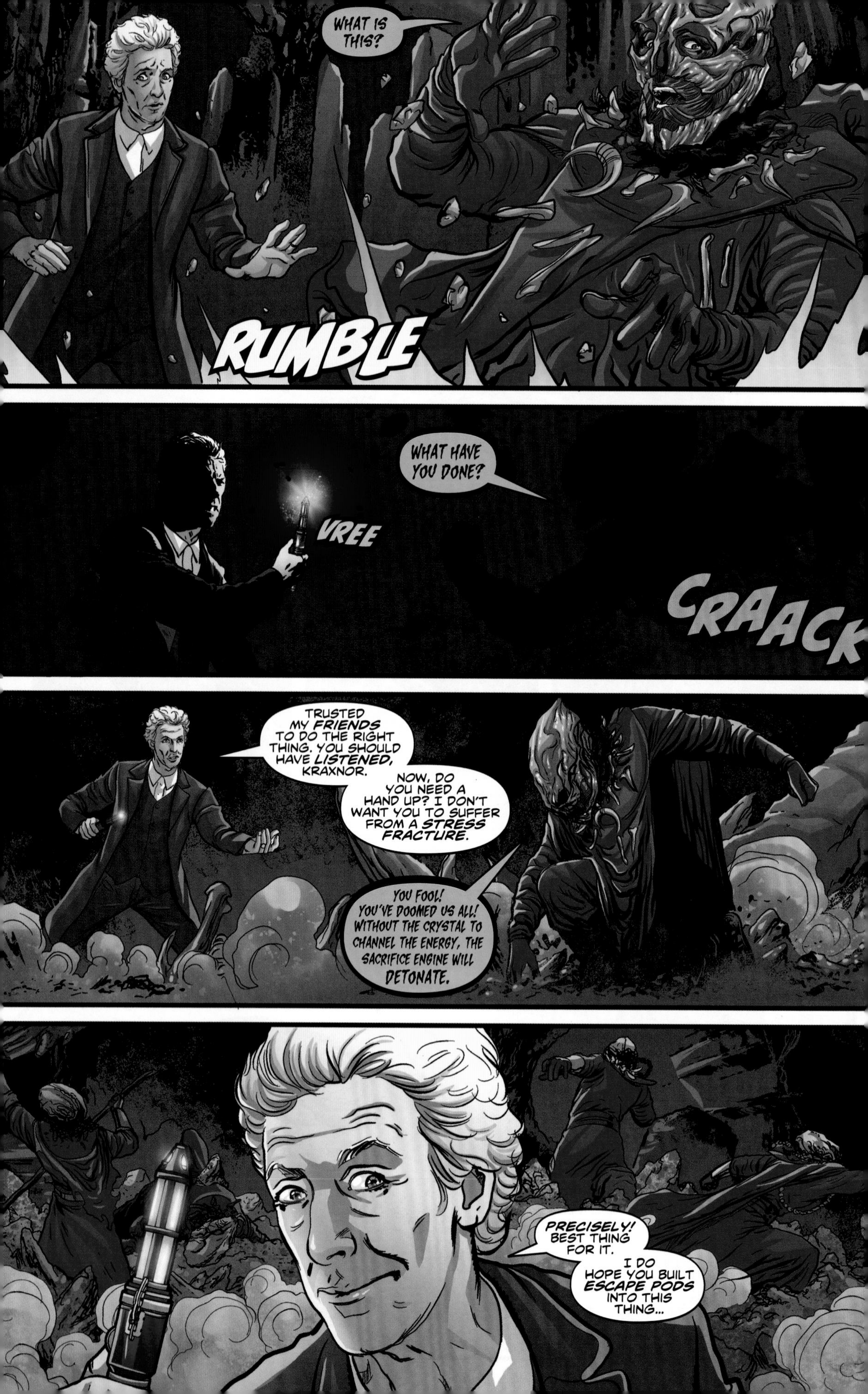
WHAT IS THIS?
RUMBLE
WHAT HAVE YOU DONE?
VREE
CRAACK
TRUSTED MY FRIENDS TO DO THE RIGHT THING. YOU SHOULD HAVE LISTENED, KRAXNOR.
NOW, DO YOU NEED A HAND UP? I DON'T WANT YOU TO SUFFER FROM A STRESS FRACTURE.
YOU FOOL! YOU'VE DOOMED US ALL! WITHOUT THE CRYSTAL TO CHANNEL THE ENERGY, THE SACRIFICE ENGINE WILL DETONATE.
PRECISELY! BEST THING FOR IT.
I DO HOPE YOU BUILT ESCAPE PODS INTO THIS THING...

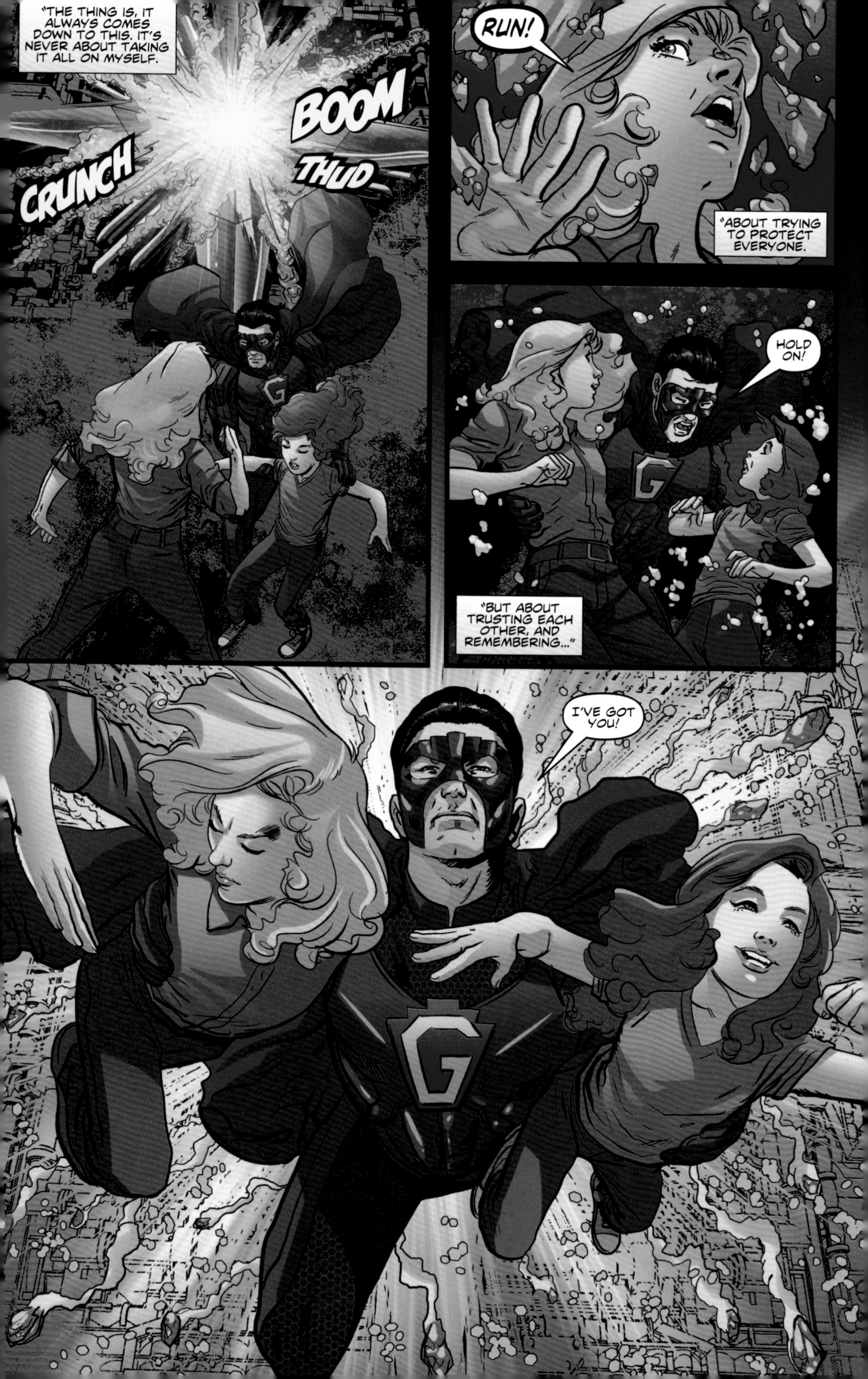
"THE THING IS, IT ALWAYS COMES DOWN TO THIS. IT'S NEVER ABOUT TAKING IT ALL ON MYSELF.
CRUNCH
BOOM
THUD
RUN!
"ABOUT TRYING TO PROTECT EVERYONE.
HOLD ON!
"BUT ABOUT TRUSTING EACH OTHER, AND REMEMBERING..."
I'VE GOT YOU!

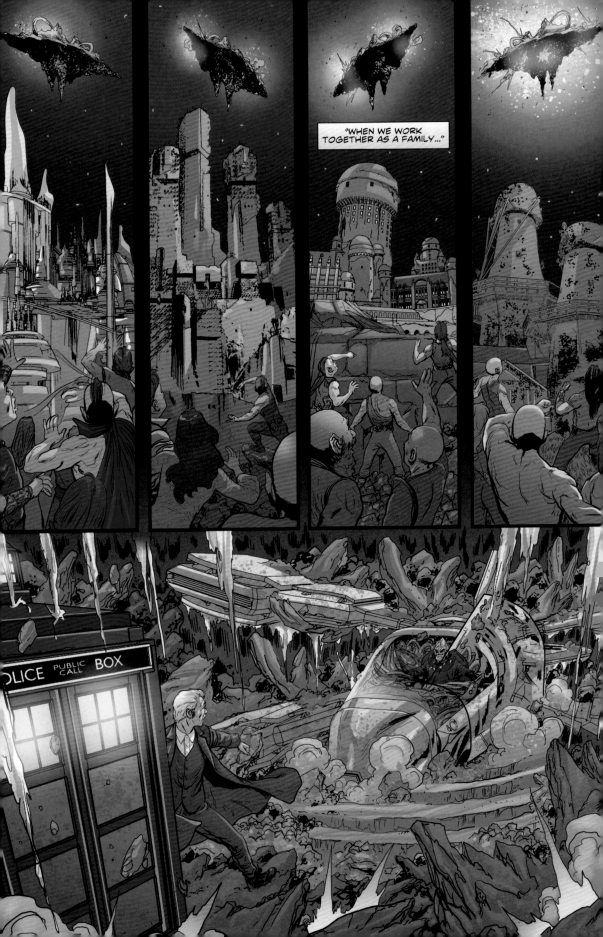

"WHEN WE WORK TOGETHER AS A FAMILY..."

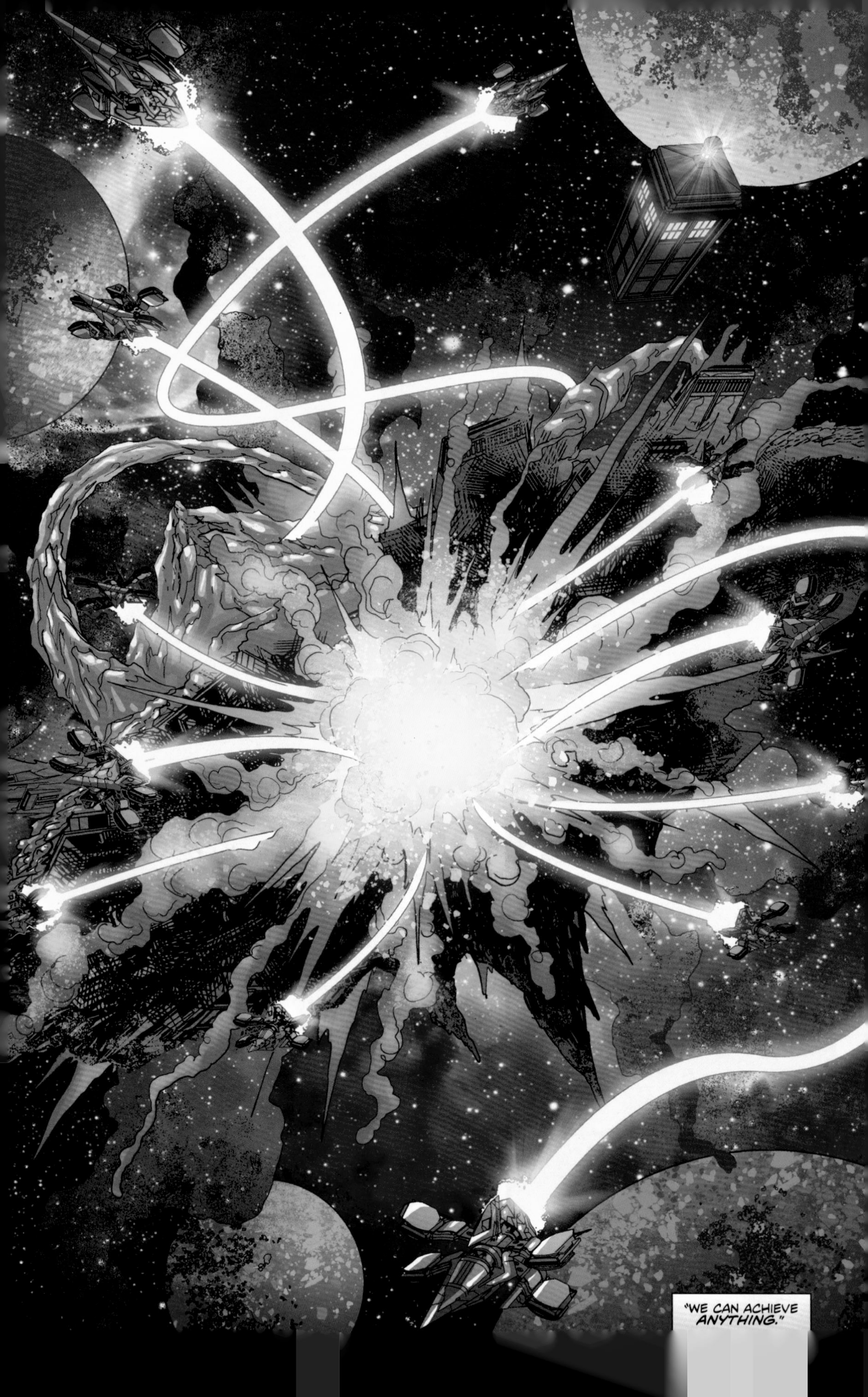
"WE CAN ACHIEVE ANYTHING."

WELL, I CAN'T SAY I'M SORRY *THAT'S* OVER.

YOU'VE GOT ALL THE MISSING CRYSTALS NOW, DOCTOR.

WHAT NOW? YOU STILL HAVEN'T TOLD US WHAT YOU'RE GOING TO *DO* WITH THEM.

APART FROM *SAVE THE UNIVERSE,* YOU MEAN?

DOCTOR...

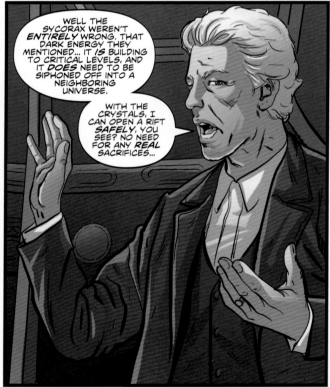

WELL THE SYCORAX WEREN'T *ENTIRELY* WRONG. THAT DARK ENERGY THEY MENTIONED... IT *IS* BUILDING TO CRITICAL LEVELS, AND IT *DOES* NEED TO BE SIPHONED OFF INTO A NEIGHBORING UNIVERSE.

WITH THE CRYSTALS, I CAN OPEN A RIFT *SAFELY,* YOU SEE? NO NEED FOR ANY *REAL* SACRIFICES...

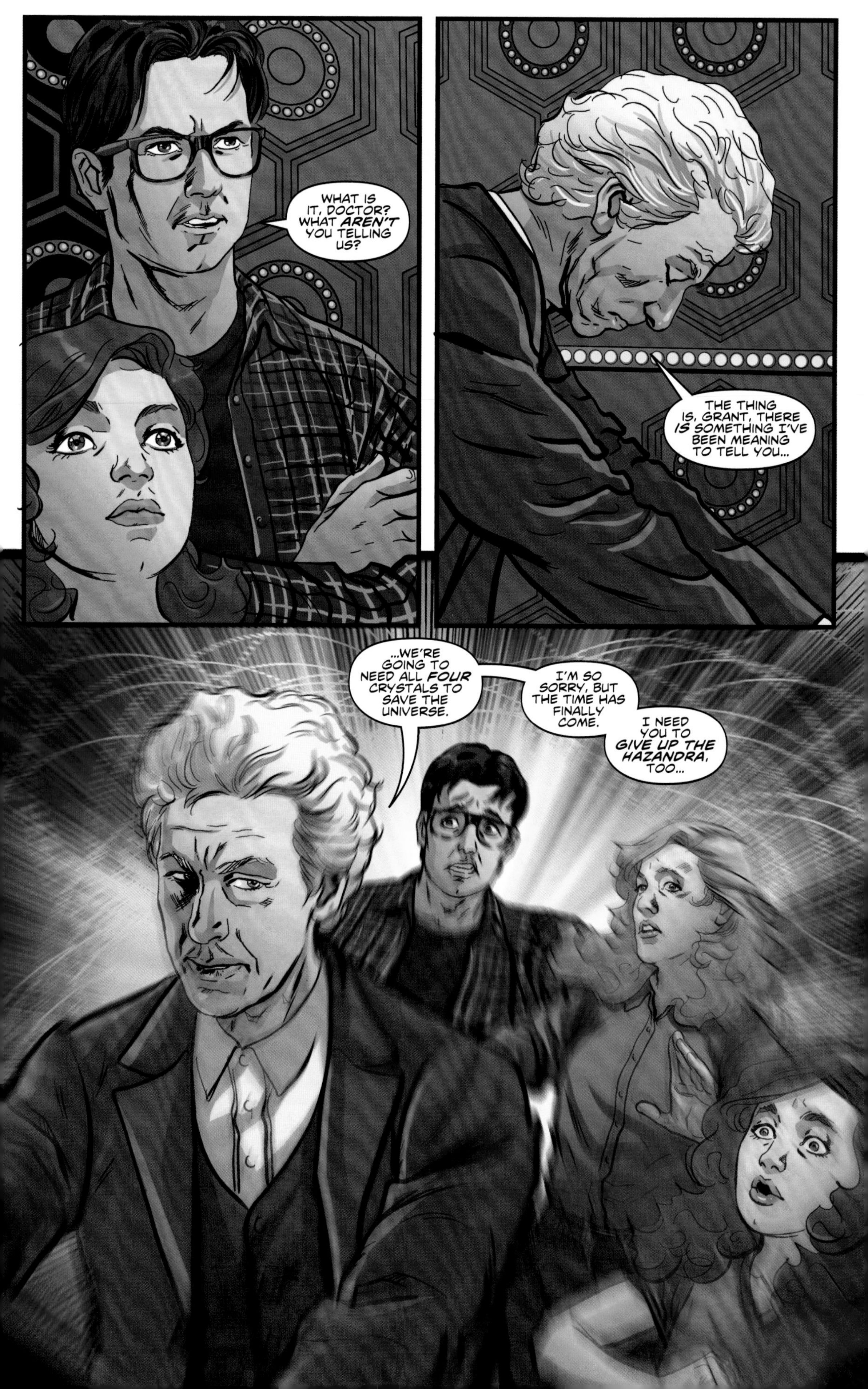
WHAT IS IT, DOCTOR? WHAT AREN'T YOU TELLING US?
THE THING IS, GRANT, THERE IS SOMETHING I'VE BEEN MEANING TO TELL YOU...
...WE'RE GOING TO NEED ALL FOUR CRYSTALS TO SAVE THE UNIVERSE.
I'M SO SORRY, BUT THE TIME HAS FINALLY COME.
I NEED YOU TO GIVE UP THE HAZANDRA, TOO...

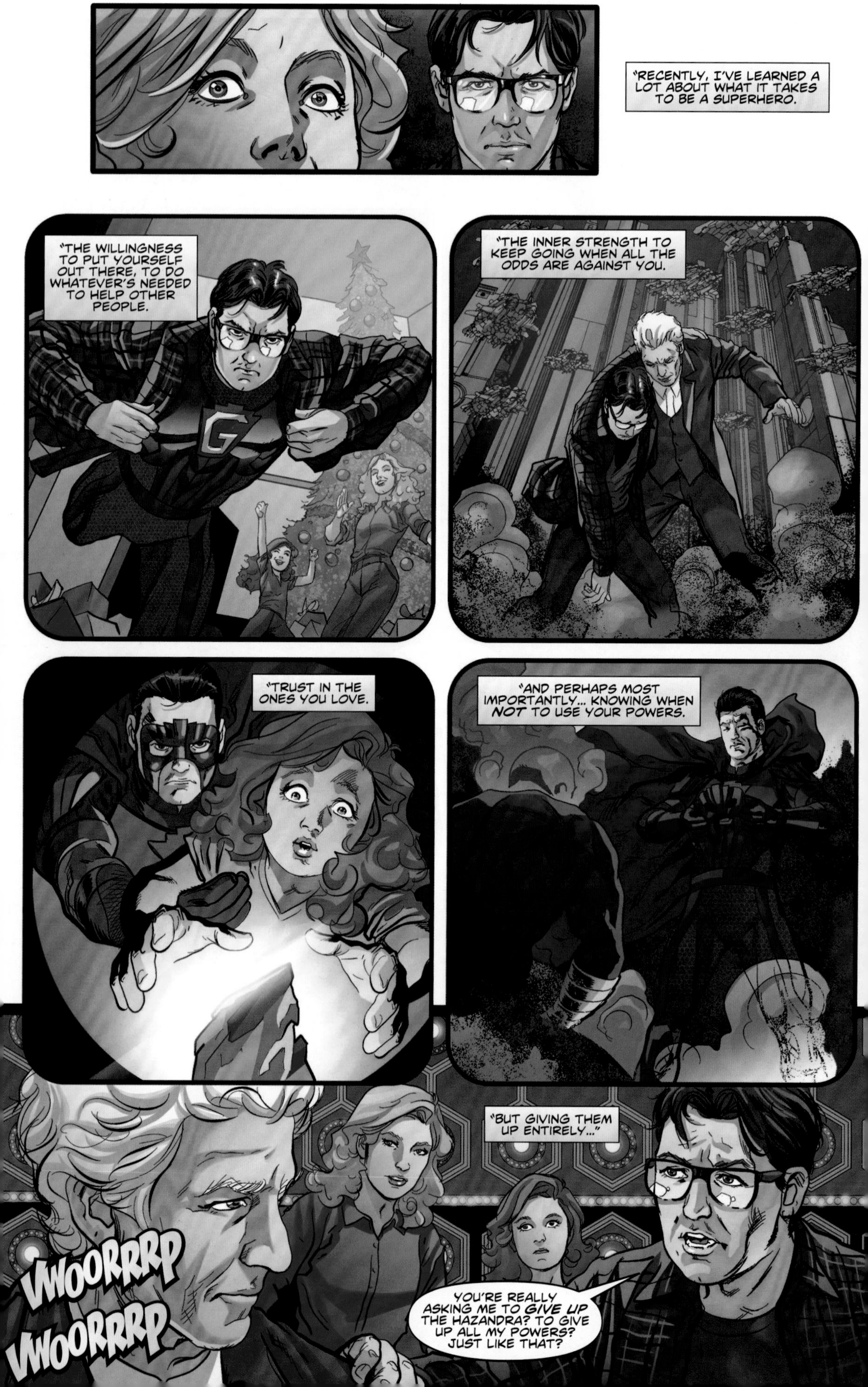
"RECENTLY, I'VE LEARNED A LOT ABOUT WHAT IT TAKES TO BE A SUPERHERO.
"THE WILLINGNESS TO PUT YOURSELF OUT THERE, TO DO WHATEVER'S NEEDED TO HELP OTHER PEOPLE.
"THE INNER STRENGTH TO KEEP GOING WHEN ALL THE ODDS ARE AGAINST YOU.
"TRUST IN THE ONES YOU LOVE.
"AND PERHAPS MOST IMPORTANTLY... KNOWING WHEN *NOT* TO USE YOUR POWERS.
"BUT GIVING THEM UP ENTIRELY..."
VWOORRRP
VWOORRRP
YOU'RE REALLY ASKING ME TO *GIVE UP* THE HAZANDRA? TO GIVE UP ALL MY POWERS? JUST LIKE THAT?

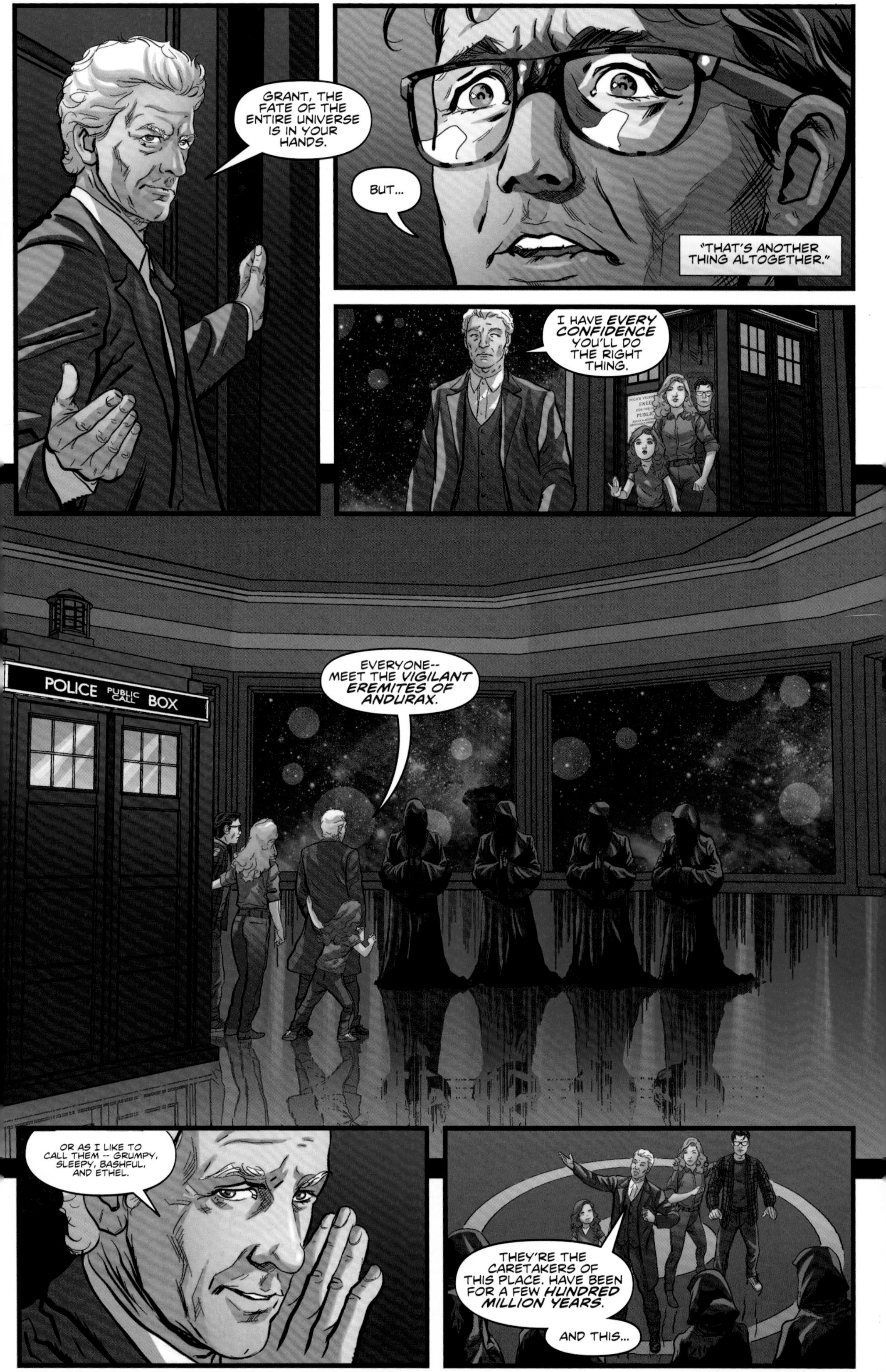
GRANT, THE FATE OF THE ENTIRE UNIVERSE IS IN YOUR HANDS.
BUT...
"THAT'S ANOTHER THING ALTOGETHER."
I HAVE *EVERY CONFIDENCE* YOU'LL DO THE RIGHT THING.
POLICE PUBLIC CALL BOX
EVERYONE-- MEET THE *VIGILANT EREMITES OF ANDURAX.*
OR AS I LIKE TO CALL THEM -- GRUMPY, SLEEPY, BASHFUL, AND ETHEL.
THEY'RE THE CARETAKERS OF THIS PLACE. HAVE BEEN FOR A FEW *HUNDRED MILLION YEARS.*
AND THIS...

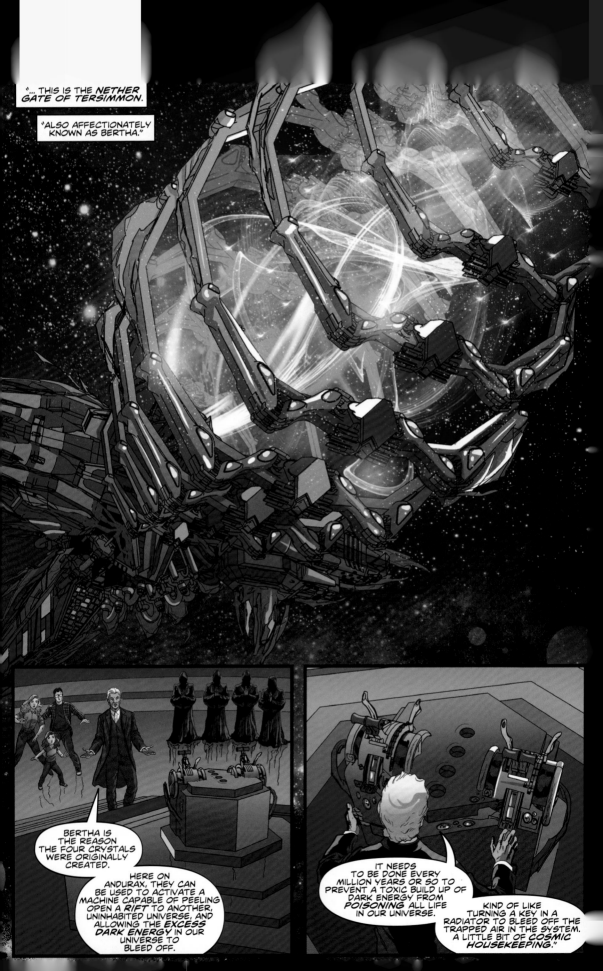

"... THIS IS THE *NETHER GATE OF TERSIMMON*."

"ALSO AFFECTIONATELY KNOWN AS BERTHA."

BERTHA IS THE REASON THE *FOUR CRYSTALS* WERE ORIGINALLY CREATED.

HERE ON *ANDURAX*, THEY CAN BE USED TO ACTIVATE A MACHINE CAPABLE OF PEELING OPEN A *RIFT* TO ANOTHER, UNINHABITED UNIVERSE, AND ALLOWING THE *EXCESS DARK ENERGY* IN OUR UNIVERSE TO BLEED OFF.

IT NEEDS TO BE DONE EVERY MILLION YEARS OR SO TO PREVENT A TOXIC BUILD UP OF *DARK ENERGY* FROM *POISONING* ALL LIFE IN OUR UNIVERSE.

KIND OF LIKE TURNING A KEY IN A RADIATOR TO BLEED OFF THE TRAPPED AIR IN THE SYSTEM. A LITTLE BIT OF *COSMIC HOUSEKEEPING*."

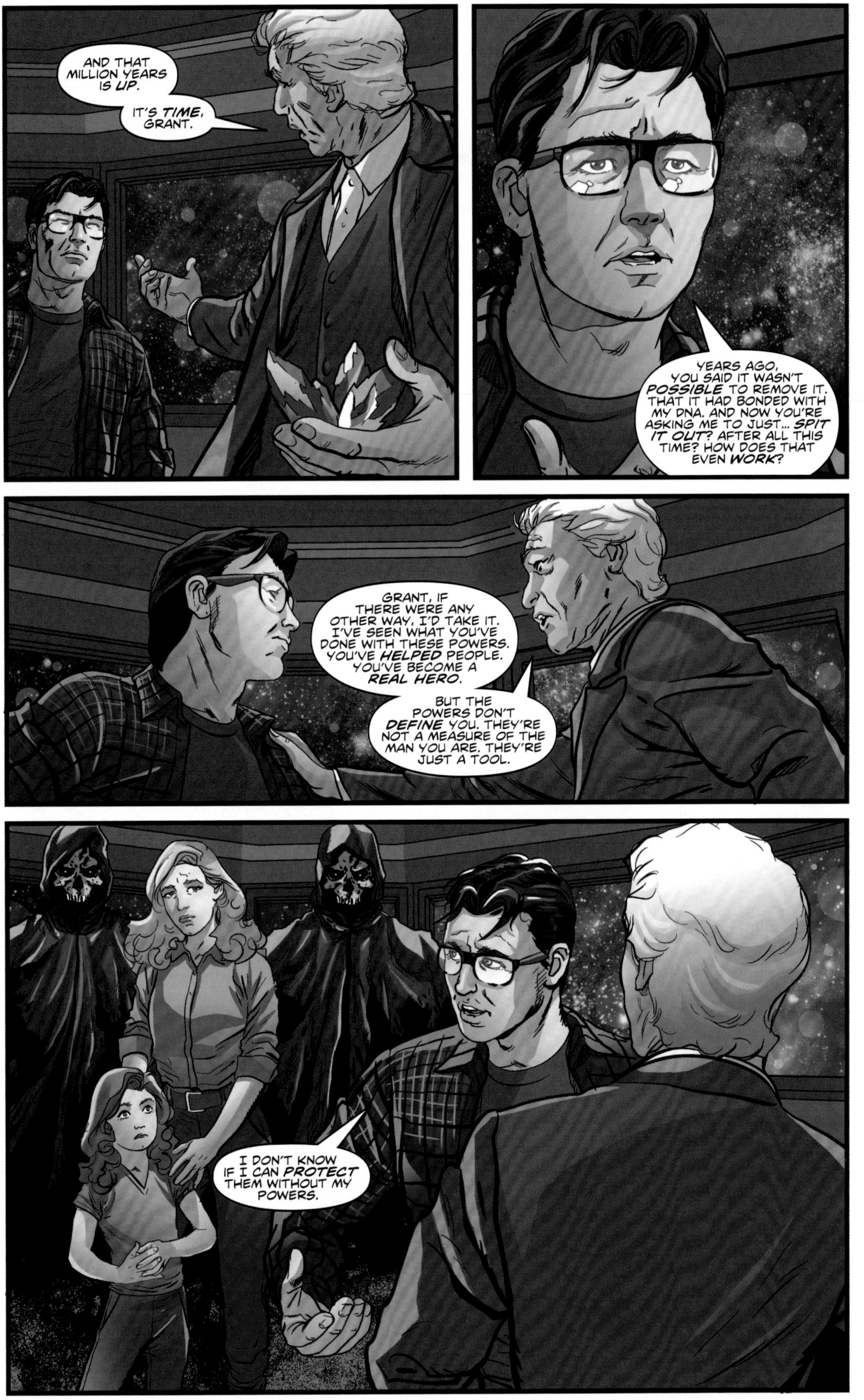
AND THAT MILLION YEARS IS UP.
IT'S TIME, GRANT.
YEARS AGO, YOU SAID IT WASN'T POSSIBLE TO REMOVE IT. THAT IT HAD BONDED WITH MY DNA. AND NOW YOU'RE ASKING ME TO JUST... SPIT IT OUT? AFTER ALL THIS TIME? HOW DOES THAT EVEN WORK?
GRANT, IF THERE WERE ANY OTHER WAY, I'D TAKE IT. I'VE SEEN WHAT YOU'VE DONE WITH THESE POWERS. YOU'VE HELPED PEOPLE. YOU'VE BECOME A REAL HERO.
BUT THE POWERS DON'T DEFINE YOU. THEY'RE NOT A MEASURE OF THE MAN YOU ARE. THEY'RE JUST A TOOL.
I DON'T KNOW IF I CAN PROTECT THEM WITHOUT MY POWERS.

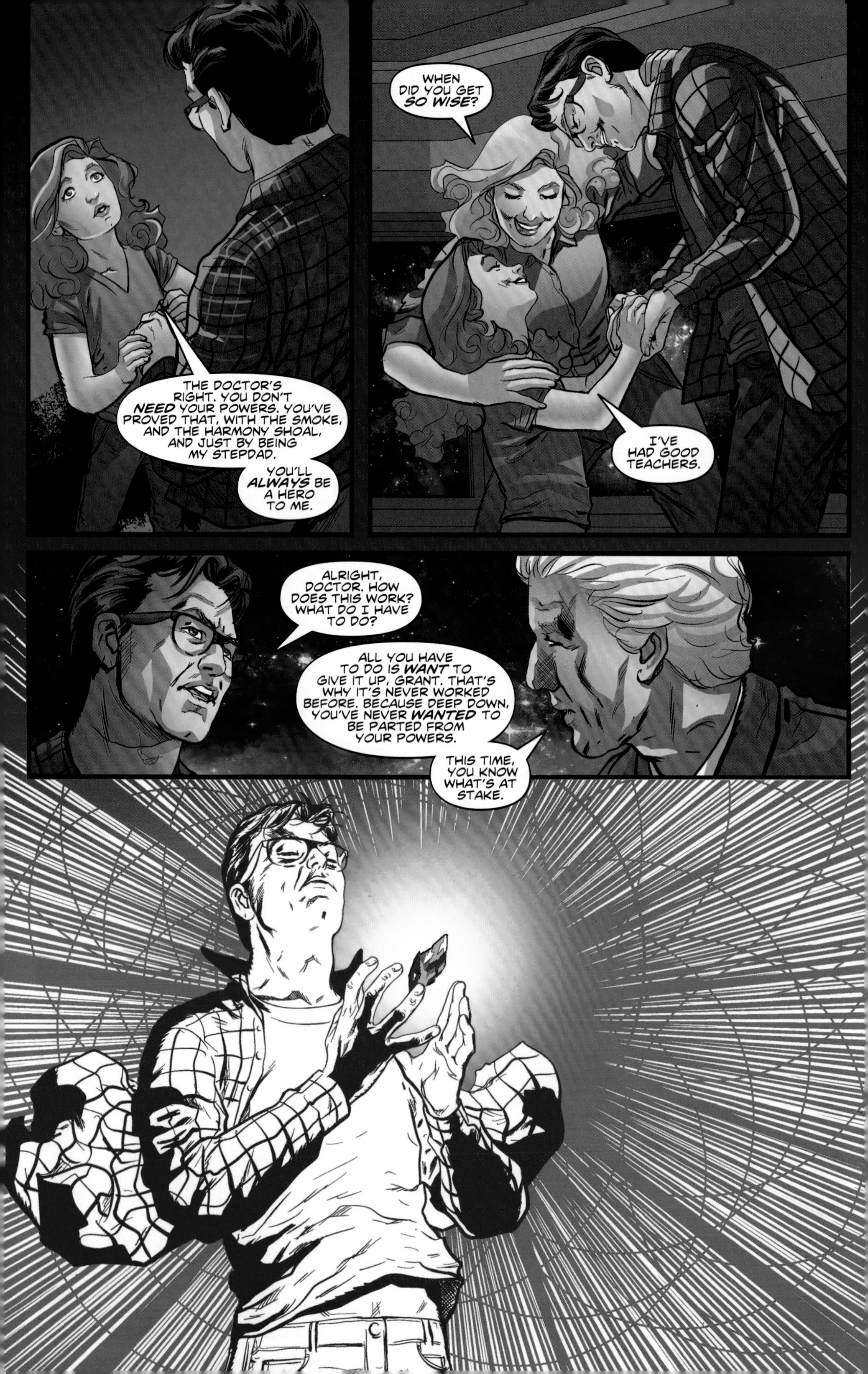
THE DOCTOR'S RIGHT. YOU DON'T NEED YOUR POWERS. YOU'VE PROVED THAT, WITH THE SMOKE, AND THE HARMONY SHOAL, AND JUST BY BEING MY STEPDAD.
YOU'LL ALWAYS BE A HERO TO ME.
WHEN DID YOU GET SO WISE?
I'VE HAD GOOD TEACHERS.
ALRIGHT, DOCTOR. HOW DOES THIS WORK? WHAT DO I HAVE TO DO?
ALL YOU HAVE TO DO IS WANT TO GIVE IT UP, GRANT. THAT'S WHY IT'S NEVER WORKED BEFORE. BECAUSE DEEP DOWN, YOU'VE NEVER WANTED TO BE PARTED FROM YOUR POWERS.
THIS TIME, YOU KNOW WHAT'S AT STAKE.

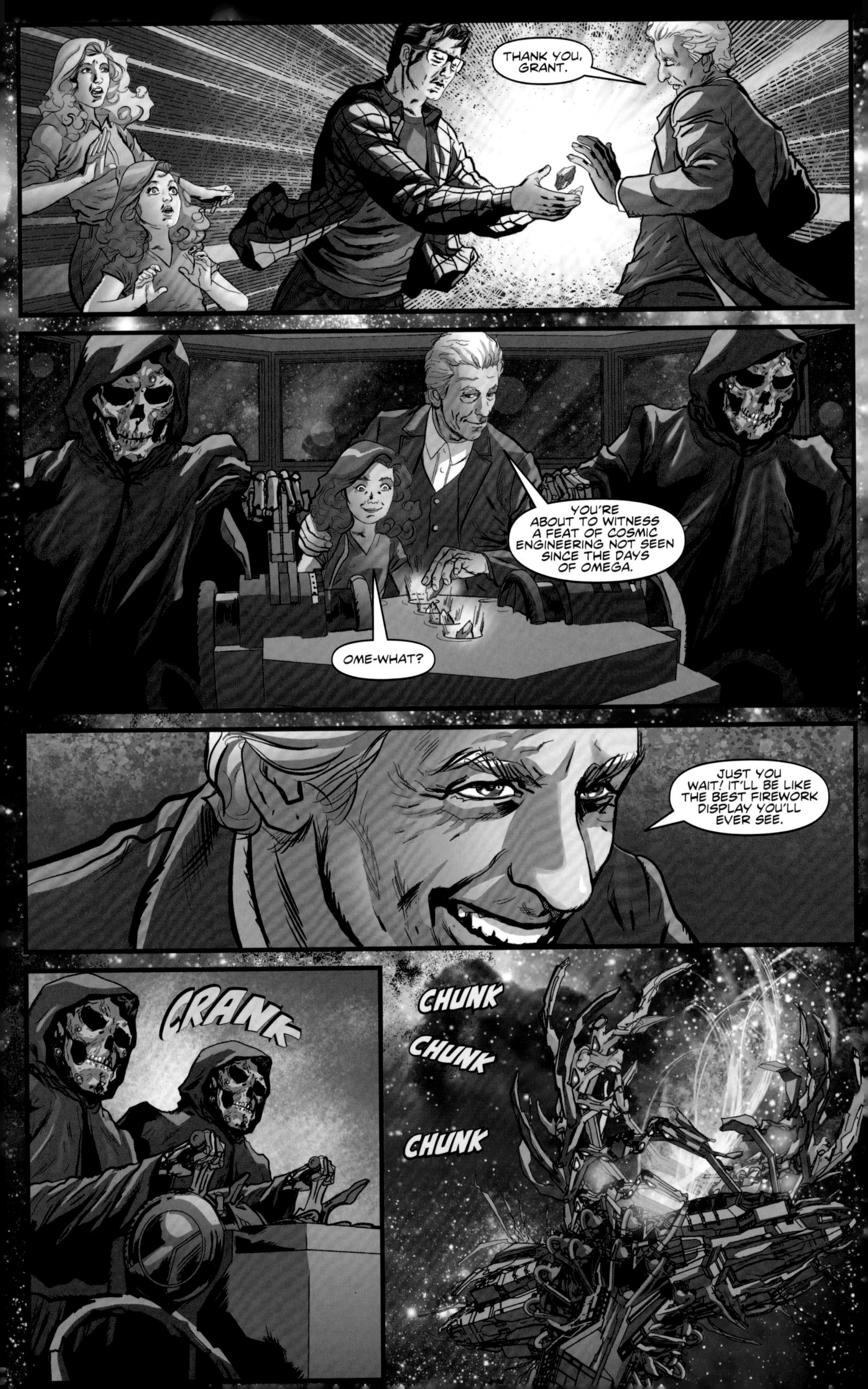
THANK YOU, GRANT.
YOU'RE ABOUT TO WITNESS A FEAT OF COSMIC ENGINEERING NOT SEEN SINCE THE DAYS OF OMEGA.
OME-WHAT?
JUST YOU WAIT! IT'LL BE LIKE THE BEST FIREWORK DISPLAY YOU'LL EVER SEE.
CRANK
CHUNK
CHUNK
CHUNK

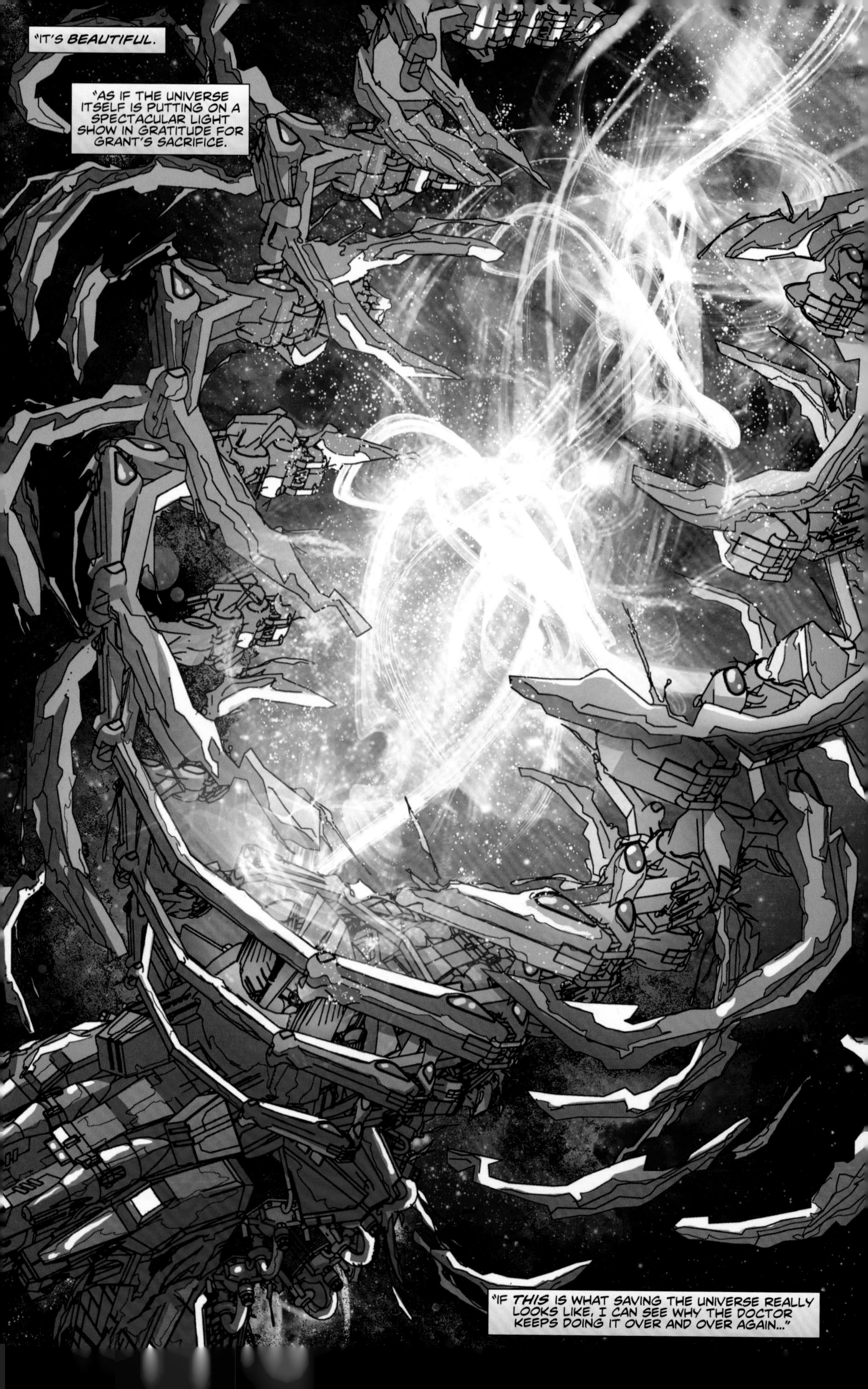
"IT'S *BEAUTIFUL*.
"AS IF THE UNIVERSE ITSELF IS PUTTING ON A SPECTACULAR LIGHT SHOW IN GRATITUDE FOR GRANT'S SACRIFICE.
"IF *THIS* IS WHAT SAVING THE UNIVERSE REALLY LOOKS LIKE, I CAN SEE WHY THE DOCTOR KEEPS DOING IT OVER AND OVER AGAIN..."

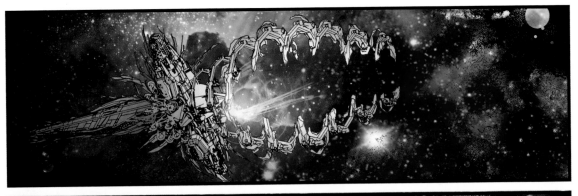

CHUNK
CHUNK
CHUNK

IT'S DONE.

JUST LIKE THAT?

JUST LIKE THAT. FOR ANOTHER MILLION YEARS, AT LEAST.

SEE YOU NEXT TIME, ETHEL.

VWOORRRP

VWOORRRP

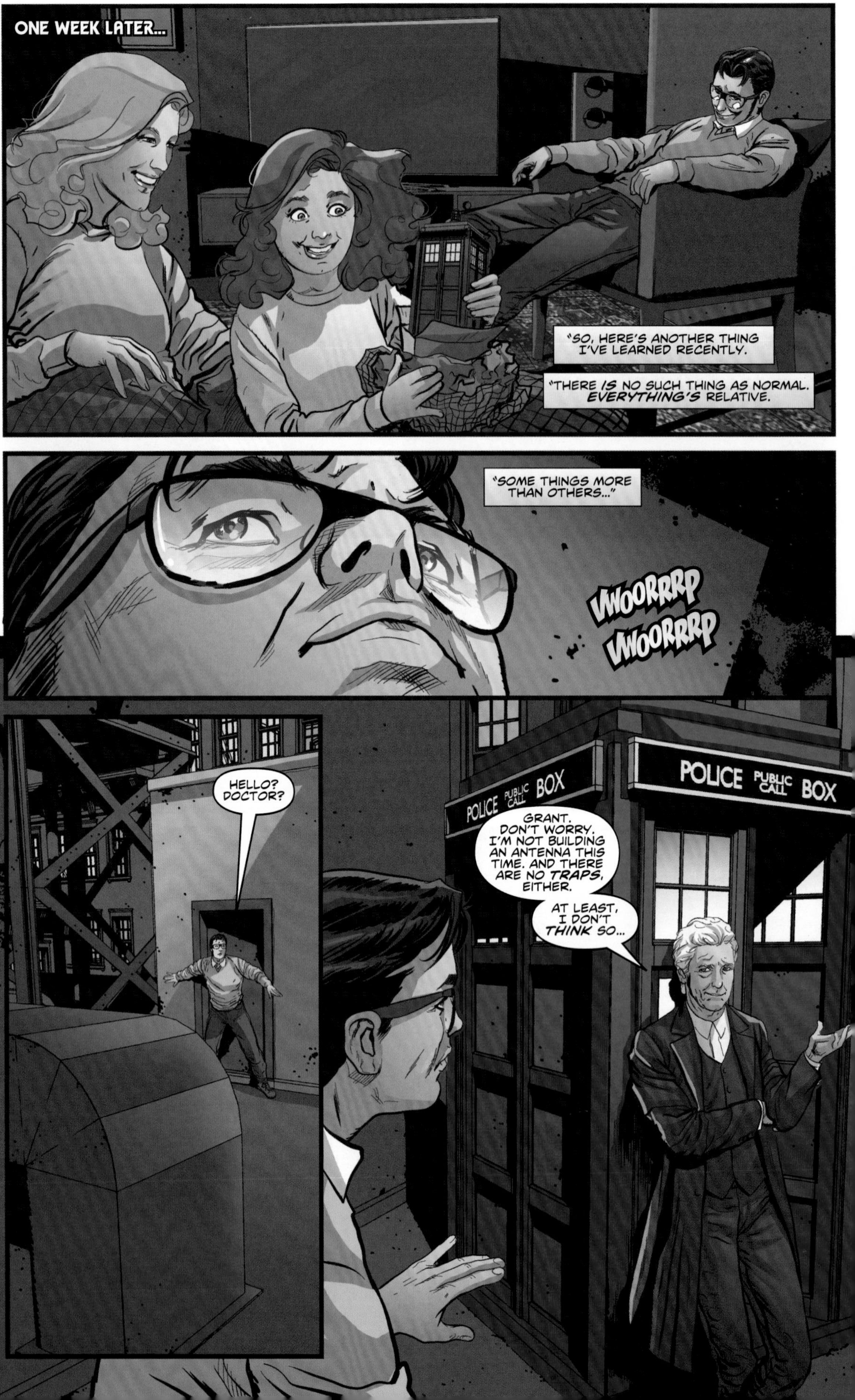
ONE WEEK LATER...
"SO, HERE'S ANOTHER THING I'VE LEARNED RECENTLY.
"THERE IS NO SUCH THING AS NORMAL. EVERYTHING'S RELATIVE.
"SOME THINGS MORE THAN OTHERS..."
VWOORRRP VWOORRRP
HELLO? DOCTOR?
POLICE PUBLIC CALL BOX
GRANT. DON'T WORRY. I'M NOT BUILDING AN ANTENNA THIS TIME. AND THERE ARE NO TRAPS, EITHER.
AT LEAST, I DON'T THINK SO...
POLICE PUBLIC CALL BOX

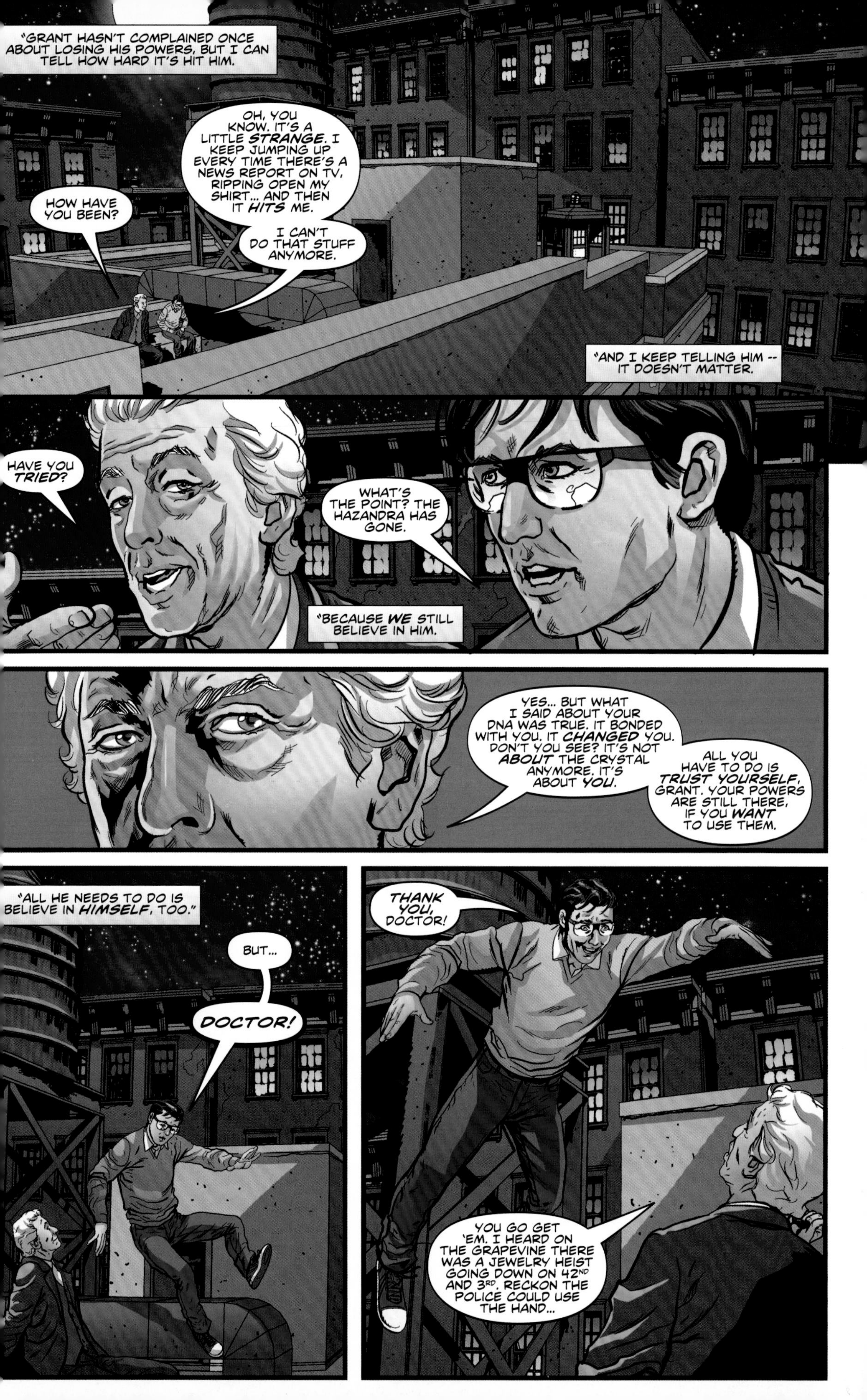
"GRANT HASN'T COMPLAINED ONCE ABOUT LOSING HIS POWERS, BUT I CAN TELL HOW HARD IT'S HIT HIM.
HOW HAVE YOU BEEN?
OH, YOU KNOW. IT'S A LITTLE STRANGE. I KEEP JUMPING UP EVERY TIME THERE'S A NEWS REPORT ON TV, RIPPING OPEN MY SHIRT... AND THEN IT HITS ME.
I CAN'T DO THAT STUFF ANYMORE.
"AND I KEEP TELLING HIM -- IT DOESN'T MATTER.
HAVE YOU TRIED?
WHAT'S THE POINT? THE HAZANDRA HAS GONE.
"BECAUSE WE STILL BELIEVE IN HIM.
YES... BUT WHAT I SAID ABOUT YOUR DNA WAS TRUE. IT BONDED WITH YOU. IT CHANGED YOU. DON'T YOU SEE? IT'S NOT ABOUT THE CRYSTAL ANYMORE. IT'S ABOUT YOU.
ALL YOU HAVE TO DO IS TRUST YOURSELF, GRANT. YOUR POWERS ARE STILL THERE, IF YOU WANT TO USE THEM.
"ALL HE NEEDS TO DO IS BELIEVE IN HIMSELF, TOO."
BUT...
DOCTOR!
THANK YOU, DOCTOR!
YOU GO GET 'EM. I HEARD ON THE GRAPEVINE THERE WAS A JEWELRY HEIST GOING DOWN ON 42ND AND 3RD. RECKON THE POLICE COULD USE THE HAND...

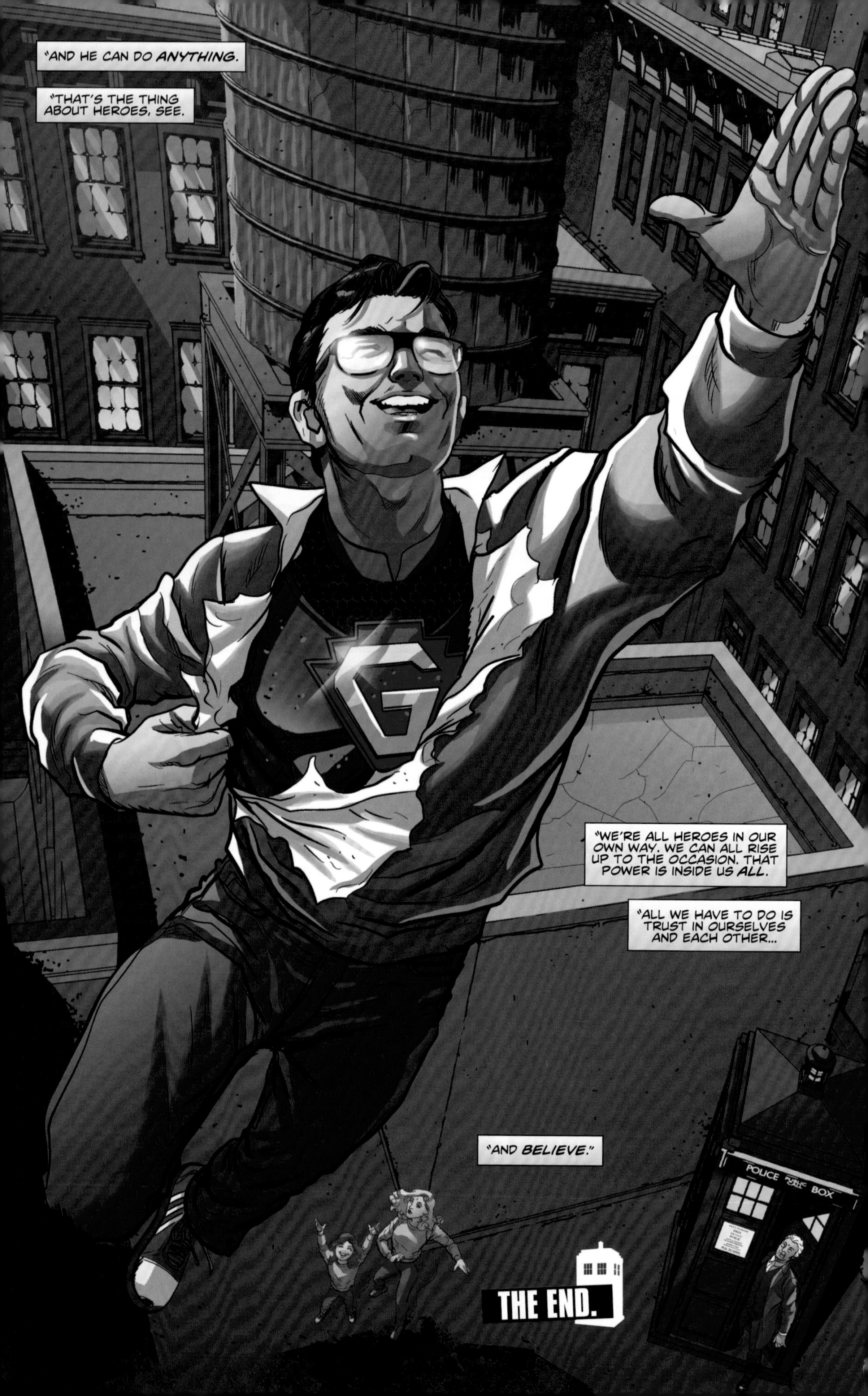
"AND HE CAN DO *ANYTHING*.
"THAT'S THE THING ABOUT HEROES, SEE.
"WE'RE ALL HEROES IN OUR OWN WAY. WE CAN ALL RISE UP TO THE OCCASION. THAT POWER IS INSIDE US *ALL*.
"ALL WE HAVE TO DO IS TRUST IN OURSELVES AND EACH OTHER...
"AND *BELIEVE*."
POLICE PUBLIC BOX
THE END.

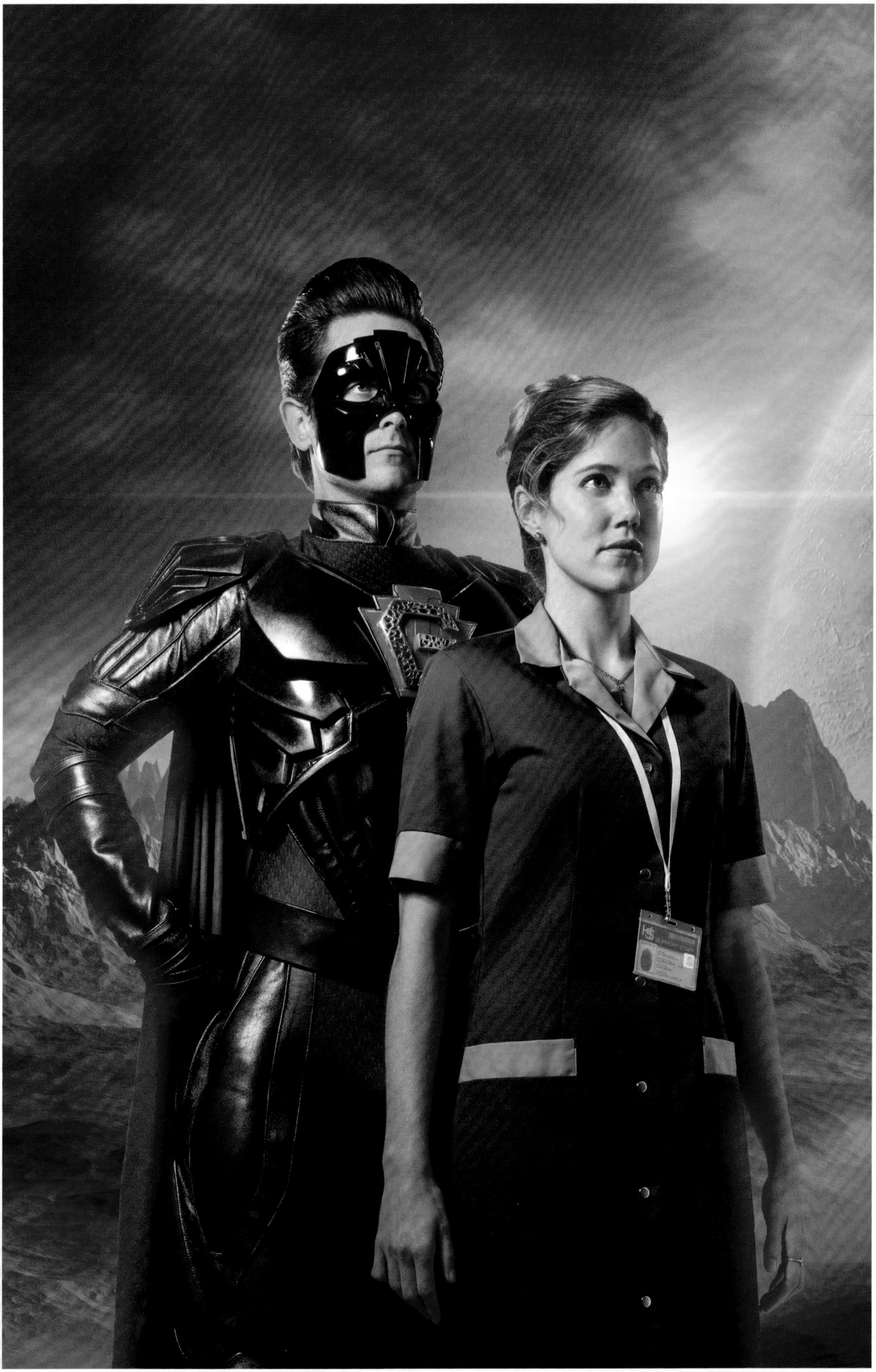

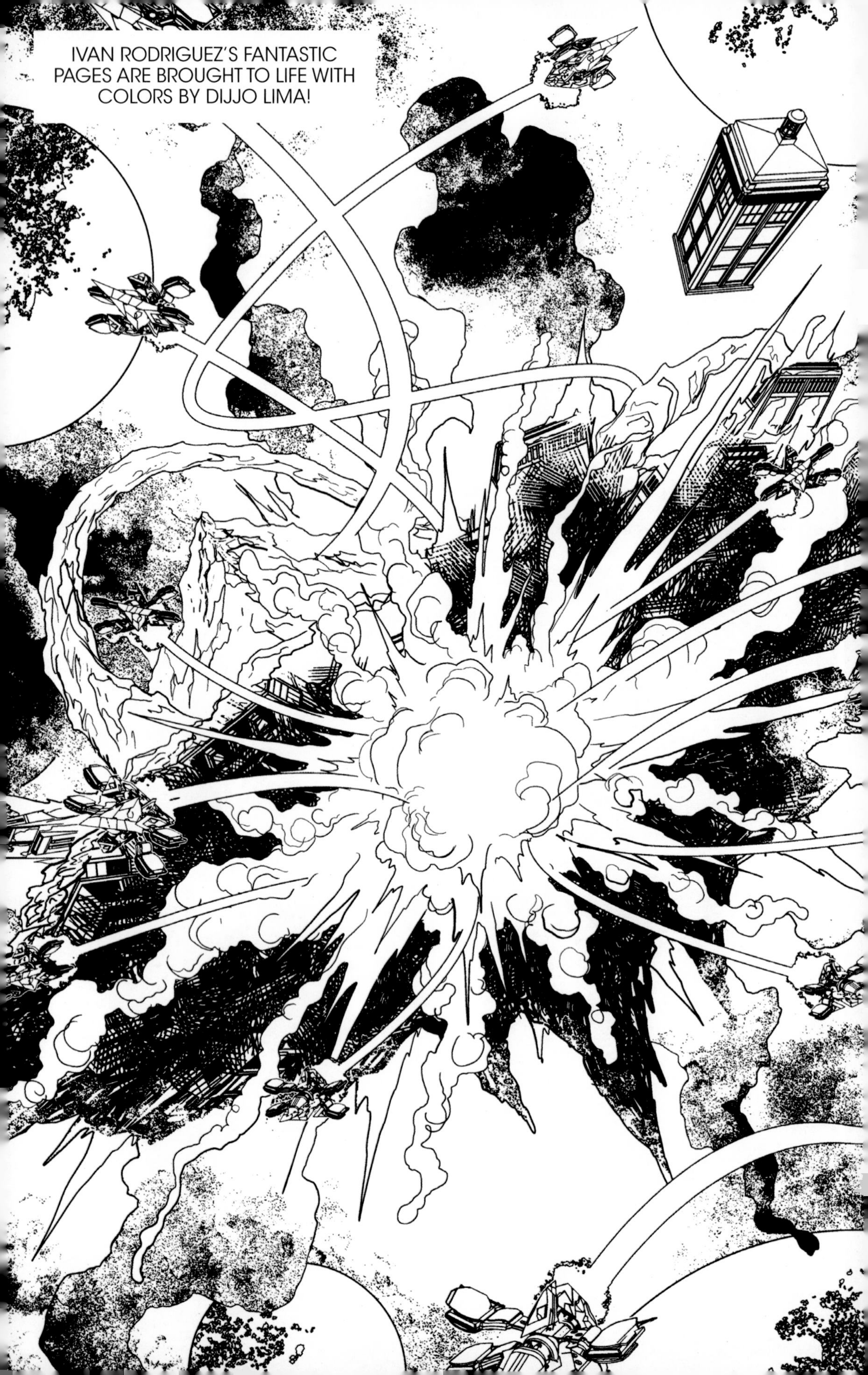
IVAN RODRIGUEZ'S FANTASTIC PAGES ARE BROUGHT TO LIFE WITH COLORS BY DIJJO LIMA!

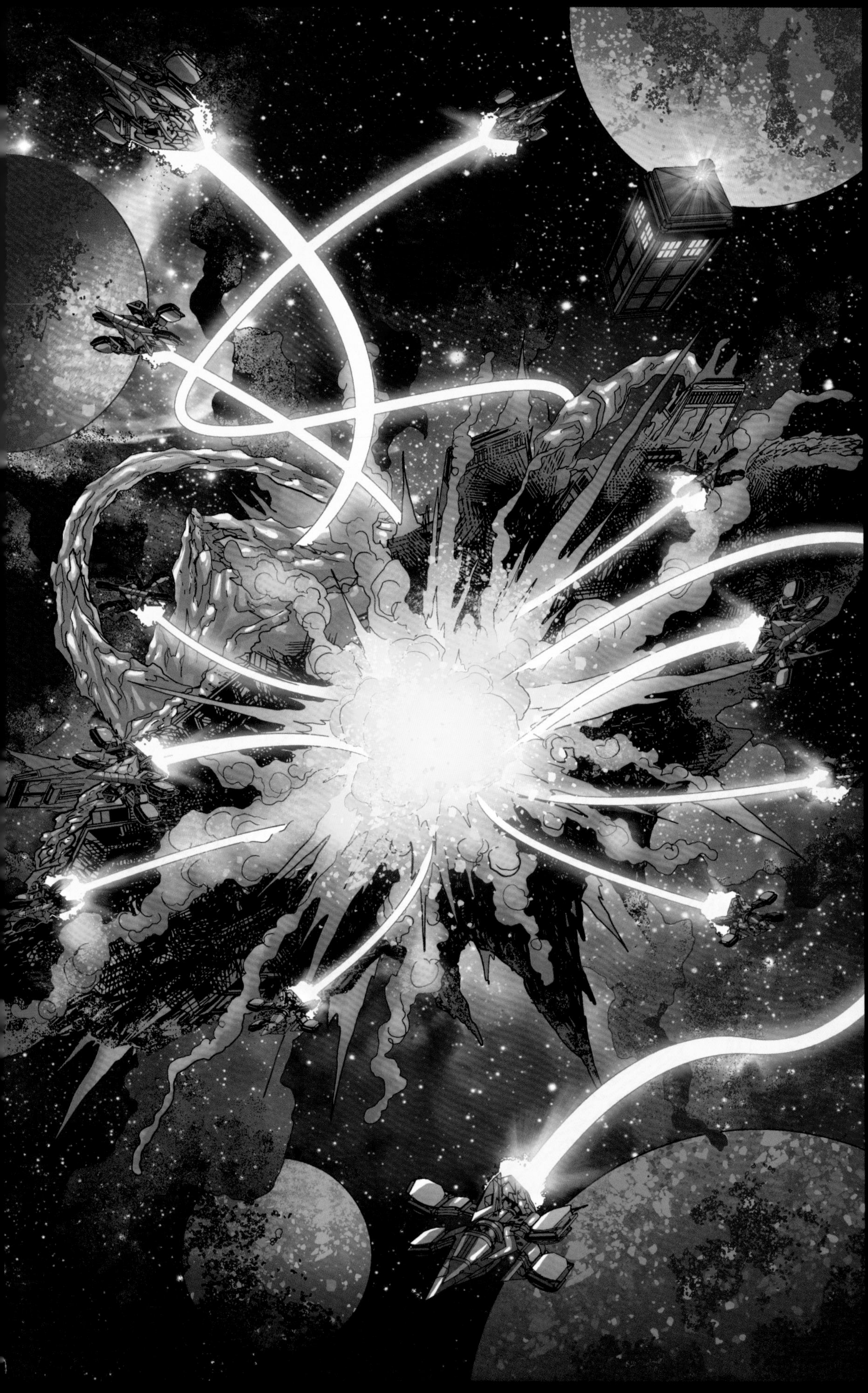

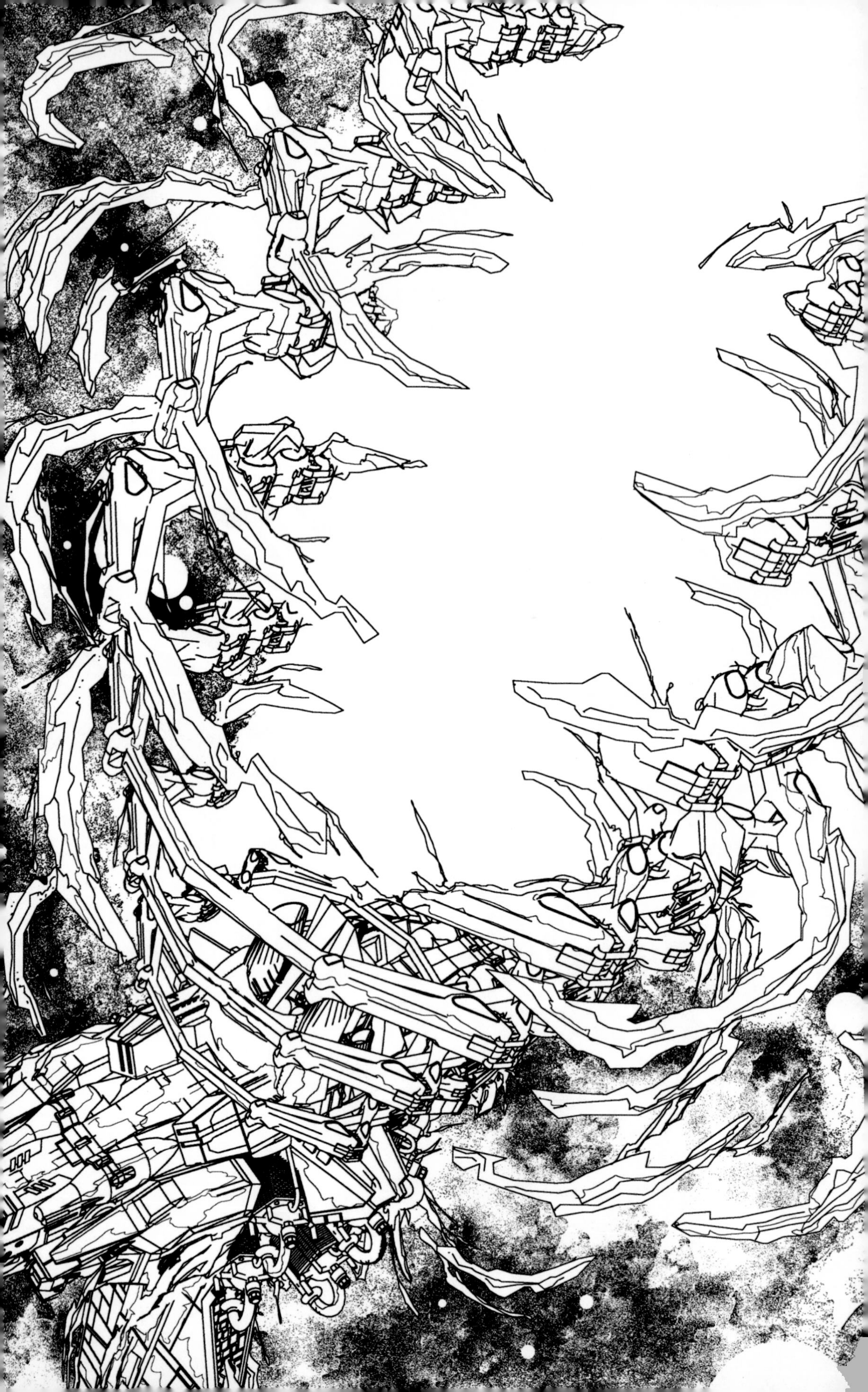

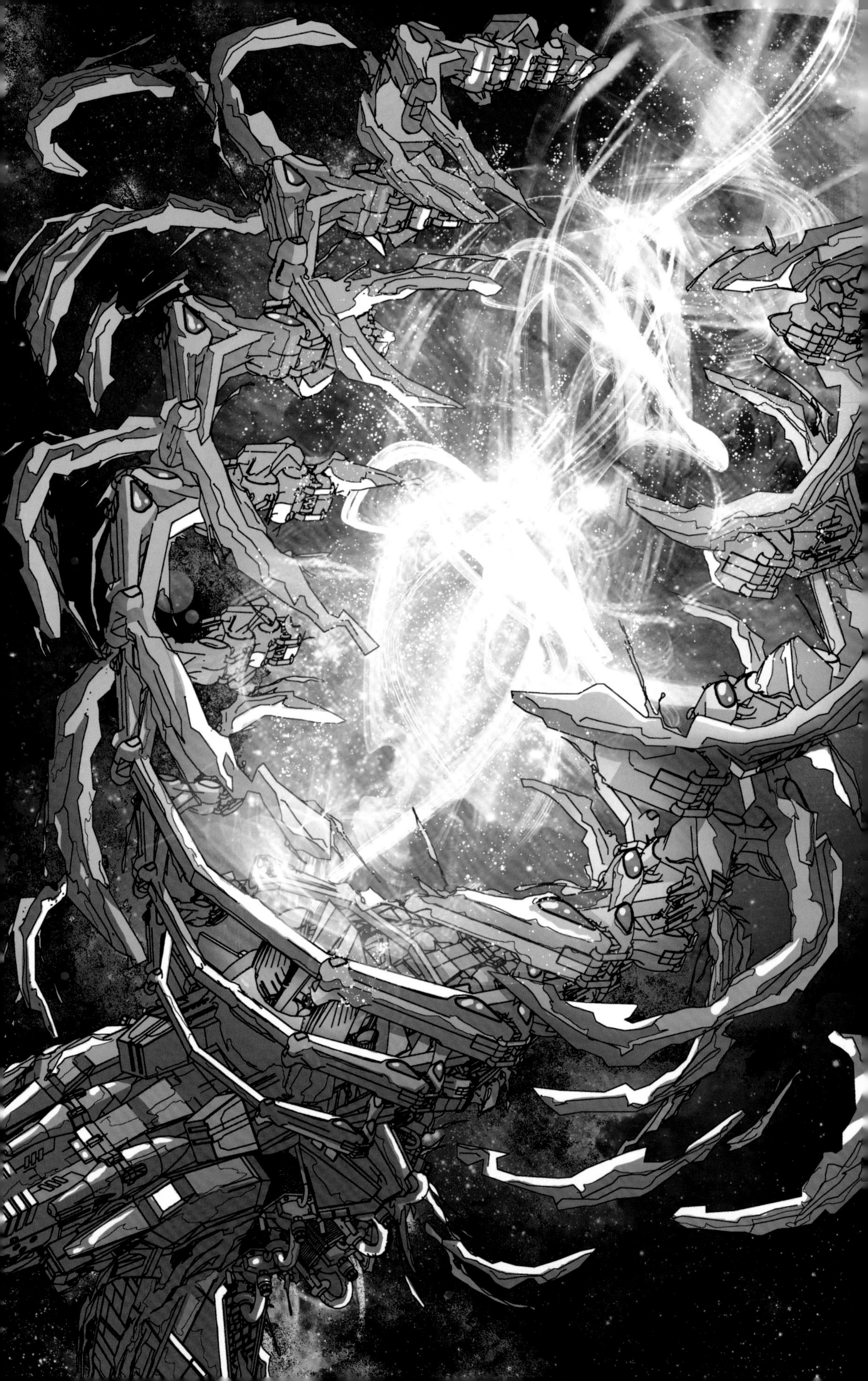

BBC DOCTOR WHO THE TWELFTH DOCTOR

COVER GALLERY

ISSUE #1

BBC
THE TWELFTH DOCTOR: GHOST STORIES
DOCTOR WHO
01 MAY '17 $3.99
COVER B AJ
TITAN COMICS
GEORGE MANN • IVAN RODRIGUEZ • DIJJO LIMA

B. AJ

COVER GALLERY

BBC
THE TWELFTH DOCTOR: GHOST STORIES
DOCTOR WHO
GEORGE MANN • IVAN RODRIGUEZ • DIJJO LIMA
TITAN COMICS

C. SIMON MYERS

BBC
THE TWELFTH DOCTOR: GHOST STORIES
DOCTOR WHO
LATER...
HERE I COME!
THE BIG CITY
GEORGE MANN • IVAN RODRIGUEZ • DIJJO LIMA
TITAN COMICS

D. ANTONIO FUSO

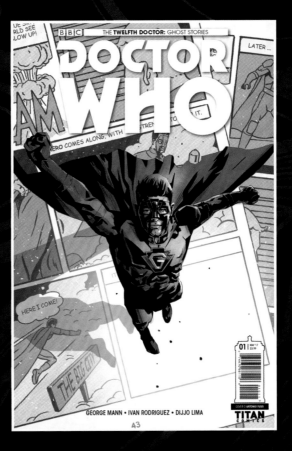

DOCTOR WHO
THE TWELFTH DOCTOR

COVER GALLERY

ISSUE #1

E. LUIS GUERRERO

BBC
THE TWELFTH DOCTOR: GHOST STORIES
DOCTOR WHO
COVER E LUIS GUERRERO
TITAN COMICS
GEORGE MANN • IVAN RODRIGUEZ • DIJJO LIMA

BBC
THE TWELFTH DOCTOR: GHOST STORIES
DOCTOR WHO
PREVIEWS EXCLUSIVE
Limited Edition
GEORGE MANN • IVAN RODRIGUEZ • DIJJO LIMA

DIAMOND UK EXCLUSIVE PHOTO COVER

BBC
DOCTOR WHO
THE TWELFTH DOCTOR

COVER GALLERY

ISSUE #2

BBC
THE TWELFTH DOCTOR: GHOST STORIES
DOCTOR WHO
02
GEORGE MANN • PASQUALE QUALANO • DIJJO LIMA
TITAN COMICS

C. ANTONIO FUSO

BBC
THE TWELFTH DOCTOR: GHOST STORIES
DOCTOR WHO
02
GEORGE MANN • PASQUALE QUALANO • DIJJO LIMA
TITAN COMICS

D. LUIS GUERRERO

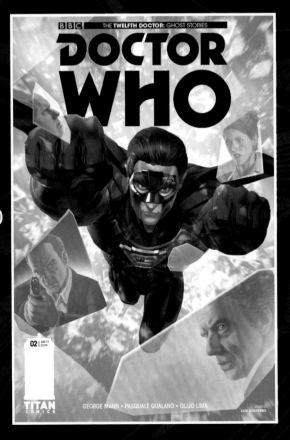

COVER GALLERY

ISSUE #3

BBC
THE TWELFTH DOCTOR: GHOST STORIES
DOCTOR WHO
PUBLIC CALL
03 | JUL '17 $3.99
COVER C
DENNIS CALERO
GEORGE MANN • DENNIS CALERO • DIJJO LIMA
TITAN COMICS

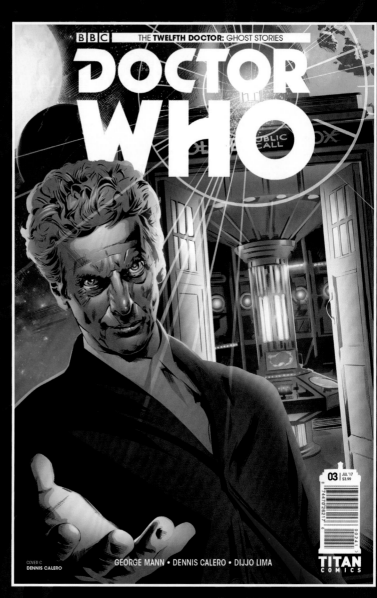

C. DENNIS CALERO

COVER GALLERY

ISSUE #4

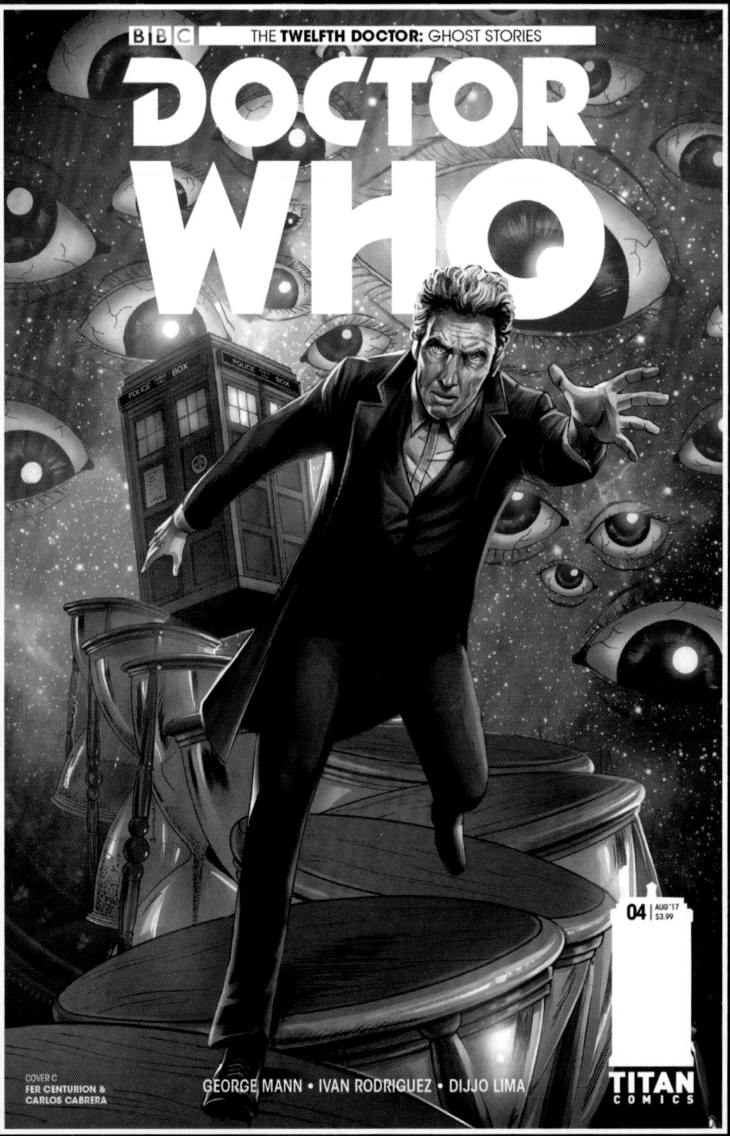
BBC
THE TWELFTH DOCTOR: GHOST STORIES
DOCTOR WHO
04 AUG '17 $3.99
COVER C
FER CENTURION &
CARLOS CABRERA
GEORGE MANN • IVAN RODRIGUEZ • DIJJO LIMA
TITAN COMICS

C. FER CENTURION &
CARLOS CABRERA

BBC

DOCTOR WHO

READER'S GUIDE

With so many amazing *Doctor Who* comics collections, it can be difficult to know where to start! That's where this handy guide comes in.

THE TWELFTH DOCTOR – ONGOING

TERRORFORMER
FRACTURES
HYPERION
THE SCHOOL OF DEATH
THE TWIST

VOL. 1: TERRORFORMER

VOL. 2: FRACTURES

VOL. 3: HYPERION

YEAR TWO BEGINS! VOL. 4: SCHOOL OF DEATH

VOL. 5: THE TWIST

THE ELEVENTH DOCTOR – ONGOING

AFTER LIFE
SERVE YOU
CONVERSION
THE THEN AND THE NOW
THE ONE

VOL. 1: AFTER LIFE

VOL. 2: SERVE YOU

VOL. 3: CONVERSION

YEAR TWO BEGINS! VOL. 4: THE THEN AND THE NOW

VOL. 5: THE ONE

THE TENTH DOCTOR – ONGOING

REVOLUTIONS OF TERROR
THE WEEPING ANGELS OF MONS
THE FOUNTAINS OF FOREVER
THE ENDLESS SONG
ARENA OF FEAR

VOL. 1: REVOLUTIONS OF TERROR

VOL. 2: THE WEEPING ANGELS OF MONS

VOL. 3: THE FOUNTAINS OF FOREVER

YEAR TWO BEGINS! VOL. 4: THE ENDLESS SONG

VOL. 5: ARENA OF FEAR

THE NINTH DOCTOR – ONGOING

WEAPONS OF PAST DESTRUCTION
DOCTORMANIA
OFFICIAL SECRETS
SIN EATERS

VOL. 1: WEAPONS OF PAST DESTRUCTION

VOL. 2: DOCTORMANIA

VOL. 3: OFFICIAL SECRETS

VOL. 4: SIN EATERS

here are currently **four** ongoing *Doctor Who* series, each following a different Doctor.
ach ongoing series is **entirely self-contained**, so you can follow one, two, or all of your favorite Doctors, as you vish! The ongoings are arranged in season-like **Years,** collected into roughly three books per Year. Feel free to start at /olume 1 of any series, or jump straight to Volume 4, for an equally-accessible new season premiere!
ach book, and every comic, features a **catch-up and character guide** at the beginning, making it easy to jump on board – and each ongoing has a very different flavor, representative of that Doctor's era on screen.

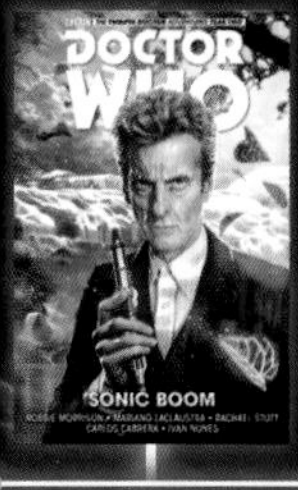
DOCTOR WHO
SONIC BOOM

VOL. 6:
SONIC BOOM

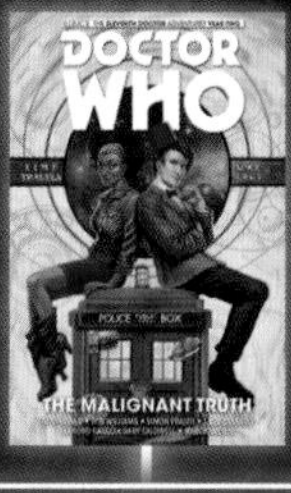
DOCTOR WHO
THE MALIGNANT TRUTH

VOL. 6:
HE MALIGNANT TRUTH

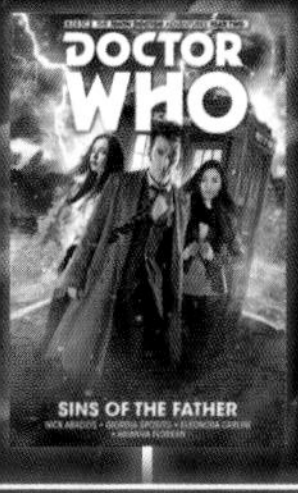
DOCTOR WHO
SINS OF THE FATHER

VOL. 6:
SINS OF THE FATHER

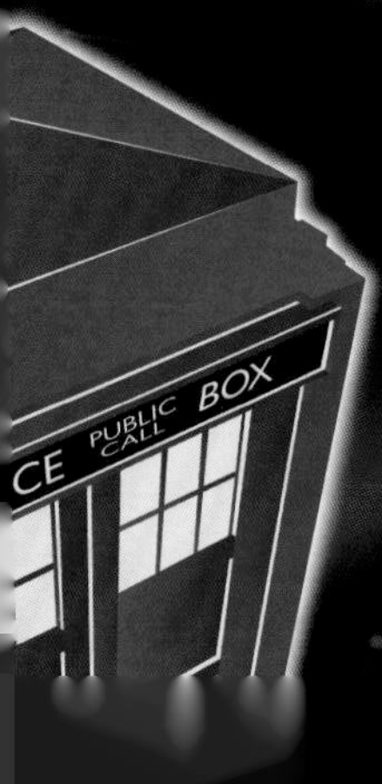
CE PUBLIC CALL BOX

THIRD DOCTOR

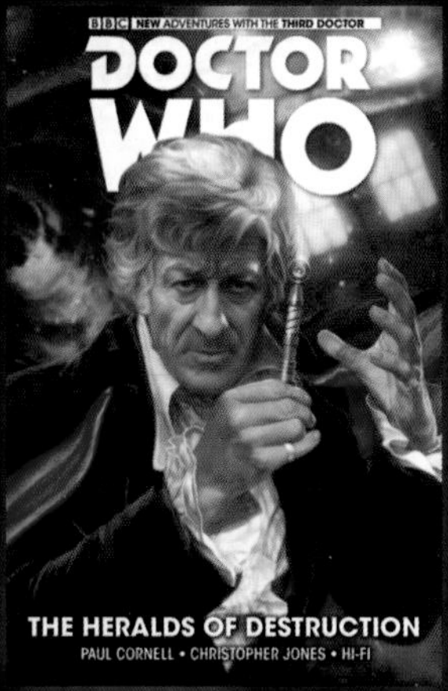
BBC NEW ADVENTURES WITH THE THIRD DOCTOR
DOCTOR WHO
THE HERALDS OF DESTRUCTION
PAUL CORNELL • CHRISTOPHER JONES • HI-FI

As well as the four ongoing series, we have published three major **past Doctor miniseries**, for the Third, Fourth, and Eighth Doctors. These volumes are each a **complete** and **self-contained** story.

There are also two fantastic **crossover event** volumes, starring the Ninth, Tenth, Eleventh, and Twelfth Doctors – the first, *Four Doctors*, sees an impossible team-up, and the second, *Supremacy of the Cybermen*, sees the monstrous cyborgs rule victorious over the universe... unless the Doctors can stop them!

FOURTH DOCTOR

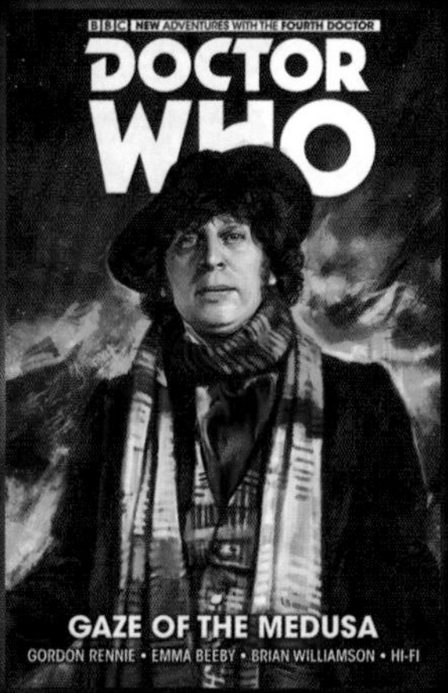
BBC NEW ADVENTURES WITH THE FOURTH DOCTOR
DOCTOR WHO
GAZE OF THE MEDUSA
GORDON RENNIE • EMMA BEEBY • BRIAN WILLIAMSON • HI-FI

FOUR DOCTORS

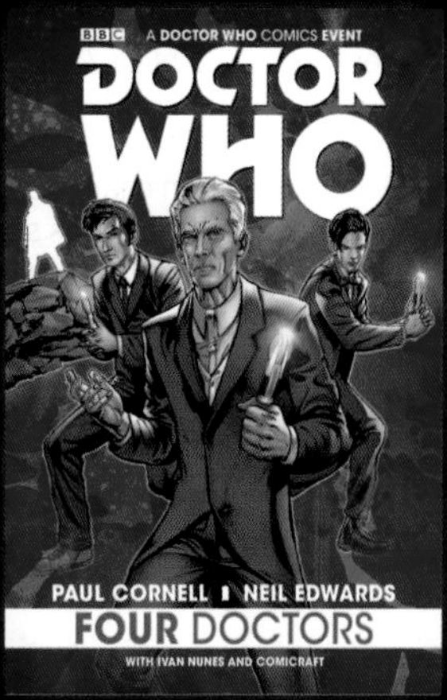
BBC A DOCTOR WHO COMICS EVENT
DOCTOR WHO
PAUL CORNELL ▮ NEIL EDWARDS
FOUR DOCTORS
WITH IVAN NUNES AND COMICRAFT

EIGHTH DOCTOR

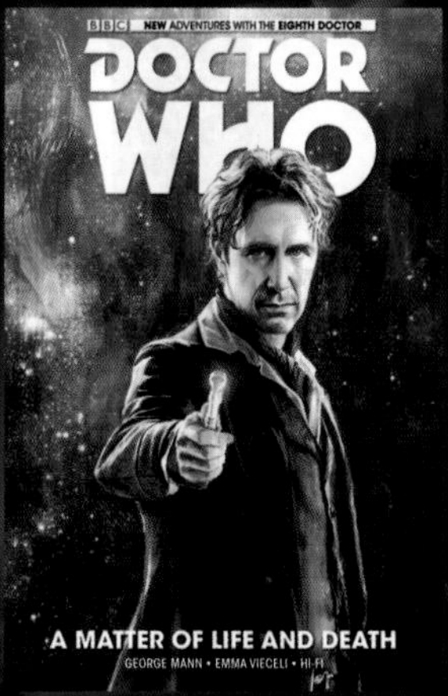
BBC NEW ADVENTURES WITH THE EIGHTH DOCTOR
DOCTOR WHO
A MATTER OF LIFE AND DEATH
GEORGE MANN • EMMA VIECELI • HI-FI

SUPREMACY OF THE CYBERMEN

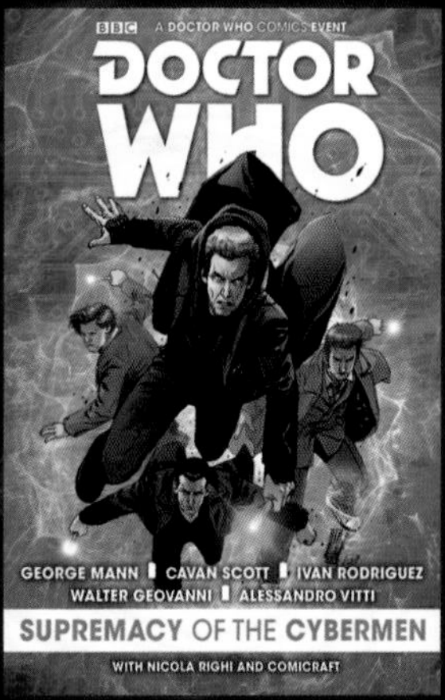
BBC A DOCTOR WHO COMICS EVENT
DOCTOR WHO
GEORGE MANN ▮ CAVAN SCOTT ▮ IVAN RODRIGUEZ
WALTER GEOVANNI ▮ ALESSANDRO VITTI
SUPREMACY OF THE CYBERMEN
WITH NICOLA RIGHI AND COMICRAFT

VISIT **TITAN-COMIC.COM**

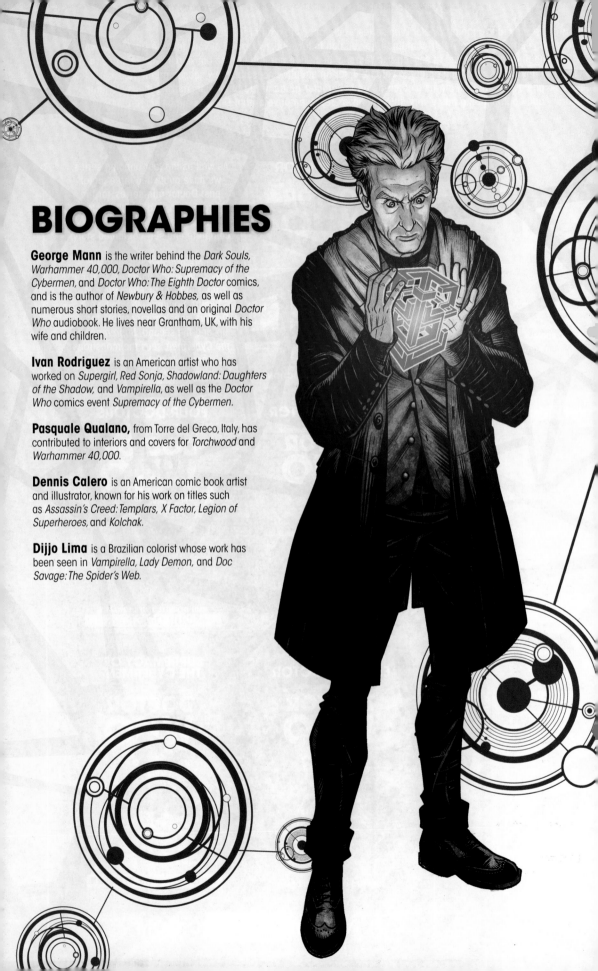

BIOGRAPHIES

George Mann is the writer behind the *Dark Souls, Warhammer 40,000, Doctor Who: Supremacy of the Cybermen,* and *Doctor Who: The Eighth Doctor* comics, and is the author of *Newbury & Hobbes,* as well as numerous short stories, novellas and an original *Doctor Who* audiobook. He lives near Grantham, UK, with his wife and children.

Ivan Rodriguez is an American artist who has worked on *Supergirl, Red Sonja, Shadowland: Daughters of the Shadow,* and *Vampirella,* as well as the *Doctor Who* comics event *Supremacy of the Cybermen.*

Pasquale Qualano, from Torre del Greco, Italy, has contributed to interiors and covers for *Torchwood* and *Warhammer 40,000.*

Dennis Calero is an American comic book artist and illustrator, known for his work on titles such as *Assassin's Creed: Templars, X Factor, Legion of Superheroes,* and *Kolchak.*

Dijjo Lima is a Brazilian colorist whose work has been seen in *Vampirella, Lady Demon,* and *Doc Savage: The Spider's Web.*